DATE DUE

The Gender Gap in College

The Gender Gap in College

Maximizing the Developmental Potential of Women and Men

Linda J. Sax

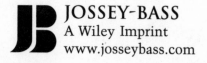

JOSSEY-BASS
A Wiley Imprint
www.josseybass.com

Published by Jossey-Bass
A Wiley Imprint
989 Market Street, San Francisco, CA 94103-1741—www.josseybass.com

Jossey-Bass books and products are available through most bookstores. To contact Jossey-Bass directly call our Customer Care Department within the U.S. at 800-956-7739, outside the U.S. at 317-572-3986, or fax 317-572-4002.

Jossey-Bass also publishes its books in a variety of electronic formats. Some content that appears in print may not be available in electronic books.

Library of Congress Cataloging-in-Publication Data

Sax, Linda J., 1967-
    The gender gap in college : maximizing the developmental potential of women and men / Linda J. Sax.
        p. cm.—(Jossey-Bass higher and adult education series)
    Includes bibliographical references and index.
    ISBN 978-0-7879-6575-4 (cloth)
    1. Sex differences in education—United States. 2.   Sexism in education—United States.
    3.   Education, Higher—United States. 4.   Educational equalization—United States. I.   Title.
    LC212.92.S29 2008
    378.1'9822—dc22
                                                                                    2008018500

Printed in the United States of America
FIRST EDITION
HB Printing   10 9 8 7 6 5 4 3 2 1

The Jossey-Bass

Higher and Adult Education Series

Contents

List of Figures and Tables

Figures

Tables

Foreword

Linda Sax has produced an encyclopedic volume comparing women's and men's development during the undergraduate years. We believe it is destined to become a classic in the higher education literature.

Sax's pioneering work marks a new phase in how the issue of gender has been treated in research on human development. Most of the early "stage" theorists ignored women altogether, basing their proposed developmental stages primarily on data collected from men. Subsequently, and partly as a consequence of the advent of the women's movement (when gender came to be recognized as a potentially important "independent" variable), researchers began to ask whether being a woman makes any difference in students' performance in college. In the third stage, research was undertaken using women-only samples in order to study women's experiences in depth, to provide information on women's development, and thus to close the information gap about gender and college.

Linda Sax's book has opened the door for the next stage of research, where environmental effects are examined separately for women and men. Her findings not only demonstrate that we can no longer afford to assume that women and men are affected in the same way by their undergraduate experience, but also suggest that future research that looks at other types of student diversity should employ similar refinements. Despite the complexity of the analyses, the book is clearly written and should be accessible to virtually all practitioners and policy makers in higher education.

While it has for some time been fashionable among educators to advocate for the individualization of instruction, researchers have to date produced remarkably little evidence to support such a policy, especially in the field of higher education. Practitioners who might be sympathetic to the notion of individualization have thus been left with little to go on beyond simple stereotypes. Sax's pioneering study represents a large first step toward remedying this lack of knowledge, and we can only hope that other researchers will follow suit.

It is true, of course, that researchers have done many studies of particular subpopulations—as defined by gender, age, race, social class, religious affiliation, and so on—but until now most of this research has been limited either to the subpopulation of interest or to simple descriptive comparisons of the characteristics of the different subpopulations. What is unique about Sax's approach is that she has gone the next step by directly examining the *interaction* between gender and a variety of college experiences, a major inquiry which allows her to address the fundamental individualization question: Do women and men respond differently to a given educational experience?

In their recent comprehensive review of the student development literature, Ernest Pascarella and Patrick Terenzini (2005) highlight the need for more research on what they call the conditional effects of college, the possibility that different types of students may respond very differently to our various policies and practices in higher education. We think it is fair to say that Sax's book represents by far the most comprehensive study ever done of the conditional effects of college on undergraduate students.

What is perhaps most remarkable about Sax's findings is the fact that more than half of the 584 different college effects that she identified are *not* the same for women and men! What this suggests, among other things, is that the growing community of scholars who study how college affects students should seriously consider looking at conditional effects as a matter of course. Considering all of the potentially important conditions that have yet to be explored in any systematic fashion, there is clearly a great deal more work that remains to be done.

One of the major impediments to further research of this type, of course, is the data required: conditional effects cannot readily be identified without large and sophisticated databases. And the more different conditions we seek to examine—gender, race/ethnicity, social class, preparation level, and so on—the more subjects we need, especially if we choose to examine more complex *combinations* of conditions (e.g., gender within social class). Furthermore, in higher education in particular, there is also an almost limitless set of *institutional* conditions—type, size, selectivity, and so on—that can and probably should be studied. Again, the data requirements for such studies are considerable, and we can only hope that funding agencies will see fit to support the creation and maintenance of the kinds of databases that make such research possible.

As we were jointly reflecting on Sax's beautifully crafted final chapter 8—where she discusses the implications of her major findings—the persistent question for us was: When it comes to the issue of gender equity, are college women faring better today, given four decades of legislation, affirmative action, and consciousness raising? While her conclusions point to certain areas, such as college finances and faculty-student interaction, where significant questions of educational equity remain, the equity implications of many of her other findings are more complex. But we remain certain of one thing: If higher education faculty, staff, and policy makers familiarize themselves with the major findings and implications of this pioneering study, the cause of gender equity in American higher education will be well served.

Alexander W. Astin
Helen S. Astin
University of California Los Angeles

To my husband, Norman
And our children, Samantha and Jeremy

Preface

The idea for this book came about over fifteen years ago, when I was a graduate student and just beginning to study the gender gap in college. At that time, I was trying to figure out what role gender had played in my own educational decisions and, in particular, my experiences in math and science. Up until college, I had always been a strong student in math. Ever since my mother taught me the basic principles of addition and subtraction, I was fascinated with numbers. My affinity for math lasted clear through my high school calculus course, and I had so much fun manipulating numbers that I actually looked forward to tests and quizzes. Though I was aware of purported gender differences in math ability, I naively thought those days were in the past. After all, among the top math students in my courses, there were always equal numbers of males and females. As a teenager in the 1980s, I assumed that the women's movement had indeed leveled the playing field; I never once thought of math as a male domain.

All this changed when I went to college. I remember enrolling in a calculus course my first year at the University of California, Berkeley. I found myself in a very large lecture hall, surrounded almost completely by men. I had essentially no interaction with the professor (I'm not sure if anybody did) and experienced a sense of invisibility even in the small discussion sections led by the teaching assistant. I began to notice that issues and questions were taken less seriously when posed by women than by men. My classmates seemed generally less willing to share resources and study together than students in my social science classes. Due to the austere architecture of the math building, the competitive classroom climate, and the traditional lecture-heavy pedagogy, I began to feel that math was more cold and alienating, and less relevant to the real world, than I had previously thought. And I began to wonder whether my growing disinterest in math was a function of my own changing interests or was the result of being female in a male-dominated field.

I ultimately found my comfort zone in sociology, history, and political science, where I not only learned about ongoing social inequities but also discovered the world of social science research. It was a revelation to see the ways in which quantitative methods could be used to study issues of broader societal importance. Ultimately, this led me to pursue a graduate degree in higher education at the University of California, Los Angeles (UCLA), where I focused on women's experiences in college math and science and learned that my experiences were more universal than I had thought. I learned through research that for many women, the likelihood of persisting in math and science was shaped, just as mine was, by their interactions with faculty, by their peers, and by a perception of science as being disconnected from larger societal concerns. All this raised the question of whether the forces influencing college student development would differ for women and men across a broader range of outcomes, not just those related to math and science.

This book is an opportunity to explore that question. It reveals the ways in which the impact of college is a function of students' gender and places the study of college impact within the larger discussion of the gender gap in higher education. It is designed to serve as a resource for campus practitioners, whose efforts ought to be mindful of women's and men's unique needs, and for higher education researchers, who are in a position to further demonstrate the ways in which college impact varies for different types of students. The approach taken in this book is

exclusively quantitative, based on the survey responses of literally millions of men and women over the past four decades.
While there is strength in these numbers, we certainly cannot
understand the role of gender and college student development
through survey data alone. In fact, the qualitative works of Mirra
Komarovsky, Ruthellen Josselson, and Marcia Baxter Magolda
all demonstrate the richness of interviews as a means of revealing depth and teasing out the nuances of college women's development. Ideally, researchers will draw on both quantitative and
qualitative modes of inquiry to address the Pandora's box of new
questions raised in this book.

Acknowledgments

I am indebted to many individuals who provided various forms
of assistance and support throughout this project. I want to start
by acknowledging the time and intellect contributed by a number of graduate students over the years (many of whom have
since moved on to faculty positions of their own). Every day I
think how lucky I am to have worked with them and learned
from them.

In the early phases of this book, I benefited from the wisdom
and tenacity of Alyssa Bryant. Alyssa conducted an extensive
review of the literature on gender differences in college impact
and cowrote chapter 3 with me. She also played the chief role
in constructing the longitudinal database used in this study. She
chronicled every data decision that we made (and unmade . . .
and remade), which turned out to be an invaluable resource as
different students worked on the project over the years. Alyssa
was part of a talented team of graduate students—including
Frank DiCrisi, Casandra Harper, and Victor Saenz—who conducted the majority of the statistical analyses included in this
book, as well as scores of other data manipulations that did not
make it into this final version. Additional assistance creating tables
and reviewing chapter drafts was provided by stellar UCLA

graduate students Jennifer Curley and Julie Park, as well as Dalia Gefen, a graduate student at the City University of New York who offered valuable feedback on chapter 5.

I also want to acknowledge the role that Casandra Harper played during the arduous process of writing up the findings. She read every draft chapter and provided the sort of critical feedback that one expects from seasoned scholars, not young graduate students. My working relationship with Casandra can be thought of as an adviser-advisee relationship turned on its head: just as I pushed and challenged her with her dissertation, she pushed and challenged me with this book.

In the book's final stages, I was fortunate to work with my newest graduate student, Casey Eznekier. Casey helped make substantial revisions to chapter 2, a chapter she coauthors, and provided technical and editorial support throughout the final months of writing. She has also been crucial in helping me consider the broader implications of my work for the field of student affairs.

Another key player on this project is Emily Arms, my valued colleague at the University of Southern California. She collaborated with me on the many iterations of chapter 2 and contributed a wealth of knowledge on gender issues in the broader educational context.

This study could not have been conducted without the participation of millions of college students in the Cooperative Institutional Research Program over the past forty years. Though they may not know it, their honest survey responses have contributed to hundreds of research studies and have helped improve the college experience for subsequent generations of students. I am also indebted to the professionals on each campus for their part in administering these surveys, and to Bill Korn of the Higher Education Research Institute for his wizardry in managing survey operations and for his part in creating the invaluable databases used in this book.

I want to thank David Brightman, my editor at Jossey-Bass, both for his patience and for pushing me to make the book

more relevant to campus practice and generally more accessible to a wider audience. Instrumental in helping me accomplish that goal has been Kathy Wyer, director of the Sudikoff
Family Institute for Education & New Media. As a Sudikoff fellow, I have benefited immensely from the editing and coaching
Kathy has provided me. She has taught me strategies for making complex findings more accessible, for bringing the reader
into the narrative, and for communicating and emphasizing key
insights. Kathy's fresh perspectives and enthusiasm about this
book have helped me remember why I started writing it in the
first place.

I also want to express my gratitude to Sandy and Lena Astin,
my longtime mentors whose collective work lays the foundation
for the new questions raised in this book. They have cheered
me on throughout this process and have provided insightful
feedback about the big issues I encountered while doing the
research. I am honored that they have written the Foreword for
this book, thus solidifying the lasting legacy of their perspectives
on issues of gender and college impact.

My appreciation also extends to Ernie Pascarella and Pat
Terenzini, in part because their reviews of college impact
research were an essential resource in writing this book, but
also because they periodically reacted to my ideas for advanc-
ing the study of conditional college effects. Thank you, Ernie,
for reading the first full draft of this manuscript! And special
thanks go to Shannon Gilmartin, a friend and colleague whose
wisdom and wit I have relied on over the years. Shannon was,
in fact, the person who convinced me that this book *needed* to
be written.

This project has taken much longer to complete than I had
anticipated. Like many of the women represented in this book,
I extend myself across a wide range of commitments: my work,
my family, and my community. The countless hours that I have
spent writing—and rewriting—this book have been interlaced
with the time I have spent cheering on my children in sports,

volunteering in their school, taking oh-so-necessary family vacations, and meeting my friends for coffee. By attempting to maintain a sense of balance in my life, some things just take longer to finish. I am forever thankful to my friends for helping me stay connected and remember what really counts in life.

Most important, I am grateful to my family. I am lucky to have had a mother and father whose expectations of me were never influenced by gender-based stereotypes. They always encouraged me to pursue what I enjoy doing, and I have actually taken that advice. And my mother deserves special thanks for the time she spends taking care of my children while I am at work. I am truly blessed to have her in my life.

And finally, Norman and the kids. Norman played a major role in my academic development, first as my study partner in high school chemistry and calculus, and later as my husband, whose unwavering support and dry sense of humor have helped keep this book—and all my other professional trials and tribulations—in perspective. Our children, Samantha and Jeremy, have also enriched this process by asking questions about what this book is about and offering their own unique take on the gender gap. Their love, energy, and just plain silliness are what I most look forward to every day.

About the Author

Linda J. Sax is an associate professor in the Graduate School of Education & Information Studies at UCLA, where she serves as founding faculty director of the master's program in student affairs. Dr. Sax's research focuses on gender differences in college student development, with a focus on how institutional characteristics, peer and faculty environments, and forms of student involvement differentially affect male and female college students. She is currently principal investigator on a nationwide study of the effects of single-sex secondary education, and coprincipal investigator on a project to increase women's pursuit of graduate degrees in the physical sciences and engineering.

Dr. Sax received her BA (1990) in political economy from the University of California, Berkeley, and her MA (1991) and PhD (1994) in higher education from UCLA. Between 1994 and 2005, she served as director of the Cooperative Institutional Research Program and associate director of the Higher Education Research Institute at UCLA. She has authored over fifty publications in the field of higher education and has served on numerous editorial boards. Dr. Sax was selected as a 2007–2008 fellow for the Sudikoff Family Institute for Education & New Media. She is also the recipient of the 2005 Scholar-in-Residence Award from the American Association of University Women and the 1999 Early Career Award from the Association for the Study of Higher Education.

The Gender Gap in College

1

INTRODUCTION

On July 9, 2006, the front page of the *New York Times* read, "At Colleges, Women are Leaving Men in the Dust." The story described growing gender gaps in college enrollment and academic performance and raised questions about what, if anything, should be done about "the new gender divide." Reaction to this article was widespread, with some applauding women's academic successes, and others lamenting the seemingly dismal state of affairs for today's young men.

We have indeed reached a critical juncture in the history of women and men in higher education. Today—decades after the women's movement started what became monumental gains for female students in terms of access, equity, and opportunity—the popular notion is that gender equity has been achieved. Some higher education statistics do paint a rosy picture for women, who now make up the majority of undergraduates (up to 58 percent nationally), earn better college grades than men do, and are more likely than men to complete college. In recent years, these gender gaps have raised concerns that we have reached a crisis point for men (Hoff Sommers, 2000; Mortenson, 2003).

Although it is easy to view these trends as a clear indication of women's progress—and of the challenges now facing men—interpretations of those trends depend on how deeply we look at them. According to reports by the American Council on Education and the Education Sector, the growing gender gap in college enrollments is attributable primarily to increases in college attendance among women from groups historically underrepresented in higher education—namely, African Americans,

Latinas, older students, and those of lower socioeconomic status (King, 2006; Mead, 2006). This fact is important because it demonstrates that the sociodemographic composition of female students is becoming increasingly different from that of male students. That is, male and female college students differ from each other not only based on their gender; they are becoming more distinct in terms of their demographic makeup.

Notable educational gains made by women also must be understood in the context of significant gender gaps that favor men. For example, women continue to score lower than men on standardized tests used for college admissions and remain underrepresented in the majority of scientific and technical fields, especially at the master's and doctoral levels. Female college students also report higher levels of stress and lower levels of self-confidence than their male counterparts. This is not to suggest that college is *responsible* for such gender differences. In fact, sex differentials stem primarily from the precollege years, when women and men develop different values, confidences, aspirations, and patterns of behavior (Sax & Harper, 2007). Yet, for the most part, these gender differences persist—and may even grow larger—during college. In fact, a major nationwide study of students shows that nearly every gender difference observed at college entry widens over time:

> Even though men and women are presumably exposed to a common liberal arts curriculum and to other common environmental experiences during the college years, it would seem that their educational programs preserve and strengthen, rather than reduce or weaken, stereotypic differences between men and women in behavior, personality, aspirations, and achievement. (Astin, 1993c, p. 406)

However, less is known about *how* college contributes to these differences. Do gender gaps at the end of college result from differential reactions to academic and social experiences? Do women's and men's exposure to faculty, peers, the curriculum, or extracurricular activities affect them in different ways? For the most part, the college curriculum and cocurriculum do not consider these potential gender differences in the impact of college. Though some campus practitioners may anticipate differential needs from and developmental patterns among their male and female students, these considerations tend to be shaped by personal experiences, anecdotes, and gut instinct—not by empirically driven research.

Theoretical perspectives certainly support the notion that college women's development should be considered as potentially distinct from men's. Traditional theories of cognitive, moral, and identity development contributed by Perry (1970), Kohlberg (1975), and Erikson (1968) have long been criticized for their lack of attention to developmental differences based on gender. Critiques of traditional male-based theories have given rise to feminist theoretical approaches that view women's development as uniquely dependent on their relations with individuals and on fostering a "care orientation" (Chodorow, 1978; Gilligan, 1982; Josselson, 1987). Based on these perspectives, one might expect women's development in college to be more strongly tied to their interactions with others—such as peers, faculty, and family—or to their involvement in the community than is the case for men. Conversely, it may be that relationships and a sense of connectedness are important for *both* women and men, but that their influence depends on the developmental outcome in question. The vast body of empirical research on college student development scarcely addresses such potential gender differences. In fact, our understanding of how college affects students has generally derived from studies of students in the aggregate.

The seminal works of Feldman and Newcomb (1969), Trent and Medsker (1968), Astin (1977, 1993c), Pascarella and Terenzini (1991, 2005), and countless others have shaped this field's conception of how college environments and experiences contribute to various dimensions of cognitive and affective development. What is clear from this ever-expanding scholarship base is that students stand to benefit from forging meaningful connections on campus, whether with people, places, or programs. This sense of connection is characterized in a number of ways, and among the most popular are "involvement" (Astin, 1999), "engagement" (Kuh, 2001), and "integration" (Tinto, 1987; Weidman, 1989). And yet little is known about the extent to which such important forces in college might operate *differently* for women and men. Indeed, as Pascarella (1984) noted more than two decades ago, "It is unlikely that all students will benefit equally from the same institution, program, or instructional emphasis" (p. 47). Thus, by considering "college impact" generically—without addressing how women and men may differ in their reactions to college—we run the risk of misapplying knowledge about how college affects students.

Responding to this gap in the research, some higher education scholars have begun to address what are known as "conditional" effects, or the ways in which aspects of college—such as classroom climate, peer culture, or extracurricular activities—differentially affect groups of students as defined by race, gender, or other characteristics. Pascarella and Terenzini (1991, 2005) emphasize the importance of studying the conditional effects of college and present a thorough review of what we know regarding college impact for different types of students. They note that although the study of conditional effects has grown, particularly over the past decade, conclusions about conditional effects are typically based on single studies that are in need of replication. This gap in the knowledge base provides higher education researchers with an important research agenda, but unfortunately, it leaves today's campus practitioners without information to guide them in developing programs and services that maximize the benefits of college for all students. Given the role that college impact research has had in transforming and improving the practice of student affairs, it is now incumbent on researchers to extend our understanding of college impact by uncovering *which* types of students benefit from *which* college experiences.

Intention of This Book

This book seeks to advance the study of college impact by addressing whether and how the impact of college differs for women and men. It draws from the nation's largest and longest-running study of American higher education to address the following fundamental questions:

- In what ways do women and men differ when they enter college? How has the gender gap shifted over the past four decades?

- To what extent do gender differences expand or contract over four years of college?

- Do the experiences in college that influence student development differ between the sexes? Are some college environments and experiences important for both genders but perhaps more salient for women or men? If so, is there a discernable pattern across the results that can inform long-standing theories of college student development?

In answering these questions, this book provides insights into how we can improve the college-going experience for both genders. It helps us understand that men and women experience college differently, even when they are enrolled in the same classes, live in the same residence halls, and join the same clubs. It reveals that certain aspects of college—such as living away from home, interacting with faculty, and learning about diversity—contribute in unique ways to women's and men's development.

The book also points the way toward new research questions that can further illuminate the complex role of gender in college. We find, for example, that interacting with professors influences stress and self-image among women, while it contributes to political and social activism among men. We also learn that sports and exercise promote academic achievement among women but have the opposite effect among men. These and other intriguing findings suggest important avenues for future research. They also underscore the practical value of thinking about the *differential* effects of college for different types of students, whether defined by gender, race, ethnicity, class, sexual orientation, or any other characteristic that may influence how a student experiences college.

And though this book is not the first to address gender differences in the college-going experience, it is perhaps the first to examine this issue in such a systematic and comprehensive fashion. It is intended to determine whether there exist fundamental differences in the impact of college on women and men. And while it does reveal more differences than similarities, such "conditional" effects of college do not arrange themselves as coherently and thematically as one might hope—or as some theoretical perspectives might suggest. Instead, understanding the "gendered" effects of college is unchartered, complex terrain; it does not lend itself to one big, unifying message. This book moves the agenda forward by revealing literally hundreds of ways in which college affects women and men in unique ways, with each difference suggesting potential implications for practice and avenues for further research.

Who Should Read This Book?

The topic of the "gender gap" in higher education garners attention in numerous circles, including researchers, practitioners, faculty, students, policy makers, and the media. Individuals within any one of these groups may be interested in the role of gender in college because it informs their professional work or perhaps because it shapes their thinking about their own college experience. Indeed, all readers are encouraged to recall their own college experiences when reading this book as a way of gaining insights into their own choices and dispositions.

Though this book provides valuable information to a wide range of individuals, it is geared primarily toward two major audiences. The first is practitioners working in any capacity in a college setting. If you are a professional affiliated with student affairs, academic affairs, or other campus units, your ability to most effectively serve students benefits from knowing the ways in which college can yield differential effects on different types of students—in this case, women and men. While reading this book, you should consider how the findings can help you improve your practice. Do the results suggest ways in which one gender or the other is potentially benefiting—or being shortchanged—by programs and services under your purview? How can your professional work benefit from an awareness of the experiences that women and men have in services outside your domain? How might you facilitate the creation of programming and services that maximize the potential of both genders? Though the book offers numerous implications for practice, you, through your own experiences, will have a better idea of the real-life implications of the results presented here.

This book's other major audience includes researchers, graduate students, and other scholars interested in the interplay between gender and higher education. Those who are familiar with the literature on the impact of college may appreciate the ways in which this book confirms much of what we know of as "general" effects of college as well as the ways it adds much-needed new knowledge on gender-based "conditional" effects of college. Researchers will find a large number of fertile avenues for future research. Indeed, scholars may wish to replicate the findings generated in this book and/or to address the dozens of new research questions that emerge. As readers will see, these new research questions are not inconsequential. They force us to reconsider all our assumptions about how college affects students, at least if we aim to understand how college affects some students *differently* than others.

Gearing this book to these two major audiences also presents an opportunity to enhance the connection between scholars and practitioners. Ideally, researchers aiming to advance knowledge about gender differences in the impact of college will also aim to convey it in a way that provides relevant information to those who can use it. And while practitioners can apply these findings to their practice, they also have an opportunity to further shape the research agenda on gender in higher education by raising awareness of persistent and emerging gender differences in their interactions with students. Ultimately, greater collaboration between researchers and practitioners will enhance their mutual goal of improving the student experience for both genders.

Studying Gender Difference: An Ethical Dilemma

Readers of this book may also wish to reflect on an important ethical question: What are the consequences of studying gender difference? The answer to this question is a matter of scholarly debate. At first glance, identifying differences between college women and men would seem to be a useful mechanism toward improving the college experience for *both* genders. Surely, if we understand how women and men are unique in their backgrounds, aspirations, preparation, interests, expectations, and goals, it seems logical to conclude that we could use such information to better serve women and men as they prepare for, enroll in, and graduate from college.

However, there is a legitimate argument that the study of gender difference primarily reinforces gender differences. In fact, despite decades of research documenting so-called "statistically significant" differences between males and females, the actual size of the gender gap tends to be quite small (Hyde, 2005). In fact, differences *among* men or women tend to be much larger than differences *between* the sexes (Tavris, 1992). Focusing our attention on gender gaps—no matter how small—may lead us to overstate sex differences, thereby fueling public misconceptions about differences between males and females. An overgeneralized perception of sex differentials can have nontrivial consequences for students, as their academic, occupational, and personal decisions are shaped by years of socialization by parents, teachers, the media, and other sources of influence.

In my view, the benefits of uncovering gender differences far outweigh the potential drawbacks, especially since the alternative is to ignore gender differences altogether. What is important, however, is to engage in thoughtful reflection on the magnitude and meaning of the differences that do exist. Indeed, this book highlights scores of "significant" differences between the sexes, both in students' characteristics and experiences as they enter college and in how they change during college. Further, the very large samples make it fairly easy for sex differentials to be deemed significant from a statistical standpoint. For that reason, this study has adopted stringent standards for determining statistical significance and readily acknowledges that the differences observed between women and men may be only the tip of the iceberg. In fact, while this study advances our understanding of conditional effects of college, one could argue that assessing just one condition (i.e., gender) minimally detects conditional effects.

Thus, this book is a first step in understanding the extent to which college yields *nonuniform* effects on women and men and opens up the door for future research to examine conditional effects *within* gender. In other words, if a college experience relates to a particular outcome for women but not men, we must then ask: Does the experience predict this outcome equally for all women or just certain types of women? Which women are more strongly affected and why? How do race, ethnicity, class, and other factors further shape women's college-going experiences? This sort of questioning and probing of conditional college effects ought to become second nature not only to those of us engaged in research on college impact but also to campus practitioners and decision makers whose everyday efforts should be guided by maximum enlightenment about the ways in which college affects different types of students in different ways.

Who Is Included in the Study?

This book is based on the survey responses of undergraduate women and men attending colleges nationwide over the past four decades. These students participated in surveys conducted by the Cooperative Institutional Research Program (CIRP) at the University of California, Los Angeles. The CIRP is a nationwide program of research designed to study the characteristics and experiences of college students and the ways in which college contributes to students' personal and academic development.

The CIRP is probably best known for its annual Freshman Survey. Initiated in 1966 by Alexander Astin and his colleagues at the American Council on Education, the Freshman Survey is designed to collect a wide range of information on the characteristics of students just as they arrive at college. The data are intended to serve as a baseline for assessing changes in students during the college years. The four-page questionnaire includes questions on students' precollege characteristics, including family background, academic experiences, values, attitudes, life goals, self-ratings, academic major and career aspirations, and expectations for college. Each year, the CIRP collects data on three hundred fifty thousand to four hundred thousand students who constitute the entering first-year classes at approximately six hundred fifty two- and four-year colleges and universities nationwide.

In the forty years since the CIRP's inception, dozens of longitudinal follow-up studies of varying lengths have been conducted. CIRP data have informed seminal books on college students (e.g., Astin, 1977, 1993c; Bowen & Bok, 1998; Pascarella & Terenzini, 1991, 2005) as well as hundreds of studies focusing on issues such as racial/ethnic diversity, gender, retention, civic engagement, and dozens of other critical issues in higher education. Publications based on CIRP data have had an undeniable impact on the field of higher education research and, perhaps more important, the practice of higher education. For an account of CIRP's origins, history, and major trends, see Astin (2003); Pryor, Hurtado, Saenz, Santos, & Korn (2007); and Sax (2003).

This study benefits from two invaluable CIRP databases. The first includes more than 8 million students who participated in the Freshman Survey between 1966 and 2006 at more than one thousand baccalaureate institutions nationwide. The responses of men and women over the past forty years allow us to examine long-term trends in the gender gap. The second major data source is a longitudinal file of students who entered college in 1994 and were followed up in 1998 via the College Student Survey (CSS). The CSS is similar in format to the Freshman Survey and includes information on students' college experiences and their perceptions of college, as well as post-tests of dozens of the items that appear on the Freshman Survey. These longitudinal data enable us to assess how women and men change over the course of college and to explore how college might differentially contribute to those changes.

Organization of This Book

To open up the discussion of college and the gender gap, chapter 2 ("Gender Differences Among Entering College Students") examines male-female differentials among a very recent cohort of students—those who entered college in fall 2006—and discusses present-day gender gaps in the context of long-term trends dating back forty years. Specifically, the chapter focuses on gender differences in the following areas: demographic and financial background; family ties; academic self-confidence and engagement; leisure time; psychological and physical well-being; degree, major, and career aspirations; community orientation; and political and social attitudes.

Chapters 3 and 4 lay the theoretical and methodological groundwork to move the conversation from "How do women and men differ in college?" to "How are women and men differentially affected by college?" Chapter 3 ("Gender and College Student Development") offers theoretical frameworks that can be used to understand the development of college women as potentially distinct from that of men. The chapter also discusses the state of empirical research on gender differences in the impact of college. Chapter 4 ("Approaches to Studying Gender and College Impact") describes how the research for this book was conducted and introduces a model for studying the "conditional" effects of college.

Chapters 5 through 7 tackle this book's central question: Does college affect women and men differently? These chapters are divided into three broad outcome areas: "Personality and Identity" (chapter 5), "Political and Social Values" (chapter 6), and "Academic Outcomes" (chapter 7). These categories bear some similarity to outcome classifications used by Astin (1993c) and Pascarella and Terenzini (1991, 2005) to facilitate the reader's comparison of the findings from this study with the results of earlier work, which was conducted almost exclusively on combined samples of women and men. These three chapters examine a total of twenty-six outcomes of college. For each of the outcomes, regression analyses were conducted separately by gender to compare the magnitude and direction of effect for eighty-six college environments and experiences. Though the results are based on complex statistical analyses, they are presented in a way that readers unfamiliar with statistics should be able to access and understand.

Finally, chapter 8 ("Where Should We Go from Here? Implications of the Gender Gap for Campus Practice and Future Research") brings together the major findings from the book in an attempt to discern patterns of gender difference in the impact of college. It encourages practitioners to consider how they can use these results in their own work and proposes a scholarly agenda to further advance our understanding of gender differences in the impact of college.

2

GENDER DIFFERENCES AMONG ENTERING COLLEGE STUDENTS

Each fall, over 1 million students set foot on campuses across the country to begin their first year of college. They bring with them powerful personal histories—an immense range of experiences with family, education, community, jobs, sports, hobbies, and other interests—that continually shape their choices during college. They also bring with them confidence, doubts, beliefs, values, and hopes—traits that may not be apparent to others but which nevertheless shape their reactions to college. This array of characteristics varies widely across students in any entering class and, ideally, makes for a diverse and vibrant student body.

What campus personnel may not know is the extent to which college men and women differ across these various domains. Too often the focus is on the relative numbers of women and men on campus—with women constituting nearly 60 percent of student bodies nationwide—and not on how college-enrolled women and men differ from each other in potentially important ways. Though they are enrolled in classes together, use the same campus services, and often live in the same residence halls, the backgrounds and needs of college women and men are not the same. Information about these student characteristics is valuable to the campus because it enables planning and programming that addresses incoming students' needs and interests. Knowing, for example, that certain percentages of women or men plan to get involved in volunteer work, seek personal counseling, or play intramural sports allows campuses to distribute resources more efficiently and, ideally, more equitably. Indeed, despite the academic successes of today's college women and policies aimed at promoting gender equity (e.g., Title IX), gender equity has not been fully realized. There continue to be fundamental differences in the backgrounds, values, beliefs, and aspirations of college women and men, all of which have consequences for the opportunities available to students after college. In an effort to inform the gender equity debate, this chapter describes the myriad ways in which women and men differ at college entry as well as how such gender gaps have shifted over the past forty years.

The opportunity to examine the wide range of differences between women and men as they enter college is made possible by the nationwide survey of entering college students conducted by the Cooperative Institutional Research Program at the University of California, Los Angeles (UCLA). To provide an overview of gender differences, this chapter draws on the responses of 271,441 students who participated in the 2006 Freshman Survey at 393 four-year colleges and universities nationwide (Pryor, Hurtado, Saenz, Korn, Santos, & Korn, 2006). Additionally, long-term trends between 1966 and 2006—based on the responses of over 8 million women and men from over 1,000 baccalaureate institutions—are presented for survey questions that display particularly interesting shifts over time for women, men, or the nature of gender differences. (See Pryor, Hurtado, Saenz, Santos, & Korn (2007) for additional trends and details on data collection.)

Discussion of male-female differentials and the implications of this gender gap is organized throughout this chapter around the following thematic areas: demographic and financial background; family ties; academic self-confidence and engagement; leisure time; psychological and physical well-being; degree, major, and career aspirations; community orientation; and political and social attitudes.[1]

Demographic and Financial Background

As already discussed, a rapidly growing female enrollment depicts gender as a major force in shifting college student demographics. We also know that the college student population has become more variable in terms of students' age and more diverse in terms of students' racial/ethnic and economic backgrounds. However, as this section demonstrates, several of these demographic trends take on unique trajectories when examined separately for women and men.

Age

Though the majority of both women and men enter four-year colleges and universities at the traditional age of seventeen or eighteen, male students tend to be older than female students, a gender gap that has widened over the past four decades. Today, approximately one in three men enter a four-year college for the first time at age nineteen or older, compared to only one in four women.[2] Interestingly, this age differential is not a function of men taking more time off between high school and college; in fact, the vast majority of both genders enter four-year colleges and universities directly from high school. Instead, the age gap likely stems from the fact that boys are more likely than girls to be held back a year in the elementary and secondary grades or to start school a year later than girls, a practice known as kindergarten redshirting (Mead, 2006; West, Meek, & Hurst, 2000). While there is some research on the effect that delayed kindergarten entry has on elementary school students—generally revealing mixed results (Stipek, 2001)— little is known about the impact of this age differential on students as they transition from high school to college. Future research will need to address whether and how the presence of a slightly older male population affects the experience of college women and men.

Race

Though the majority of men and women in four-year colleges and universities identify themselves as white/Caucasian, over the past four decades the proportion of students in this category has declined from over 90 percent to about 75 percent (see table 2.1). Though the relative decline in the number of white/Caucasian students has been similar for women and men, the growing racial/ethnic diversity in the student population has not manifested itself in the same ways for the two genders. Since the early 1970s, for example, increases in the proportional representation of African American/Black and Asian American/Asian students have been greater among males than females. Also, relative gains in the proportion of students identifying themselves as Chicano/Latino have been larger among women than men. Presently, women are more likely than men to identify themselves as African American/Black, Chicano/Latino, American Indian/Alaska Native, or "other," while men are more likely than women to be Asian. These gender differences in racial composition are consistent with those reported in other research on traditional-age college students (King, 2006). They signify that among today's college students, women are more likely than men to come from racial/ethnic groups that have been historically marginalized in education and tend to come from lower-income backgrounds, as we'll soon see.

Financial Background

One of the most important student trends is the emergence of an economic gender gap. Whereas median family income was once equivalent for male and female students, family income for men entering college in 2006 was about $12,000 higher than for female students (see figure 2.1). Perhaps even more telling is that since 1966, median family incomes for male students have increased by approximately 42 percent, relative to a 16 percent increase among the women. These results extend and highlight

Table 2.1 Racial/Ethnic Composition of First-Year Students, 1971-2006

	Women						Men					
	1971	1976	1986	1996	2006	1971	1976	1986	1996	2006
White/Caucasian	90.0	85.3	83.8	78.3	75.5	91.8	87.2	86.4	79.3	77.8
African American/Black	8.5	11.7	11.0	12.1	11.2	6.6	9.2	8.0	9.5	9.6
Asian American/Asian	0.5	1.1	2.8	5.0	8.3	0.6	1.2	3.2	6.4	9.2
Chicano/Latino[a]	0.5	1.1	1.9	5.0	9.0	0.6	1.2	1.8	4.8	7.3
American Indian	1.0	1.0	1.0	2.5	2.3	0.9	1.0	0.9	2.2	2.2
Other	1.0	1.3	1.5	2.6	3.8	1.0	1.5	1.6	2.7	3.4

Note: Weighted national figures abstracted from Pryor et al. (2007). This table begins in 1971 because the Freshman Survey assessed racial background differently between 1966 and 1970. Columns do not sum to 100 because some respondents marked more than one race/ethnicity.

[a]Includes Mexican American/Chicano, Puerto Rican, and other Latino.

Figure 2.1 Median Family Income of Entering First-Year Students, 1966-2006 (in Constant 2006 Dollars)

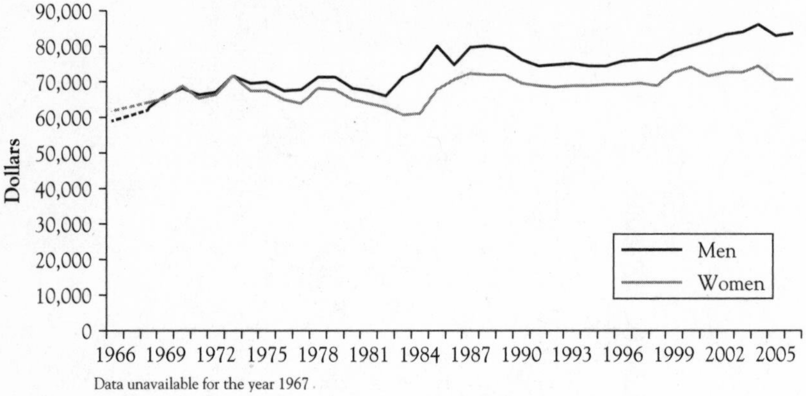

Data unavailable for the year 1967

Note: Calculated from weighted national figures in Pryor et al. (2007).

findings reported by Lindholm, Astin, Choi, and Gutierrez-Zamano (2002), who found that "the greatest growth in enrollments for women has occurred among low-income women" (p. 34). In fact, whereas women are the majority of college students nationwide, they are a slight *minority* among students from high-income families.

Women's socioeconomic status relative to men's also can be seen by examining trends in parental education. Although women attending college in the 1960s were more likely than men to have college-educated mothers and fathers, this trend reversed in the late 1970s, and the gap continues to widen (see figures 2.2 and 2.3). Today, 56.4 percent of men and 50.1 percent of women have fathers who graduated from college, and 55.5 percent of men and 50.5 percent of women have mothers who graduated from college. In other words, just as we have witnessed a growing gender gap in family income that now favors men, we have also seen emerging disparities in levels of parental education, with men more likely than women to report that their parents graduated from college.

From a campus perspective, it is important to know that low-income, first-generation college students are now more

**Figure 2.2 Mother's Education, 1966-2006: Percentage
with College Degree or Higher**

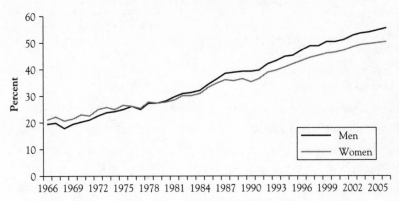

Note: Weighted national figures abstracted from Pryor et al. (2007).

**Figure 2.3 Father's Education, 1966-2006: Percentage
with College Degree or Higher**

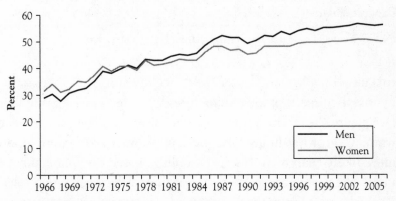

Note: Weighted national figures abstracted from Pryor et al. (2007).

likely to be women than men and that this trend seems likely to
continue. For one thing, it suggests that campuses need to be
prepared to meet the needs of women who are struggling financially while in school. In fact, as shown in table 2.2, first-year
college women are particularly worried about how they are going
to finance their college education. Approximately 70 percent of
women have "some" or "major" concerns about their ability to pay
for college, compared to 58 percent of men. Gender differences on

Table 2.2 Gender Differences in Financial Background Among First-Year Students, Fall 2006

	Women (%)	Men (%)	Diff. (W – M)
Finances			
Concern about financing college (some or major)	69.5	57.5	+12.0
Reasons for choosing this college (very important)			
Offers of financial assistance	37.2	30.7	+6.5
Graduates get "good jobs"	51.8	46.1	+5.7
Reason for going to college (very important)			
Make more money	66.6	71.9	−5.3
Future activity (very good chance)			
Get a job to help pay for college	50.2	36.5	+13.7
Goals (very important or essential)			
Be well-off financially	72.4	74.6	−2.2
Be successful in own business	37.9	46.7	−8.8

Note: Weighted national norms abstracted from Pryor et al. (2006).

this item have widened over the years, revealing net increases in financial concern among women and net decreases among men (see figure 2.4). The process of choosing a college also reflects women's growing financial concerns. Women, for example, are more likely than men to select a college based on financial assistance offers or because graduates of that college get "good jobs." As such, it is clear that women place greater importance not only on financing college but also on their employment options after graduation.

Given these trends, it is not surprising that women are more likely than men to anticipate getting a job during college. The expectation to seek employment while attending school produces one of the more interesting trends in the Freshman Survey's history. Since 1976, when women and men were equally likely to anticipate employment during college, the increase in anticipated

Figure 2.4 Financial Concern, 1966-2006: Percentage Reporting "Some" or "Major" Concern

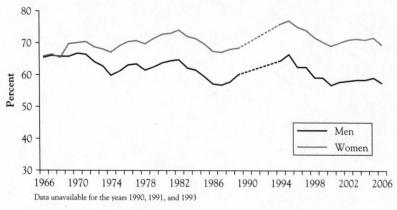

Data unavailable for the years 1990, 1991, and 1993

Note: Weighted national figures abstracted from Pryor et al. (2007).

employment has been substantially higher for women. Presently, half of all college women think there is a very good chance that they will seek employment while in college, compared to just over one-third of the men. Although one might easily attribute this to women's lower family income, gender differences are readily apparent across *all* income levels, with women at each level notably more inclined than men to report a "very good chance" that they will get a job to help offset college costs (see table 2.3), a fact that has become more pronounced over time.

Table 2.3 Gender Differences in Income and Employment Expectations Among First-year Students, Fall 2006: Percentage Reporting a "Very Good Chance" That They Will Have to Get a Job to Pay for College Expenses

Family income	Women	Men	Diff. (W – M)
$100,000 or more	34.9	25.4	+9.5
$60,000–99,999	54.6	41.4	+13.2
$30,000–59,999	60.0	46.0	+14.0
Less than $30,000	59.9	45.1	+14.8

Figure 2.5 Goal: Being Well-Off Financially, 1966–2006: Percentage Reporting "Very Important" or "Essential"

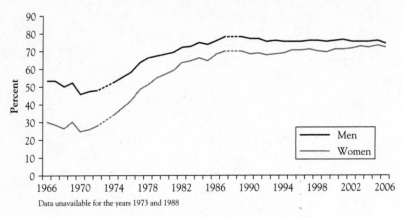

Data unavailable for the years 1973 and 1988

Note: Weighted national figures abstracted from Pryor et al. (2007).

Finally, consistent with the increase in women's immediate financial concerns, women are becoming more concerned about their long-term financial well-being. Whereas interest in being very well-off financially was markedly higher among men than women in the 1960s, by 2006 women had nearly caught up to men on this item (see figure 2.5). Despite these shifts, men continue to hold more entrepreneurial aspirations than women, with 46.7 percent of men and only 37.9 percent of women entering college with a commitment to becoming successful in a business of their own.

As more men and women from diverse backgrounds enter college, campus personnel should be aware of, and responsive to, students' changing financial needs. Gender differences are particularly important to acknowledge because women's financial concerns and need for employment are higher than men's. Thus, the ongoing shift in federal financial aid from grants to loans and work-study may present a particular challenge to female students. Also, campus staff and faculty should be mindful that many women have continuing—and *unpaid*—responsibilities to their families.

Family Ties

Parents play an important role in students' college lives, both before and during college. They might encourage their children to pursue a college preparatory curriculum, help them through the college application process, and guide them in selecting a particular college. Some parents may play a less active role in their child's transition to college, especially if the parents did not attend college themselves. One question is whether the role of family is *different* for male and female students. Only a few items on the survey shed light on this question, though they provide some evidence that women college students have a stronger connection to family than do men.

First, women are more likely than men to attend college to satisfy their parents' wishes; 48.9 percent of women note this as an important reason for attending college versus 43.3 percent of men. Second, women are more likely than men to select a particular college to live near home, although the numbers are fairly small for both genders (21.5 percent of women versus 14.4 percent of men). Interestingly, despite the greater value women place on living near home, there is practically no gender difference in the distance students travel to attend college, whether it's less than ten miles (10.8 percent of women versus 10.4 percent of men) or as much as three thousand miles (13.4 percent of women versus 13.6 percent of men). Thus, it appears that while women and men are equally likely to live near home, proximity to family is more *important* to women. Finally, women students are more likely than men to assist the family with household and/or childcare duties in the year before starting college (65.5 percent of women versus 51.7 percent of men).

Other research has also demonstrated a stronger connection to family among women students relative to men.[3] An important question is how women's relationships with family members influence their development during college. Though the research on this question is sparse, some evidence suggests that especially close relationships with family members can be *mal-*adaptive for women students because they impede those students' self-assessed emotional adjustment in the first year of college (Sax, Bryant, & Gilmartin, 2004). In other words, while women and their parents may aim to stay highly connected during college—a goal easily attainable via cellular phones and e-mail—it may not be in the students' best interests. Colleges can thus serve an important role by guiding female students and their families in how to stay connected without compromising the students' autonomy and sense of independence. Because parents may be more protective of their daughters and grant more autonomy to their sons (Lundgren & Rudawasky, 1998), it is crucial that student affairs units support programming that helps female students create a sense of self-reliance. For example, campus health centers or psychological services can offer students seminars or one-on-one counseling on how to develop independence while at college. Although evidence suggests that men's development of autonomy is less strongly tied to their family connections, the same advice may also be relevant to them.

Parent programs are another way in which campus practitioners have responded to parents' increased desire to stay connected to their children. Parent orientation sessions provide information that can help ease fears and educate parents about the services offered on campus to support students and to provide them with space to grow during college. Parent-specific portals on university Web sites are another way to keep parents informed about specific campus resources, such as student psychological services or women's centers. These resources often provide a range of programs—including one-on-one counseling, self-defense programs, mentoring programs, and support groups—for different types of women, including mothers and women of color.

Academic Self-Confidence and Engagement

As women have come to dominate enrollments on campuses nationwide, they are often portrayed as an academic success story. Popular conceptions of today's youth tend to characterize women as achievers and men as slackers. However, women's seemingly strong academic orientation is tempered by a comparatively low academic self-concept. Campus personnel should be mindful of the potential disconnect between women's performance and their self-confidence.

Indeed, first-year college women rate themselves lower than men on nearly every self-rating related to academic or intellectual confidence: just over half of women consider themselves to be "above average" or "highest 10 percent" in intellectual self-confidence, compared with over two-thirds of the men. Women also express less confidence than men in their mathematical ability and academic ability. Only in the area of writing ability do women report higher levels of confidence than do men, and the differences here are fairly small (see table 2.4).

These results are consistent with decades of research on gender and self-confidence, but why do women underestimate their skills and abilities? Do women actually view themselves as less academically capable than men, or are they simply more modest in their self-assessments? Prior research, for example, has shown women to indicate lower levels of mathematical confidence than men, even when their *demonstrated* math abilities are equal to or greater than men's (Marsh, Smith, & Barnes, 1985; Sax, 1994c; Sherman, 1983). Sadker and Sadker (1994) also discuss a phenomenon by which "girls, especially smart girls, learn to underestimate their ability" (p. 95) and more often attribute their intelligence to hard work than to innate ability. Conversely, adolescent boys have been shown to exhibit a sometimes outsized sense of self that's not always commensurate with their academic achievement (Sadker & Sadker, 1994).

Table 2.4 Gender Differences in Academic Self-Confidence and Engagement Among First-Year Students, Fall 2006

	Women (%)	Men (%)	Diff. (W – M)
Self-ratings (above average or highest 10%)			
Intellectual self-confidence	52.2	68.8	−16.6
Mathematical ability	35.9	53.1	−17.2
Academic ability	65.9	71.9	−6.0
Writing ability	49.3	45.7	+3.6
Reasons for going to college (very important)			
Gain a general education	69.9	57.5	+12.4
Learn more about things that interest them	80.6	72.1	+8.5
Reason for choosing this college (very important)			
Academic reputation	61.4	52.4	+9.0
Time allocation			
Studying or homework 6+ hours per week	37.6	26.9	+10.7
Student clubs/groups 3+ hours per week	37.0	25.8	+11.2
Talking with instructors 1+ hours per week	51.1	43.8	+7.3
Classroom engagement (frequently or occasionally)			
Was bored in class	39.3	43.0	−3.7
Came late to class	59.2	62.3	−3.1
High school grades			
A or A+	24.9	18.3	+6.6
A−	26.0	21.7	+4.3
B+	21.9	21.2	+0.7
B	18.7	23.2	−4.5
C+ or B−	7.7	13.7	−6.0
C or lower	0.7	2.0	−1.3

Note: Weighted national norms abstracted from Pryor et al. (2006).

Perhaps women's lower self-ratings stem from the way these questions are posed on the survey, where students are asked to rate their abilities as "compared to the average person your age." Women may be more reluctant to report their skills as higher than others because doing so may denote a competitive orientation that may be unappealing to many women. In fact, historically the largest gender difference observed across all self-rating measures has been on competitiveness, with 70 percent of men and only 45 percent of women rating themselves highly on this item.[4]

Despite women's lower academic self-confidence at college entry, other survey items point to a stronger academic orientation relative to men. When it comes to motives for attending college, women are more likely than men to rate the following as "very important" reasons for attending college: to gain a general education and appreciation of ideas, to learn more about things that interest them, and to improve their study skills.[5] Further, when selecting a *particular* college, women place more importance than men on academic reputation.

In addition to being more academically oriented when they arrive at college, women also exhibit more consistent patterns of academic engagement. Women spend significantly more time studying or doing homework in the last year of high school than men; 37.6 percent of them studied six or more hours per week, compared to only 26.9 percent of men. It is worth noting, however, that study time for both genders has decreased substantially over time. Women are also more likely than men to talk with their high school teachers outside class and to participate in student clubs and groups. Men, on the other hand, are slightly more likely than women to feel bored in class or to come late to class—patterns of behavior that persist from high school to college

Women's greater time on task appears to pay off in terms of their grades: 50.9 percent of women earned at least an A- in high school, compared with 40.0 percent of men. Figure 2.6 shows that as students spend more time studying, their grades improve and that women earn higher grades than men *regardless* of how much time they spend studying. The gender gap in high school grades has a long history on the survey, even as grades have risen dramatically for all students (see figure 2.7). Clearly,

Figure 2.6 Percentage Earning an A- or Higher High School GPA, by Time Spent Studying, Fall 2006

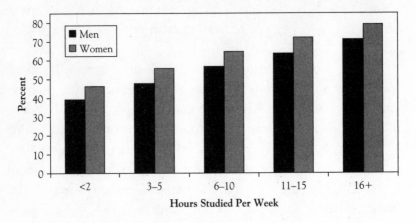

Figure 2.7 Percentage Earning A and C Grades in High School, 1966-2006

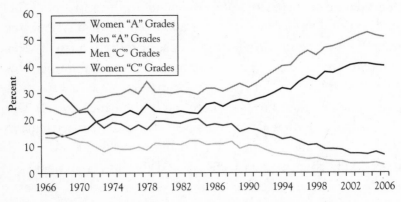

Note: "A" grades include A−, A, A+, "C" grades include C or C+. Weighted national figures abstracted from Pryor et al. (2007).

men and women are equal beneficiaries of "grade inflation," a phenomenon witnessed at both the high school and college levels (Rosovsky & Hartley, 2002; Sax, 2003).

What should we make of the results presented in this section? On the one hand, women reveal comparatively low academic and intellectual self-confidence. On the other hand, women are achieving at higher levels than men and are more strongly oriented toward the academic aspects of college life. Clearly, campus practitioners must be attuned to the differential needs and experiences of both genders. In particular, they should encourage a stronger sense of self-confidence in female students because getting good grades does not guarantee that women will make favorable academic or intellectual self-assessments. In other words, competence does not always translate into confidence. Thus, faculty and practitioners should not discount the concerns of female students who, despite a string of academic successes, doubt their ability to do well in their classes, thrive in their major, or pursue graduate school. Academic counselors and others who help students with academic decision making should know that low self-confidence—whether genuine or a facade—can inhibit students' academic aspirations and motivations.

Campus personnel also need to consider strategies to engage men more in the academic aspects of college. To do so, they must question what leads men to spend less time studying and to skip class more often. Does this reflect the relatively lower value that men place on the intellectual benefits of college, as reported earlier? Does men's stronger sense of confidence lead them to underestimate the importance of studying or attending class? How do men spend their time that might account for their lower grades and, as reported in other studies, higher college dropout rates? The next section provides some clues to these questions.

Leisure Time

How do men and women choose to spend their free time? Admittedly, it is difficult to pinpoint exactly what constitutes a leisure-time activity. Certainly, watching television and drinking beer are easy to characterize as leisure activities, but other behaviors included in this section—such as participation in sports—are not necessarily free-time activities. Nevertheless,

Figure 2.8 Time Spent Exercising or Playing Sports, 1987-2006: Percentage Reporting 6 or More Hours Per Week

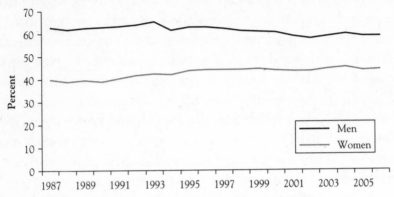

Note: Weighted national figures abstracted from Pryor et al. (2007).

women's and men's choices about how to use their out-of-class time reveal important differences that may explain some of the gender differences in academics discussed in the prior section.

A clear and long-standing gender gap is evident when it comes to the amount of time that students devote to sports and exercise. Though the gender gap has narrowed somewhat over time, men continue to spend significantly more time than women exercising or playing sports (see figure 2.8). A report by the American Association of University Women (AAUW) also documents differences between women and men in physical activity, a difference that is considered to have negative implications in other areas since physical activity is associated with the chance to develop competitive and leadership skills, "higher self-esteem, positive body image, and lifelong health" (AAUW Educational Foundation, 1998, p. 20). Furthermore, physical activity clearly reduces stress, and as we will find later in the chapter, college women report higher levels of stress than college men.

Men also report spending significantly more time than women in front of the television and playing video or computer games. In fact, a full 22 percent of college men devote six or more hours per week to video and computer games, compared to only 3.8 percent of women. Though some would rightly argue that men ought to spend less time playing video games and more time studying, it is also worth noting that playing computer and video games contributes to a sense of comfort and familiarity with technology, thereby strengthening students' interest in computer science and other technical fields (Margolis & Fisher, 2002). Thus, to the extent that women opt out of the video game culture—due in part to the fact that games tend to be designed for male users—one consequence is the long-standing and vast underrepresentation of women in technological fields, as demonstrated later in this chapter.

Drinking and smoking represent another dimension to students' leisure time. As they enter college, men and women report fairly similar rates of cigarette smoking and wine and alcohol consumption. However, men report significantly higher rates of beer drinking (37.3 percent for women versus 48.5 percent for men) and other forms of partying. Approximately half of men report drinking beer in their last year in high school, relative to just over one-third of women (see table 2.5). While

Table 2.5 Gender Differences in Leisure Time Among First-Year Students, Fall 2006

	Women (%)	Men (%)	Diff. (W − M)
Activities (6+ hours per week)			
Exercising or sports	44.0	58.9	−14.9
Watching TV	22.6	30.8	−8.2
Reading for pleasure	12.2	8.5	+3.7
Partying	18.9	25.6	−6.7
Playing video/computer games	3.8	22.0	−18.2
Activities (frequently or occasionally)			
Drinking beer	37.3	48.5	−11.2
Drinking wine/liquor	47.8	49.6	−1.8
Smoking cigarettes	4.9	5.7	−0.8

Note: Weighted national norms abstracted from Pryor et al. (2006).

both college women and men may benefit from campus alcohol and drug abuse awareness programs, practitioners may want to consider whether they want to adopt different approaches for male and female students.

To summarize, some of the largest gender differences in leisure time are that men spend more time than women partying, drinking beer, playing sports, and watching television. These findings partially answer the question raised in the prior section about what men are doing when they are not studying, doing homework, or attending classes. It could be said that men are finding more time to simply have fun and let loose in college. Though these behaviors can bring about potentially negative consequences, they also can yield psychological benefits, such as reducing stress, as the next section highlights. The challenge for campus practitioners is to create programming that provides healthy outlets for all students. Men, for example, should be persuaded to participate in more positive out-of-class activities, such as community service. And women should be encouraged to strike a healthier balance between academics and leisure. This is a valuable lesson for women to learn because these gendered behavior patterns are not exclusive to college; they often appear in the larger population as well.

Psychological and Physical Well-Being

In the past ten years, much attention has been devoted to adolescents' low self-esteem. Research studies and popular books have documented what researchers call the "self-esteem slide" (Sadker & Sadker, 1994, p. 77), which is said to occur among preadolescent and teenage girls (AAUW Educational Foundation, 1992; Deak, 2002; Orenstein, 1994; Pipher, 1995). It is argued that, on the brink of womanhood, many of today's girls succumb to society's messages about the importance of social success and physical attractiveness. If girls buy into this message, they open the door to a whole host of potential consequences, including a loss of self-esteem, depression, and eating disorders.

Research on adolescent boys, too, has found them at risk for low self-esteem, underachievement, and dropping out of school. Advocates for boys argue that the consequences for boys are often much more extreme or violent (Hoff Sommers, 2000; Kindlon & Thompson, 1999; Pollack, 1999). Rather than take sides in a zero-sum game, let us acknowledge that research seems to suggest that both girls and boys experience a loss of self-confidence during adolescence that can impact both their psychological well-being and their academic achievement. What do we find as these young women and men reach college?

First, just as we found for academic self-ratings, women rate themselves lower than men on a number of psychological measures. For example, 48.5 percent of women rate their emotional health as "above average" or "highest 10 percent" versus 62.2 percent of men, a gender gap among first-year students that has remained stable in recent decades (see table 2.6).

Consistent with their lower ratings on emotional health, women report higher levels of stress than men, with more than twice as

Table 2.6 Gender Differences in Psychological Well-Being Among First-Year Students, Fall 2006

	Women (%)	Men (%)	Diff. (W – M)
Self-ratings (above average or highest 10%)			
Emotional health	48.5	62.2	−13.7
Physical health	46.3	67.2	−20.9
Behaviors (frequently)			
Felt overwhelmed	38.0	17.3	+20.7
Felt depressed	9.0	5.3	+3.7
Student estimates (very good chance)			
Seek personal counseling	9.1	6.1	+3.0

Note: Weighted national norms abstracted from Pryor et al. (2006).

Figure 2.9 Percentage That Felt Frequently "Overwhelmed by All I Had to Do," 1985–2006

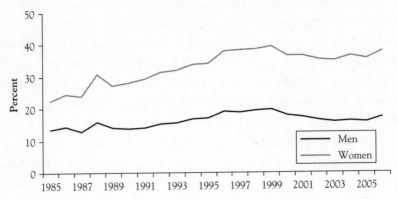

Note: Weighted national figures abstracted from Pryor et al. (2007).

many women as men reporting that they frequently feel over-whelmed by all they have to do. Notably, the gender gap in feelings of stress has grown wider over the years (see figure 2.9). Similarly, women are more likely than men to report frequent feelings of depression, although the numbers are relatively small for both groups. Other research has also found higher rates of depression among women than men (McGrath, Keita, Strickland, & Russo, 1990), a difference that seems to emerge in early or middle adolescence (Nolen-Hoeksema & Girgus, 1994). Additionally, while the difference between men and women is small, women are more likely to anticipate seeking out personal counseling in college.

Related to students' sense of psychological well-being is their sense of physical well-being. At college entry, women rate their physical health significantly lower than men, with more than two-thirds of men—and less than half of women—believing that their physical health is "above average" or in the "highest 10 percent" relative to their peers. As with other measures of self-confidence discussed thus far, it is concerning that women have—or choose to report—weaker self-concepts than men regarding their physical well-being. In this case, we must also consider the standards that men and women use in assessing physical well-being. For example, as we will see in chapter 5, men's sense of physical health is more strongly tied to sports and exercise than it is for women. To some extent, then, men's stronger sense of physical health is a function of the greater amount of time they spend exercising or playing sports.

Thus, campuses must be prepared for the fact that as the number of women entering college has grown, so too have the number of students with health and wellness concerns. This probably comes as no surprise to those working in student counseling and psychological services, who have witnessed an increase in the number of students seeking out these services (Kitzrow, 2003). Campuses must also be on the lookout for those students who might benefit from such services but do not seek them out.

Practitioners should be even more proactive in educating students about the services offered on campus, not just at orientation, but also throughout students' years at college. Resources provided through residential life, the student health clinic, recreation departments, student psychological services, academic advising, and career centers should continually remind students about where to go for help with stress, depression, poor body image, or other health concerns. Each of these units should think independently, as well as collaboratively, about what programming could provide students of both genders with ideas to alleviate stress in productive and healthy ways. UCLA's Fitwell program, for instance, offers students a comprehensive and integrated fitness, nutrition, and stress management program that educates and empowers them to make healthy lifestyle choices throughout their college career.

Degree, Major, and Career Aspirations

Historically, college students' major choices and degree aspirations have closely related to the career opportunities available to them. Gendered patterns in career choice were accentuated during the 1950s and 1960s, but the wide disparities in choice of major, degree attainment, and career aspirations began to narrow dramatically during the 1970s and 1980s. This was due in no small part to federal legislation regarding equal pay as well as Title IX and affirmative action legislation. Today, with more women pursuing graduate and professional degrees and nontraditional occupations, the public perception seems to be that the gap in opportunities between college men and women has all but disappeared. As we'll see, the data indicate a significant convergence of the gender gap when it comes to level of degree aspiration, but not always when it comes to the specific academic and career fields students plan to pursue.

Degree Aspirations

Marking a significant shift over the past few decades, women are now more likely than men to plan to attend graduate or professional school. As shown in table 2.7, currently 32.3 percent of women and 29.0 percent of men plan to earn doctoral degrees, including the PhD, MD, and JD. This marks a substantial shift

Table 2.7 Gender Differences in Degree Aspirations Among First-Year Students, Fall 2006

	Women (%)	Men (%)	Diff. (W − M)
Degree aspirations			
Bachelor's (BA, BS, etc.)	21.8	25.5	−3.7
Master's degree (MA, MS, etc.)	42.6	42.2	+0.4
PhD or EdD	17.3	16.4	+0.9
MD, DDS, DVM, or DO	10.4	7.7	+2.7
LLB or JD (law)	4.6	4.9	−0.3
Reason for going to college (very important)			
Prepare for graduate school	63.1	51.0	+12.1
Reason for choosing this college (very important)			
Graduates admitted to top graduate schools	33.3	26.3	+7.0

Note: Weighted national norms abstracted from Pryor et al. (2006).

in the gender gap over the past forty years, as only 8.6 percent of women entering college in 1966 aspired to doctoral degrees, compared to 28.3 percent of men at that time. Today's male and female students almost equally aspire for master's degrees, with 42.6 percent of women and 42.2 percent of men planning to earn a master's. Given women's growing interest in earning graduate degrees, it is not surprising that women are more likely than men to indicate that they are attending college to prepare for graduate or professional school and to select their college because the school's graduates are admitted into top-ranked graduate and professional schools. Yet, while their degree aspirations have surpassed men, women still tend—with a few notable exceptions—to choose sex-stereotyped majors and careers.

Intended Major

The Freshman Survey includes a list of eighty-two academic majors, which have been grouped into eighteen different categories (see table 2.8). At college entry, women are significantly more likely than men to plan to major in education, psychology, and health fields, but they are much less likely than men to major in engineering and business. For the most part, these results reflect long-standing sex differences in major selection that are well documented in other studies (e.g., Astin, Oseguera, Sax, & Korn, 2002; Gati, Osipow, & Givon, 1995; Jacobs, 1986, 1996; Little, 2002; Morgan, Isaac, & Sansone, 2001; Sax, 1996; Stickel & Bonett, 1991). They also may reflect women's reported lower confidence in their mathematical abilities, as discussed earlier. In particular, elementary education and engineering stand out as two major areas that reveal an enduring gender gap over the years.

However, in some cases, choice of major signals a reversal of historical patterns. For example, in the 1960s and 1970s, male students predominated the biological sciences. Interest in biology converged among the sexes in the 1980s, and during the 1990s, a new pattern of female predominance in the biological sciences emerged. By 2000, U.S. women earned over 80 percent

Table 2.8 Gender Differences in Major Selection Among First-Year Students, Fall 2006

	Women (%)	Men (%)	Diff. (W − M)
Engineering	2.5	14.5	−12.0
Business	13.6	23.6	−10.0
Computer science	0.4	3.0	−2.6
History or political science	4.5	5.7	−1.2
Physical sciences	2.0	2.8	−0.8
Agriculture or forestry	0.4	0.9	−0.5
Architecture/urban planning	0.4	0.7	−0.3
Mathematics or statistics	0.6	0.9	−0.3
Technical/applied majors	1.1	1.3	−0.2
Fine arts	5.5	4.8	+0.7
Social sciences	3.3	2.6	+0.7
Undecided	7.8	6.4	+1.4
Humanities/English	5.2	3.7	+1.5
Biological sciences	9.2	7.4	+1.8
Journalism/communications	5.1	3.0	+2.1
Psychology	6.6	2.6	+4.0
Education	12.5	5.9	+6.6
Health professions	15.7	6.2	+9.5

Note: Weighted national norms abstracted from Pryor et al. (2006).

of the master's degrees in the health professions and related sciences and over 40 percent of degrees in medicine (U.S. Department of Education, 2004).

Career Aspirations

Gender differences in career choice mirror those found for major preferences. Upon entering college, women are more likely than men to plan to become elementary school teachers, health professionals, and nurses, while men are more likely than women to aspire toward careers in engineering, business, and computer programming. These differences generally reflect historical trends in men's and women's relative career aspirations. Women's continued preference for less financially lucrative careers, however, is perplexing given their self-reported financial concerns and their goal to get a "good job," as reported earlier. Clearly, gender-based socialization continues to drive certain career choices. (See table 2.9 for gender differences across career categories.)

Table 2.9 Gender Differences in Career Aspirations Among First-Year Students, Fall 2006

	Women (%)	Men (%)	Diff. (W − M)
Engineer	2.0	11.7	−9.7
Business professional	11.6	20.7	−9.1
Computer programmer	0.3	3.4	−3.1
Military	0.4	2.1	−1.7
Law enforcement officer	0.5	2.0	−1.5
Farmer/forester	0.3	0.8	−0.5
Architect	0.5	1.0	−0.5
Clergy	0.2	0.5	−0.3
Research scientist	1.7	2.0	−0.3
College teacher	0.4	0.6	−0.2
Business clerk	0.6	0.8	−0.2
Homemaker	0.1	0.1	0.0
Lawyer	4.0	3.8	+0.2
Secondary teacher	5.4	4.8	+0.6
Undecided	14.4	13.5	+0.9
Social worker	1.5	0.3	+1.2
Doctor/dentist/physician	7.9	6.4	+1.5
Psychologist	2.2	0.7	+1.5
Artist	9.1	7.3	+1.8
Health professional	8.9	4.5	+4.4
Nurse	6.8	0.8	+6.0
Elementary teacher	7.9	1.0	+6.9

Note: Weighted national norms abstracted from Pryor et al. (2006).

Figure 2.10 Career Aspiration: Lawyer, 1966-2006

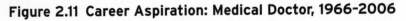

Data unavailable for the years 1973–1975

Note: Weighted national figures abstracted from Pryor et al. (2007).

However, it is important to point out several careers in which gender gaps have been eliminated over time. In nearly all cases, these include careers that have been historically male dominated, such as careers in law and medicine that converged in the 1980s and 1990s, respectively (see figures 2.10 and 2.11). These trends reflect the dramatic narrowing of the gender gap in law and medical degrees conferred in the United States over the past several decades (U.S. Department of Education, 2003).

Figure 2.11 Career Aspiration: Medical Doctor, 1966-2006

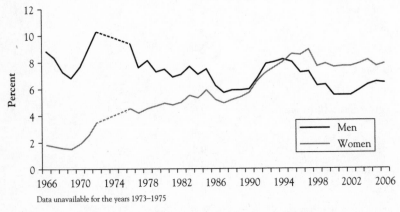

Data unavailable for the years 1973–1975

Note: Weighted national figures abstracted from Pryor et al. (2007).

Figure 2.12 Career Aspiration: Secondary School Teacher, 1966-2006

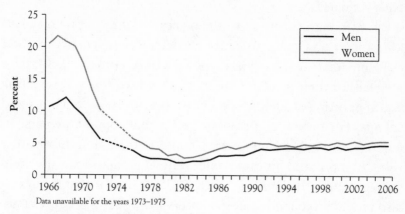

Data unavailable for the years 1973-1975

Note: Weighted national figures abstracted from Pryor et al. (2007).

In one instance, the genders have converged on a career choice that was once dominated by women: secondary education. As shown in figure 2.12, when the survey began in 1966, women were approximately twice as likely as men to express an interest in secondary education, a gap that has nearly converged. Incidentally, gender differences with regard to elementary education have also narrowed over the survey's history, but women remain far more likely to aspire toward that career than do men.

Campus personnel—most notably academic advisers, career counselors, and faculty—need to be aware of women's and men's shifting career interests. Professionals in such roles should advise students that *no* career is inappropriate for their gender but that they ought to prepare for the realities that they may face in their chosen field. For example, though women increasingly possess the interest and academic preparation to succeed in computer science and engineering, they often are not prepared for the unwelcoming climate that those fields offer (Margolis & Fisher, 2002; Seymour & Hewitt, 1997). By the same token, men should be encouraged to keep an open mind regarding careers traditionally dominated by women, such as nursing—a field that faces staff shortages, provides flexible work hours and competitive salaries, and stands to benefit from increased interest among both genders.

To debunk gender-based stereotypes about appropriate careers for women and men, students need to feel supported in their academic endeavors, especially if they have chosen a field that's atypical for their gender. One way to achieve this is by creating and supporting academic student groups for specific majors and careers. For example, a student group that supports women in engineering is a valuable tool for retaining and motivating women interested in that field. These groups not only help women meet other students with similar career interests but can also provide role models, foster interviewing skills, offer resume-building advice, and more. Such a valuable network of information can allow students in sex-atypical careers and majors a way to succeed in their chosen field. Further analysis and discussion of students' pursuit of sex-atypical career choices appears in chapter 7.

Community Orientation

Much of the literature over the past twenty years on women's development depicts women as having a stronger sense of community and "other orientation" than men. Theorists such as Chodorow (1978) and Gilligan (1982)—as well as later studies by Josselson (1987), Holmbeck and Wandrei (1993), and Belenky, Clinchy, Goldberger, and Tarule (1997)—noted the importance of attachment, connection, and communion with others as central to understanding women's development.

Indeed, several items on the Freshman Survey illustrate these types of gender differences (see table 2.10). From a list of nearly two dozen life goals, the largest gender difference is in students' commitment to helping others in difficulty, a goal deemed "very important" or "essential" by 73.1 percent of women versus only 58.9 percent of men. Women are also significantly more

Table 2.10 Gender Differences in Community Orientation Among First-Year Students, Fall 2006

	Women (%)	Men (%)	Diff. (W − M)
Goals (very important or essential)			
Help others in difficulty	73.1	58.9	+14.2
Influence social values	45.2	39.2	+6.0
Participate in community programs	30.8	22.4	+8.4
Promote racial understanding	36.0	31.5	+4.5
Self-rating (above average or highest 10%)			
Understanding of others	68.7	64.5	+4.2
Activities (frequently or occasionally)			
Performed volunteer work	85.8	77.5	+8.3
Tutored another student	54.9	49.7	+5.2
Future activity (very good chance)			
Volunteer or community service work	34.6	17.0	+17.6

Note: Weighted national norms abstracted from Pryor et al. (2006).

likely than men to commit to influencing social values, participating in community action programs, and promoting racial understanding.

Women's stronger commitment to improving the lives of others, as expressed in terms of their more compassionate value orientations, translates directly into action. Women are more likely than men to perform volunteer work or tutor other students in the year before college. They are also twice as likely as men to anticipate getting involved in volunteer or service work during college.

These findings present both opportunities and challenges for campus practitioners. On the one hand, the vast majority of women and men enter college with volunteer or community service experience under their belts, which is an opportunity for campuses wishing to promote civic engagement among their students because prior service is the best predictor of subsequent service (Astin, Sax, & Avalos, 1999). On the other hand, campuses are challenged to engage more men in service activities. Campuses must be proactive in encouraging men to seek out service opportunities and may need to be mindful of how best to engage them. Although helping others may not be a strong factor in motivating men toward involvement in community service, perhaps understanding the individual benefits service provides, such as an increased likelihood of graduating from college and the acquisition of important job skills, would entice them (Astin, Sax, & Avalos, 1999). Another way to involve more men in service is to incorporate service-learning into courses taken by large numbers of men, such as in business and engineering fields. Such opportunities would not only enhance men's commitment to their communities but also relate to other important outcomes, such as improved grades, writing skills, and critical-thinking skills (Astin, Vogelgesang, Ikeda, & Yee, 2000).

Political and Social Attitudes

There has been much media attention regarding the political gender gap in the past ten years, with women increasingly leaning to the left of the ideological spectrum (Edlund & Pande, 2002). Indeed, gender differences in college students' political orientations have an interesting history on the survey. Although college students as a whole have become more conservative since the height of student liberalism in 1972, when 44 percent of men and 38 percent of women identified themselves as liberal, the conservative shift has been more pronounced among men. This has resulted in a polarization of men's and women's political orientation that reflects differences found in the general U.S. population as well (Box-Steffensmeier, De Boef, & Lin, 2004). Figure 2.13 illustrates this trend by showing the extent to which students' political orientations lean to the left or to the right, as determined by subtracting the percentage of students marking "conservative" or "far right" on the survey from the

Figure 2.13 Left-Right Political Balance, 1970-2006

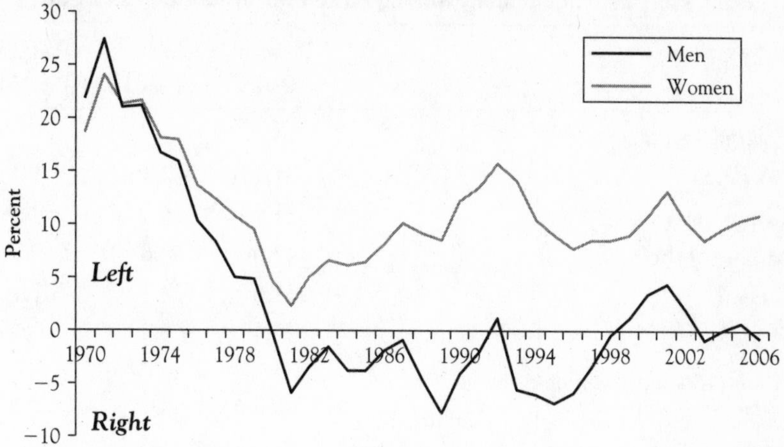

Note: Weighted national figures abstracted from Pryor et al. (2007).

percentage marking "liberal" or "far left." Women with liberal orientations have consistently outnumbered women with conservative orientations, but men's left-right differential has been more balanced over the past twenty-five years. However, as shown in table 2.11, the most popular political label among both genders is "middle of the road."

Gender differences are also apparent when it comes to students' political engagement, with women's interest in politics consistently lower than men's. In particular, women report less interest than men in keeping up to date with political affairs and influencing the political structure and are less likely than men to spend time discussing politics.

How do the attitudes of women and men compare on specific political and social issues? Table 2.11 shows the percentages of men and women who agree "somewhat" or "strongly" with a wide range of items. Noteworthy attitudinal gender differences emerge regarding the perceived role of the federal government, as women are more likely than men to demand greater federal efforts to control the sale of handguns, to control environmental pollution, to protect criminals' rights, and to provide national

Table 2.11 Gender Differences in Political/Social Attitudes and Political Engagement Among First-Year Students, Fall 2006

	Women (%)	Men (%)	Diff. (W − M)
Political orientation			
Far right	1.1	2.4	−1.3
Conservative	21.9	26.2	−4.3
Middle of the road	42.9	43.6	−0.7
Liberal	31.6	24.5	+7.1
Far left	2.4	3.3	−0.9
Goals (very important or essential)			
Keep up to date with political affairs	34.8	40.1	−5.3
Influence the political structure	20.5	25.5	−5.0
Political engagement			
Frequently discussed politics	31.3	36.8	−5.5
Views (agree somewhat or strongly)			
There should be laws prohibiting homosexual relationships	19.3	33.4	−14.1
Realistically, an individual can do little to bring about changes in our society	23.7	31.0	−7.3
Racial discrimination is no longer a major problem in America	15.2	23.8	−8.6
Federal government should raise taxes to reduce the deficit	23.1	31.0	−7.9
Abortion should be legal	56.3	57.3	−1.0
A national health care plan is needed to cover everyone's medical costs	76.5	68.7	+7.8
Federal government is not doing enough to control environmental pollution	80.8	74.4	+6.4
Federal government should do more to control the sale of guns	80.6	65.6	+15.0
Marijuana should be legalized	33.1	42.0	−8.9
There is too much concern in the courts for the rights of criminals	53.3	59.1	−5.8

Note: Weighted national norms abstracted from Pryor et al. (2006).

health care. Men, on the other hand, are more likely than women to believe that "an individual can do little to bring about changes in our society." This latter view is particularly disconcerting and may help explain men's lower levels of community engagement, as noted earlier.

In addition to gender gaps in political attitudes, college men and women differ on items measuring attitudes on social issues. First, men are more likely than women to believe that racial discrimination is no longer a major problem in America, a finding consistent with their lower overall commitment to promoting racial understanding (see table 2.10). Second, on the topic of sexuality, 33.4 percent of men agree that homosexual relations should be prohibited versus 19.3 percent of women. Women, however, are more conservative in their views on drug use; in fact, they are less likely to think marijuana should be legalized. Yet there is little difference between women's and men's beliefs that abortion should be legal, with more than half of each gender advocating pro-choice positions.

The numerous gender differences across a wide range of political and social attitudes provide a useful lens through which campus personnel can consider the motivations and behaviors of college women and men. Awareness of such differences may help an instructor prepare for potentially different reactions to issues that are presented in class. Understanding men's and women's different opinions may also be useful in designing student programs, clubs, and organizations. While it would be inappropriate for colleges to imbue students with particular perspectives, the campus can benefit from knowing students' perspectives and how they differentiate by gender.

Summary

At college entry, significant gender differences are observed across numerous aspects of students' background, self-confidence, behaviors, goals, and aspirations. Some of the largest gaps are found in the area of self-confidence, with women rating their intellectualism, mathematical ability, and competitiveness all at much lower levels than men. Sizable gender differences are also revealed in terms of women's social attitudes, as entering female college students indicate more progressive attitudes when it comes to homosexuality and married women's roles but hold a more conservative stance on the topic of legalizing marijuana. Gender differences also manifest themselves behaviorally, with women tending toward academic achievement, community service, and family responsibilities, while men are more likely to prioritize partying, exercising, watching television, and playing video games. Women also are more concerned about how they will pay for college and thus expect to spend more time than men working for pay while attending school. Given these patterns, it is perhaps not surprising that women enter college with higher levels of stress than men.

The objective of this chapter has been to demonstrate the extent to which gender gaps exist on U.S. college campuses today. As shown by the data, today's college student population is much different than it was forty years ago, with more women enrolling in college and pursuing traditionally male majors and careers, such as medicine and law. Despite these gains for women, there continue to be fundamental differences in attitude and outlook between college men and women, as reflected in their values, beliefs, experiences, and aspirations. Simply put, significant gender gaps remain on today's U.S. college campuses.

This chapter has aimed to provide campus personnel with insights into gender differences among college students with the ultimate goal of maximizing both genders' college success. However, we must also question what happens to these gender differences over the course of college. Does college reinforce differences between the sexes, or does it minimize the gender differential? Further, does the same set of factors influence women's and men's development during college? Do certain college experiences contribute to changes for one sex but not the other? These questions are examined in the chapters that follow.

Notes

1. Due to the very large sample size, differences as small as 2 percent are deemed statistically significant. However, to highlight gender differences with practical relevance, the presentation of results focuses primarily on differences of at least 4 percent or 5 percent.

2. These figures reflect students at four-year colleges and universities. Research incorporating data from all institutions (including two-year colleges) shows women to be particularly overrepresented among college attendees over the age of twenty-five.

3. See, for example, the work of Josselson (1987); Kenny and Donaldson (1991); Lapsley, Rice, and Shadid (1989); and Lopez, Campbell, and Watkins (1986).

4. Results for competitiveness come from 2001, the last year this item was included on the survey.

5. Results for study skills come from 2003, the last year this item was included on the survey.

3

GENDER AND COLLEGE STUDENT DEVELOPMENT

The prior chapter demonstrates the variety of ways in which women and men differ when they begin their first year of college. Some of these reflect long-standing sex differentials, such as women's heightened sense of stress and lesser conceptions of their academic abilities. Other differences—like the growing economic gender gap—are new revelations. Although campuses that aim to most effectively serve their students should be aware of these gender differences, too often our discussions about gender and college are limited to these sorts of descriptive comparisons or to an accounting of the relative numbers of women and men on campus.

To move the conversation forward, we must also focus our efforts on how the *impact* of college may differ for the two sexes. Do women and men receive the same benefits from their engagement with the campus environment? Do their interactions with peers and faculty lead to similar outcomes? Are women and men affected in the same ways by their membership in student clubs, participation in sports, or exposure to racial, ethnic, or cultural diversity? We currently do not have the answers to these questions because our understanding of college impact is largely based on research in which women and men are grouped together into one large category of "college students."

Intuitively, we might suspect that a student's gender shapes how aspects of college affect him or her. In fact, feminist theoretical perspectives would suggest that women's development, more so than men's, evolves in conjunction with relationships and connectedness to others. Thus, we might expect the quality of women's college experience to depend more on their interactions with family, friends, and faculty than is the case for men. However, such theoretical positions have gone largely untested in the expansive body of empirical research on college impact. Instead, research that has explored gender differences in the impact of college has produced scattered and often contradictory findings that collectively neither support nor refute feminist theoretical frameworks. Though some research has revealed that women and men change in different ways during college, we lack an understanding of *why*.

To lay the groundwork for this book's exploration of the gendered effects of college, this chapter reviews what theory and research suggest about women's development during the college years. Though feminist developmental theories are not specifically tested in this book (due to the nature of the data available), they provide a useful context for examining and interpreting gender differences in college impact.

Perspectives on Women's Development

On what basis can we presume that the dynamics of college impact differ for women and men? For many years, the concept of gender was scarcely considered in theoretical work on human development, not to mention college student development. Traditional theories of intellectual, moral, and identity development contributed by Perry (1970), Kohlberg (1975), Erikson (1968), and others paid little or no attention to differences based on gender. Traditional male-based theories assumed a linear path of development that is achieved as individuals move from one stage to the next, with higher stages reflecting more complex intellectual capacities and a sense of autonomy. Since the 1970s, however, a significant body of theoretical work and qualitative inquiry has proposed that women's developmental processes differ from those of men and that autonomy, separation, and individuation do not reflect higher-order achievements for women.

In particular, feminist theoretical approaches have often viewed women's development in the context of relationships with others and a sense of connectedness.

In her landmark book, *In a Different Voice*, Gilligan (1982) expressed concern that traditional theories of moral development, such as those offered by Freud and Kohlberg, characterize women as deviant from the norm, with the norm defined solely from the perspective of male development. Gilligan noted that "when women do not conform to the standards of psychological expectation, the conclusion has generally been that something is wrong with the women" (p. 14). She argued that women's development is reliant on their sense of attachment, responsibility, and care and does not depend on achieving separation or autonomy, as traditional male-based theories might suggest. Gilligan's conclusion resonates with the work of Chodorow (1978), who viewed the formation of female identity as tied to early caregivers, primarily women. Girls' connection with their mothers is seen as the foundation for self-understanding, whereas for boys, identity development is viewed as dependent on achieving a sense of independence and separateness.

Belenky, Clinchy, Goldberger, and Tarule (1997) also emphasized a sense of connectedness as central to women's intellectual, moral, and identity development. Based on the results of in-depth interviews with women, they described five "ways of knowing" that define women's outlook on their own lives. First is Silence, which is characterized by "an extreme denial of self and a dependence on external authority for direction" (p. 24). Second is Received Knowledge, which represents women's reliance on information generated by others and lack of confidence in their own ideas as a source of knowledge. Third is Subjective Knowledge, in which women have beliefs and perspectives that are shaped by their own intuition and life experiences but a sense of truth that remains somewhat dualistic (i.e., black and white). Next is Procedural Knowledge, which is characterized by a deliberate accounting of both internal and external sources of knowledge. Procedural Knowers are further defined in terms of having "separate" or "connected" self-conceptions, depending on whether they view themselves as primarily autonomous individuals or in relation to other people and objects. The final way of knowing is Constructed Knowledge, which recognizes that "all knowledge is constructed and the knower is an intimate part of the known" (p. 137). Constructed Knowers are comfortable with the notion that truth is relative and that conceptions of truth emanate from interactions with others. Placing value on Constructed Knowledge, the authors concluded, "Educators can help women develop their own authentic voices if they emphasize connection over separation, understanding and acceptance over assessment, and collaboration over debate" (p. 229).

Josselson also supported the notion that identity development among women depends on their relationships with others. Based on interviews with women during and after college, Josselson (1987) described women's identity in terms of four categories originally introduced by Marcia (1966):

Foreclosed: Those who are foreclosed are strongly committed to the ideologies, values, and expectations of their parents without question or scrutiny. They have not undergone serious crisis or self-exploration and, in essence, have never, metaphorically speaking, "left home."

Moratorium: Individuals in moratorium are enmeshed in crisis as they reevaluate their childhood identity and actively seek new ways in which to define themselves. They have not yet made occupational or ideological commitments but are engaged in the process of searching.

Identity achieved: Once identity is achieved, the individual has successfully overcome crisis and formed both occupational and ideological commitments.

Identity diffused: Diffused individuals have neither experienced crisis nor formed commitments. They effectively avoid the process of identity formation.

Josselson viewed this process of identity development as dependent on how women anchor themselves to their families, husband/children, friends, and to a lesser extent, careers. In the process of identity development, women face the challenge of "becoming different and maintaining connection at the same time" (p. 171).

College-going women were also the focus of a study by Komarovsky (1985), who examined the development of identity and career aspirations among female students attending a women's college. During the college years, the women in her sample exhibited an increased identification with the goals of the women's movement and a "striking rise in career commitment" (p. 120). Komarovsky described a process by which different types of women seek out different types of college experiences and explained that these variations in chosen environments reinforce initial differences among women. A major contribution of Komarovsky's study is the identification of six distinct patterns in college women's occupational decision making: constants (who remain committed to a particular career over four years); shifters (who are continually uncertain about their career plans); crystallizers (who move from several career options to a specific career choice); radical changers (who shift from one career choice to a different, unrelated career choice); discoverers (who move from general indecision to a particular career choice); and changers to relative certainty (who home in on one or two career choices). Within each of these patterns, such influences as family, peer groups, and romantic attachments shape career choices and commitments. For example, constants are described as having strong support from parents and peers regarding their occupational interests, whereas the uncertainty that characterizes shifters is attributed to indifference from families and lack of interaction with and support from faculty.

Holland and Eisenhart's (1990) ethnography of women college students also focused on how peer groups and romantic attachments influence women's college experiences. They studied African American and white women's orientation toward college and academic achievement at two institutions (one historically black college and one predominantly white institution). The women who participated in their study were described as preoccupied with social relations and relatively less invested in their academic learning and preparation for careers. Romance was found to be paramount: "Relationships with women, although valued and enjoyed, almost always revolved around relationships with men" (p. 85). Sexual attractiveness to men was perceived as central to women's prestige, a finding the authors interpreted as unique to women, given that other areas of achievement, such as sports and politics, can influence men's prestige.

Although academics reportedly took a backseat to social relations with the women in the Holland and Eisenhart study, the authors did observe that the women approached their college education in different ways. Some women took an instrumental approach to college and therefore focused on completing college as a means of getting to the next stage in life. These women viewed schoolwork as something to get through and did not make a strong intellectual or emotional investment in their education. Other women, particularly those who did well in school, approached schoolwork as a means of demonstrating a continued pattern of success. Doing well was paramount to these women, and they tended toward courses and majors that maximized their chances of earning high grades. If they experienced academic difficulties, "they began to search for alternative ways to prove themselves in college and, as a consequence, became even more vulnerable than they had been to pressures to succeed in the peer system" (Holland & Eisenhart, 1990, p. 174). A third but smaller category of women included those who viewed college as an opportunity to "learn from experts." These women focused more on intellectual development and career preparation than women in the first two groups. Overall, the women in the Holland and Eisenhart study did not view their academic and career decisions as dependent on peer influences but instead defined these resolutions as *individual* decisions. This observation differs from that reported by Komarovsky (1985), who viewed women's academic and career development as being shaped by relationships with peers, family, and others.

An important contribution to our understanding of women's *and* men's development is made by Baxter Magolda (1992) in her qualitative study of college students' intellectual development. Careful not to identify distinctively male or female patterns of development, Baxter Magolda described "gender-related" patterns of knowing. Paralleling the work of Belenky et al. (1997), she demonstrated that during the college years, the most dramatic changes in students' epistemological development include a decline in "absolute knowing" and an increase in "transitional knowing" and "independent knowing." Specifically, college is a time when students move away from a dualistic approach to knowledge and become aware that knowledge is relative and that there are a variety of perspectives on what constitutes truth. This transition is presumed to occur regardless of gender, though men and women tend to approach the transition in different ways. In other words, while "learning is a relational activity" (Baxter Magolda, 1992, p. 223) for students of both genders, interpersonal interactions, collaboration, and consensus are assumed to play a larger role in women's intellectual development than in men's.

Thus, the works of Belenky et al. (1997), Josselson (1987), Komarovsky (1985), and Baxter Magolda (1992) all speak to Gilligan's premise that women's development in college depends on the nature of their interpersonal interactions and sense of connectedness. Holland and Eisenhart's (1990) work also points to the importance of relationships in women's college experiences and outcomes, albeit because of cultural reasons (a campus culture that demanded that women focus on relationships with men) rather than a psychological imperative. With the notable excepstion of Baxter Magolda (1992), these studies did not involve men, so the extent to which relational development patterns are actually unique to women is unclear. Nonetheless, these studies are critical in laying the foundation for research that examines women and men side by side in the college context.

Gender and College Impact: The Importance of Conditional Effects

At the same time that such perspectives gained attention in scholarly circles, the field of higher education experienced a proliferation of research on the impact of college. Benefiting from new large-scale surveys of college students, technological advancements in analytical software, and a national fascination with college, new research revealed the variety of ways in which college contributes to student change and development. And yet, as noted by Pascarella and Terenzini (1991) in their first massive review of the college impact literature, most of these studies considered students in the aggregate. That is, research generally did not reveal the effects of college that were *different* for one group or another—otherwise known as the conditional effects of college. With respect to gender, Pascarella and Terenzini reported a few studies demonstrating differential effects of college on men's and women's socioeconomic outcomes but acknowledged that evidence of conditional college effects—gender or otherwise—was sorely lacking in the study of college impact.

By the late 1990s, experts began to agree that further research on student development would yield diminishing returns if it did not ask new questions or approach long-standing questions in new ways, such as how gender and other aspects of students' sociocultural background shape the college student experience (Stage & Anaya, 1996). Indeed, as pointed out by Pascarella and Terenzini (1998), most college impact research rested on "assumed homogeneity in the students being studied" (p. 162). The direction and magnitude of college influences were presumed to be consistent across the entire student population. Pascarella and Terenzini further argued that "heterogeneity . . . is a condition that can no longer be ignored in the study of college effects" (p. 162). In those authors' 2005 update of their 1991 review, they reported a steady increase in college impact research investigating conditional effects of college, but they noted that the vast majority of research in this area still provides little or no information on how findings applied to different subgroups of the student population. Too little is known about when and how college effects depend on key student characteristics (such as gender, race, or class) or on environmental characteristics (such as program, major, or place of residence). Pascarella (2006) perhaps summarized this best, noting that "limiting one's vision to general effects can frequently be misleading and mask dramatic differences in the impact of an intervention or experience for different kinds of students" (p. 512).

This book contributes to the higher education knowledge base by exploring if and how the effects of college differ for women and men. Put in methodological terms, it seeks to identify conditional or interaction effects; these occur when the influence of one variable (such as a particular college experience) depends on another variable (such as the student's gender). In other words, if the impact of a college environment on a specific student outcome is appreciably different for women and men, we would say that there is an interaction between that environment and gender.

To understand the importance of studying conditional effects, consider this fact: earlier work revealed that time spent talking with faculty predicted declines in women's mathematical confidence but demonstrated no such effect for men (Sax, 1994b). Here we would say that there is an interaction between students' gender and time spent with faculty, or that students' gender is a condition influencing the effect that faculty had on students' self-confidence. Evidence of interaction effects also emerged in a study on women's and men's career aspirations: having an orientation toward social change and an interest in raising a family deterred women, but not men, from pursuing careers in academic science (Sax, 2001). This example demonstrates an interaction between gender and values in shaping students' career orientation.

The study of interaction effects is more than an academic exercise; it is essential for effective educational policy and practice. It forces us to recognize not just that students differ from each other but that different sets of factors can influence their development. Knowing, for example, that interacting with faculty has a different effect on the math confidence of males and females forces us to consider these questions: What is the nature of student-faculty interaction, and how does it differ for women and men? In what ways do faculty subtly or intentionally discourage women's confidence in their quantitative skills? Does the faculty member's gender factor into that equation? The answers to these questions would provide practitioners with insights for improving the quality of women's interactions with their professors. Faculty could be educated about how their remarks or nonverbal gestures could result in unintended negative consequences for women. Strategies for promoting women's confidence could be discussed at the departmental level, especially in science and math disciplines. College advisers and counselors could better serve female students by understanding that women's sense of self-confidence may be linked to their interactions with faculty.

Prior Research on Separate-Gender College Effects

It is clear that knowledge of gender-based conditional effects puts us in a better position to improve campus practice, and yet the body of empirical research on gender and college faces numerous important limitations. One is that studies probing the developmental ramifications of gender often include just men or just women (primarily the latter), thus precluding direct gender comparisons. There is value, to be sure, in exploring women's experiences in their own right without constant reliance on comparisons to the "normative" male experience. Still, such studies run the risk of insinuating, without providing evidence, that women's experiences and development bear few similarities to men's. The end result may be an exaggerated depiction of gender differences that overlooks potential commonalities and glorifies alleged feminine strengths (e.g., peacefulness, connectedness, capacity for intimacy) relative to implied masculine liabilities (e.g., aggressiveness, relational detachment). Speaking to this very phenomenon, Tavris (1992) wrote:

> As soon as we start thinking of women and men as opposites (autonomous/dependent, independent/connected, care-based/ justice-based, war-mongering/peace-loving), we overlook all the other factors that influence them, such as race, class, culture, and age. We forget what philosophers call "the law of the excluded middle," which . . . is where most men and women fall in their qualities, beliefs, values, and abilities. (p. 90)

Indeed, more accurate representations of men and women rely on research that either studies both simultaneously or, when one group is studied independently, acknowledges the limitations, cautioning against assumptions that the other sex is invariably the "opposite" sex.

Even when both genders are included in empirical studies, the inclination is to focus on descriptive comparisons of women and men, rather than to focus on the environmental forces producing gender differences. That is, studies tend to compare college men and women in terms of their characteristics and abilities, such as assertiveness or mathematical competence, but pay little attention to the ways in which various experiences may contribute to those gender differences. This practice typically ends with citing the gender difference but falls short of documenting the biological, cultural, or sociological factors that may explain the observed dissimilarity.

Due in part to the small number of studies that have tested for gender-based conditional effects of college, there is no commonly accepted method for assessing differential college impact for women and men. In the rare instances when a study does focus on the gendered effects of college, it often reports the findings without using tests of significance to compare the coefficients derived separately for men and women.

In addition to the methodological and conceptual limitations in prior research on gendered college effects, noncomparability across studies limits our ability to draw generalized conclusions. Often when studies explore a similar topic, they measure variables in different ways (e.g., self-reporting versus objective measures), or the type and number of control variables they include differs. Such differences prevent direct comparisons of gender-based effects. Differences in sampling across studies also prevent direct comparisons of results. For example, findings for women attending women's colleges may not be applicable to women at coeducational institutions and are impossible to compare with men attending any institution. In addition, sample sizes vary widely across existing research, with smaller samples by default yielding fewer significant predictors. There is also considerable variation in the statistical methods used. While many studies use regression-based techniques, others rely on a range of analysis of variance techniques (see Constantinople, Cornelius, & Gray, 1988; Harris, Melaas, & Rodacker, 1999; Serex & Townsend, 1999).

Despite certain shortcomings in the empirical research on gender and college student development, it is worth highlighting a number of studies that do address this topic in methodologically sound ways. Astin and Kent (1983) were perhaps the first to use national longitudinal data to address this question head-on. They examined the ways in which college environments and experiences differentially affected women and men across aspects of self-confidence and values. Their work—based on students attending college in the early 1970s—illustrated numerous conditional effects of college. For example, they found that leadership experiences were more salient to the development of women's self-esteem than men's and that majoring in certain fields, such as the physical sciences, had differential effects on aspects of women's and men's self-confidence. Around the same time, other higher education scholars also began examining gender differences in the impact of college, sometimes in the context of how gender *and* race shape students' college experience (Pascarella, Smart, Ethington, & Nettles, 1987).

Research published in the 1990s further probed the role of gender in the college experience (e.g., Astin, 1990; Pascarella et al., 1997; Smith, Morrison, & Wolf, 1994). Evidence began to emerge that the dynamics of college impact are distinct for the two genders, especially when it comes to women's and men's orientation toward math and science (Astin & Sax, 1996; Sax, 1994b, 1994c, 1994d, 1996).

More recent studies have examined gender differences in the impact of college across a broader range of outcomes, including cognitive abilities (Whitt, Pascarella, Nesheim, Marth, & Pierson, 2003), leadership orientation (Kezar & Moriarty, 2000), gender role expectations (Bryant, 2003), and emotional health (Sax, Bryant, & Gilmartin, 2004). Appendix A provides summaries of these and dozens of other studies on gender differences in the impact of college.

Collectively, research in this area makes clear that there are gender differences in the impact of college. Yet such differences are more scattered than thematic. In fact, the literature does not provide evidence of gender-determined patterns of college impact, as we might expect based on the works of Belenky et al. (1997), Chodorow (1978), Gilligan (1982), Josselson (1987), and others. In particular, we find no clear evidence that women's development during college depends more on a sense of connectedness or relations with others than is the case for men. Rather, the importance of interactions with faculty, peers, and others is demonstrated for students of *both* genders. While it is certainly possible that there are not consistent, measurable differences in how college affects women and men, such a conclusion is premature given the fairly nonevolved state of research on the topic and the existence of highly regarded theoretical positions suggesting that women's development is distinct from men's. In other words, given limitations in the literature on gendered college effects, there is not enough evidence to conclude that women's development in college is—or is not—distinct from men's.

Summary

The question of how college affects women and men has received only minimal attention in the college impact literature, and inconsistent methodologies and scattered, nonthematic results limit the quality of the research that does exist. For those reasons, it is difficult to know whether clear patterns of gender-related effects are nonexistent or whether they simply remain undetected.

As the following chapters will demonstrate, significant differences do exist in the ways in which men and women develop during college, as well as in the experiences that influence their development. The findings, however, do not lend themselves to clearly differentiated patterns for women and men. Notably, women's development during college does *not* appear to rely more on connections and relationships than is the case for men. This finding, though important, is tempered by the fact that the data used in this study were not designed specifically to test the theoretical propositions of Gilligan or other feminist scholars. Instead, this study finds interpersonal relationships and campus experiences to be relevant to both genders, though not always in the same way.

By revealing the complexity of gender and college impact, this book opens the door for several new lines of inquiry. Each illustration of how some aspect of college differentially affects women and men raises new questions for research and offers scholars the opportunity to make an important contribution to the study of gender and college impact. Yet, despite the complexity of this issue, the findings in this book also point to a simple fact: women and men change in different ways and for different reasons over the course of college. This alone underscores the need for campus practitioners to be mindful of the gendered consequences of their work.

4

APPROACHES TO STUDYING GENDER AND COLLEGE IMPACT

As we saw in chapter 3, the work of Gilligan (1982) and other feminist scholars would suggest that men and women develop differently during college and that such differences are rooted in the relative salience of relationships and connectedness for the two genders. And yet, with some notable exceptions, empirical research tends not to address the forces contributing uniquely to women's and men's development in college. Prior research certainly provides examples of differential effects of college on women and men but has not revealed clearly differentiated patterns of college impact for the two genders.

This chapter focuses on this book's approach to determining whether college impact depends on the student's gender. It describes how college impact is considered conceptually, as well as how it is assessed methodologically. Although books often relegate a discussion of methods to an appendix, all readers of this book—whether practitioners or scholars—should familiarize themselves with this approach. Readers interested in a more technical overview of these methods should consult appendix B.

Introducing a Conditional Model of College Impact

Several models in the field of higher education provide a framework for considering how college affects students, though none specifies how gender influences the nature of college impact. Among the most well known are Astin's input-environment-outcome (IEO) model (1968, 1993a), Pascarella's general model for assessing change (1985), Tinto's model of student departure (1987), and Weidman's model of undergraduate socialization (1989). A thorough description of these models appears in Pascarella and Terenzini (2005).

The most straightforward of these models, and therefore most easily applied to the present study, is Astin's IEO model. The basic function of the IEO model is to provide a framework for considering the impact of college while taking into account students' characteristics and predispositions before college. As shown in figure 4.1, the model is divided into three blocks. Inputs are defined as students' characteristics at college entry, including educational and family background, skills, abilities, goals, aspirations, and values. Environments include structural characteristics of the institution—such as size, type, and selectivity—as well as characteristics of the peer and faculty environment. The environment also includes students' behaviors, such as academic engagement, interactions with family and friends, employment, and extracurricular activities. Finally, outcomes include students' measurable characteristics after exposure to the college environment. Astin emphasized the importance of assessing a wide variety of student outcomes, ranging from cognitive to affective and from psychological to behavioral, so that the multidimensional nature of college impact may be considered.

Figure 4.1 Astin's Input-Environment-Outcome Model of College Impact

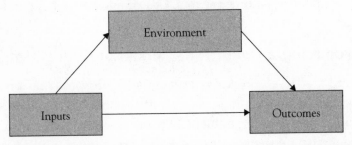

Source: Astin (1993a). Reproduced with permission of Greenwood Publishing Group, Inc., Westport, CT.

Other major college impact models are rooted in the basic structure of IEO. For instance, what Astin refers to as "inputs" is reflected by Tinto as "preentry attributes," by Pascarella as "student background/precollege traits," and by Weidman as "student background characteristics." Accounting for background factors, or inputs, is critical because such characteristics and predispositions lead students to select certain environments when they arrive on campus. If an analysis does not consider these background factors, it is impossible to determine the extent to which student characteristics at the end of college are attributable to what the students did *during* college versus what the students were like *before* college.

A consideration of precollege attributes is vital to this study's assessment of the differential impact of college on women and men. To illustrate, let us consider how participating in volunteer work during college affects men and women. It is insufficient simply to compare college outcomes for men and women who did and did not perform volunteer work because students' experiences and dispositions before college lead some (and not others) to participate in volunteer work during college (Astin & Sax, 1998). Further, there may exist gender differences in the reasons why men and women become involved in volunteer work during college. Such differences might account for gender differences in the *outcomes* related to volunteerism. Therefore, to the extent possible, it is critical to control for men's and women's different precollege orientations before determining whether gender differences exist in the impact of college environments and experiences on student outcomes.

Because existing college impact models encourage us to consider student characteristics before college, they are useful in guiding the study of how college affects women and men. Though they do not explicitly address whether the nature of college impact *depends* on gender (or other student characteristics), they certainly do not preclude that possibility. Indeed, one might visualize two IEO models side by side: one reflecting college impact for women and the other for men. However, another way to visualize this concept is through a conditional model of college impact, as represented in figure 4.2. This model is similar in structure to Astin's IEO model but differs by visually depicting the relationships between the various blocks as unique for different groups of students. For example, two arrows—one for women and one for men—connect "College environments and experiences" with "College outcomes." The use of two arrows reflects the potential for gender differences in the relationship between college environments and student outcomes. For example, do women and men benefit in the same ways from their curricular and cocurricular experiences? Similarly, the two arrows connecting "Precollege characteristics" and "College environments and experiences" reflect the possibility that aspects of students' background—such as family and secondary school experiences—may not result in the same college experiences for women and men. Notice that neither arrow is represented by a traditional solid line, which might depict one group as the norm and the other as deviant. Instead, the two arrows are patterned and distinct from each other, reflecting the possibility that the dynamics of college impact may be justifiably different for the two groups.

Though the model proposed here uses gender to categorize students, it can easily be expanded to account for differences in

Figure 4.2 Conditional Model of College Impact

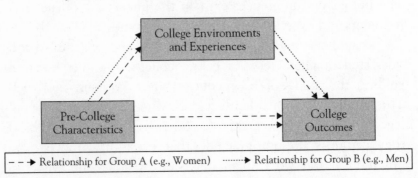

Pre-College Characteristics

College Environments and Experiences

College Outcomes

- - ▶ Relationship for Group A (e.g., Women)　·······▶ Relationship for Group B (e.g., Men)

[1]The number of arrows is determined by the number of groups being considered.

college impact that depend on race, ethnicity, class, sexual orientation, or any number of characteristics. It can also be used to study conditional effects that depend on college environments, such as major, place of residence, or type of institution. Certainly, as the number of subgroups increases, so does the number of arrows between boxes; at some point, this may become unwieldy from a visual perspective. However, from a practical standpoint, it is important to be mindful of the variety of student traits—and combinations of traits—that may shape the dynamics of college impact.

The visualization of two or more arrows between blocks is not groundbreaking from a research perspective; after all, it is common practice in structural equation modeling, where one asks, "Does the model work equally well for different groups of subjects?" The problem is that important findings from path analytic or other structural equation models are likely not reaching those in a position to make decisions about campus practice. The value of the conditional model of college impact is that it takes a well-known schematic on how college affects students and adds a simple but important concept: college may not affect all students in the same way. Thus, the model encourages practitioners to think not just about how their programs, services, or curricula will contribute to student development but also about how their efforts might result in different outcomes for different students. This mind-set may be intuitive for many campus personnel, but unfortunately, the research community has been slow to provide useful information on the nature of these conditional effects.

How Conditional Effects Are Examined in This Book

The next three chapters address the central questions posed in this study: To what extent do the dynamics of college impact differ for women and men? Do certain aspects of college have stronger or weaker effects on women than on men? These chapters are organized around three broad categories that encapsulate twenty-six outcomes of college: personality and identity (chapter 5), political and social values (chapter 6), and academic outcomes (chapter 7). These categories bear some similarity to outcome classifications used in other major studies of college impact (Astin, 1993c; Pascarella & Terenzini, 1991, 2005) to facilitate comparisons with earlier work that generally considered women and men in the aggregate.

Description of the Data

The findings presented in chapters 5, 6, and 7 are based on longitudinal data collected from students who completed the Cooperative Institutional Research Program's (CIRP) Freshman Survey in 1994 and the College Student Survey (CSS), a follow-up survey, in 1998.[1] The sample includes a total of 17,637 undergraduates (10,901 women and 6,736 men), who completed both questionnaires at 204 four-year colleges and universities across the United States.

The study is restricted to individuals who entered college as first-time, full-time students in 1994 and who completed both the CIRP and CSS at the same institution. For that reason, the study does not include transfer, part-time, or returning college students, nor does it include students attending two-year colleges. Although it would be ideal to study gender differences in college impact for the population of college students in the United States—particularly given the growing number of students attending two-year colleges, attending part-time, or transferring between institutions—the CIRP data are best suited to study the traditional-age full-time student at baccalaureate institutions. Further, the focus on this subset of the college-going population enables more valid comparisons with other major studies on college impact, since those studies have also tended to rely on data collected from traditional-age students at four-year institutions (Pascarella & Terenzini, 2005).

The longitudinal sample also is restricted to students attending coeducational institutions, a decision that may seem unusual given the important role that women's colleges play in providing a unique and generally positive environment for women (Kim, 2002; Miller-Bernal, 1989; Riordan, 1992, 1994; Smith, 1990; Smith, Wolf, & Morrison, 1995; Stoecker & Pascarella, 1991). In fact, this study originally set out to include students at single-sex institutions. However, as the study took shape, it became clear that the best way to examine the conditional effects of college—that is, environments and experiences that demonstrate different effects for men and women—is to study men and women at the same institutions. This enables us to assess how men's and women's development is affected by environments to which both genders are exposed.

The final institutional sample reflects the diversity of coeducational baccalaureate institutions nationwide in terms of size, type (four-year college versus university), control (public versus private), and selectivity (see table 4.1). However, to further improve the data, a weighting scheme was used to adjust for biases that did exist, such as the overrepresentation of high-achieving students. All analyses were conducted using the weighted data. (See appendix B for details on the calculation of weights.)

Table 4.1 Institutional and Student Samples

Institutional type	Institutional sample	Total	Women	Men
Public university	16	1,189	726	463
Private university	25	3,163	1,825	1,338
Public 4-year	19	1,320	782	538
Private nonsectarian 4-year	52	4,373	2,677	1,696
Private Catholic 4-year	28	3,721	2,291	1,430
Private other religious 4-year	64	3,871	2,600	1,271
Total	204	17,637	10,901	6,736

Methods of Analysis

Details on the statistical methodology used for these chapters are provided in appendix B; however, it is useful to briefly summarize these methods here. Following is a list of the college outcomes (i. e., dependent variables) that form the basis of the research:

Personality and Identity (Chapter 5)
- Scholar
- Social activist
- Artist
- Status striver
- Leader
- Self-rated scientific orientation
- Self-rated physical health
- Self-rated emotional health
- Feeling overwhelmed
- Cultural awareness
- Religious beliefs and convictions

Political and Social Values (Chapter 6)
- Political engagement
- Political orientation
- Classic liberalism
- Gender role traditionalism
- Permissiveness
- Raising a family
- Developing a meaningful philosophy of life
- Promoting racial understanding

Academic Outcomes (Chapter 7)
- College GPA
- Self-rated mathematical ability

- Self-rated drive to achieve
- Self-rated competitiveness
- Critical thinking and knowledge
- Degree aspirations
- Career sex-atypicality

The first step in studying these twenty-six outcomes was to compare the magnitude of senior-year gender differences with those observed at the start of college. Such a comparison indicates whether gender differences exhibited among first-year students were maintained over the course of college and reveals which gender gaps became appreciably larger or smaller over time. Details on these longitudinal comparisons are provided in appendix C.

Each of the twenty-six outcomes were also involved in a series of regression analyses conducted separately for women and men to identify gender differences in the effects of eighty-seven different college environments and experiences (after controlling for the effects of fifty-four student background characteristics). These eighty-seven college environments (i.e., independent variables) are grouped into the following categories:

- Institutional characteristics
- Residential situation
- Financial situation
- Peer group characteristics
- Major field
- Involvement in academics
- Involvement with faculty
- Involvement with peers
- Involvement in work
- Other forms of involvement (e.g., volunteering, watching television, exercising)

How Prevalent Are Gender-Based Conditional Effects?

Table 4.2 summarizes the frequency of significant relationships for men and women across each category of the college environment. Among the 584 instances when a variable is significant for at least one gender, only a quarter (27 percent) reflect variables whose effects are similar in direction and magnitude for the two genders. Thus, the majority of college effects are either stronger for one gender (18 percent), significant for only one gender (53 percent), or are opposite for the two genders (2 percent). These summary statistics provide strong validation for assessing the differential effects of college on women and men.

This table also reveals another important finding: significant effects of college are more prevalent for men than women. Indeed, among relationships that are significant and in a similar direction for both genders, more than three-quarters are stronger for men than women, most notably in the areas of institutional and peer group characteristics and involvement with academics, faculty, and peers. A similar trend was also revealed in a study of cognitive college outcomes conducted by Whitt, Pascarella, Nesheim, Marth, and Pierson (2003), who concluded that men "seemed to reap significantly greater cognitive benefits from their engagement than did their female peers" (p. 608). Together, these results raise the question of whether college experiences actually influence men to a greater extent than women, or whether the measures included on college student questionnaires are more effective at capturing the student behaviors and college environments that are relevant to men's development. It is possible that aspects of women's college experience equally influence their development but that these surveys do not measure certain important predictors. The large number of unique predictors identified in this study (157 for men and 152 for women) supports the notion that the impact of college differs for the two genders.

Table 4.2 Summary of College Effects

Independent variable category	Similar	Opposite	Stronger for men	Stronger for women	Significant for men only	Significant for women only	Total
Institutional characteristics	13	1	7	1	19	13	54
Residence	1	0	0	0	7	5	13
Finances	0	0	0	0	8	10	18
Peer group	15	3	5	0	26	19	68
Major	21	1	4	4	38	35	103
Involvement in academics	22	2	17	7	12	14	74
Involvement with faculty	21	2	16	4	11	10	64
Involvement with peers	36	2	23	3	13	19	96
Involvement in work	2	0	0	0	7	4	13
Other involvement	26	1	9	6	16	23	81
Total	157	12	81	25	157	152	584

Note: Results for career atypicality are excluded from this table due to differences in analytical approach, as discussed in chapter 7.

How the Results Are Presented

For each of the twenty-six outcomes, the tables provided throughout chapters 5, 6, and 7 list significant predictors categorized in terms of (a) those that are *common* for men and women (noting effects that are significantly stronger for one gender or the other); (b) those that are *opposite* for the two genders; and (c) those that are *unique* to one gender or the other. Findings are further organized around the various categories of collegiate variables described in the previous section. To facilitate the reader's comprehension of the large number of analyses presented, the predictive power of these college-level variables is reflected in terms of their direction of effect (either positive or negative) and only for relationships that pass a stringent test of statistical significance ($p < .0001$). Indication of "+" or "−" is omitted if the relationship is deemed nonsignificant.

The presentation of results often uses terms such as *effect* or *influence* to describe relationships between college experiences and student outcomes. Readers should keep in mind that any reported effect of college is determined after accounting for the influence of dozens of relevant student characteristics measured at the time students entered college. Though true causality cannot be determined, this approach allows us to have greater confidence in the results and encourages us to consider possible implications.

Each table also includes an indication of the proportion of variance accounted for by all variables included in the model (both college and precollege); this is known as the R^2. For readers unfamiliar with statistical jargon, the R^2 tells us how well our measures predict a particular outcome of college. An R^2 can range from 0 to 1, and the closer it is to 1, the better we are at predicting the outcome. Across these three chapters, the R^2 ranges from .17 to .65 for women, and from .18 to .66 for men, with a median of .33 for each gender.[2]

Finally, it is important to comment on the level of discussion provided in these three chapters. Given this study's exploratory nature and the hundreds of significant associations identified in the tables and text, it is neither practical nor desirable to discuss the meaning of each and every relationship. While all relationships are displayed in the tables, the text aims to summarize and highlight some of the more interesting findings, especially those that suggest implications for campus practice or that raise important questions for future research.

Summary

To set the stage for chapters 5, 6, and 7—the book's raison d'étre—this chapter reviews how the study was conducted and, perhaps more important, proposes a model for conducting research on the conditional effects of college. The conditional model of college impact offers more than just a framework for understanding this book; it represents a way of thinking about how students change and develop during college. It forces us to recognize potentially meaningful variations in how college experiences influence students and to consider such differences when developing programs and services.

Now it is time to, quite literally, roll up our sleeves and examine the data. In the three chapters that follow, gender differences in the impact of college are examined for twenty-six different student outcomes. Each of the twenty-six sections aims to highlight the most interesting findings, to identify emerging themes, and when possible, to propose implications for practice and an agenda for future research. The three chapters and their subsections need not be read in any particular order; in fact, readers may wish to skim through the findings to identify outcomes or environments that particularly interest them. Chapter 8 provides a discussion of the major themes resulting from these chapters.

Notes

1. Though it would have been ideal to use data from a more recent cohort of students, the 1994–1998 database is the most representative longitudinal CIRP database available from recent years.

2. For the most part, variables included in the separate-gender equations account for a greater share of the variance than was reported in Astin's (1993c) study on aggregated samples of women and men using a similar set of outcome measures. However, as with most research on the impact of college, the predictive power of college-level variables is small relative to the role of student background characteristics. Readers interested in a summary of the proportion of variance accounted for by the independent variables (including precollege input variables) should consult appendix D.

5

PERSONALITY AND IDENTITY

Women and men enter college with notably different perceptions of their skills, talents, interests, and sense of well-being, and these perceptions often change in different ways during college. In this chapter, we'll explore gender differences in the process of change and ask whether the experiences that influence the development of personality and identity are similar or different for the two sexes. Through an examination of eleven aspects of student personality and identity, we'll see that key forms of student engagement—such as with faculty, diversity, and religion—tap into different aspects of identity development for women and men.

Personality: Scholar

The ability to succeed in college depends in large part on having the confidence to do so. Scholarly confidence allows students to approach the educational experience believing that they can handle the rigor and pace of college academics. In this section, scholars are defined as students who exhibit high levels of self-confidence with their academic, intellectual, and writing abilities.[1] In two of these areas—academic ability and intellectual self-confidence—women's self-ratings are markedly lower than men's both at college entry and four years later. The gender gap in intellectual self-confidence actually widens over four years of college. And while first-year women do exhibit greater confidence than men in their writing ability, this gender gap disappears during college as men's writing confidence catches up to women's.

The question examined here is whether college influences changes in scholarly orientation in different ways for the two genders. Are there strategies that institutions should consider to boost their female students' confidence on this front? Table 5.1 displays the aspects of college that influence the development of a scholarly orientation.

Scholar Personality: Aspects of College That Influence Both Genders

It should come as no surprise that academic engagement during college enhances both women's and men's confidence in their scholarly abilities. Engagement can take a variety of forms, such as the time that students spend studying or taking honors classes. Regardless of gender, students' scholarly self-confidence also benefits from interactions with faculty, such as talking with faculty in and out of class and doing formalized independent study projects. Positive interactions with faculty are clearly important for both genders; in fact, feeling respected, supported, and encouraged by faculty enhances men's and women's scholarly orientation.

The only aspect of college to emerge as a negative force in developing both men's and women's scholar personality is the number of undergraduates at the institution; here, attending larger institutions is associated with lower scholarly self-ratings. This finding reflects the well-documented challenge of getting to know faculty and becoming otherwise academically engaged on larger campuses. Further, it underscores the value of many large institutions' ongoing efforts to promote academic engagement among their students via learning communities or other programming that fosters a more intimate academic experience.

Scholar Personality: Factors Influencing Women Only

In what ways does college relate to the development of scholarly orientations among women only? One is that attending institutions with a greater percentage of female faculty bolsters

Table 5.1 Gender Differences in College-Level Predictors of Personality: Scholar

	Women	Men	Variable type
Common predictors			
Number of full-time undergraduates	−	−	Institutional characteristics
Enrolled in honors/advanced courses	+*	+	Involvement in academics
Worked on independent study project	+*	+	Involvement in academics
Hours per week studying/ doing homework	+	+*	Involvement in academics
Challenged a professor's ideas in class	+	+	Involvement with faculty
General faculty support	+	+	Involvement with faculty
Hours per week talking with faculty outside class	+	+	Involvement with faculty
Tutored another student	+	+	Involvement with peers
Hours per week reading for pleasure	+	+	Other involvement
Unique predictors: Women			
Percentage of women faculty	+		Institutional characteristics
Distance from home	+		Residence
Major: English or humanities	+		Major
Attended racial/cultural awareness workshop	+		Involvement with peers
Unique predictors: Men			
Peer mean: Hedonism		+	Peer group
Percentage of bachelor's degrees in education		+	Peer group
Major: History or political science		+	Major
Major: Physical sciences, math, statistics, or computer science		−	Major
Worked full-time while a student		+	Involvement in work
Final R^2	47%	47%	

Notes: Direction of effect is noted only for variables that are significant at $p < .0001$.

Final R^2 represents the proportion of variance accounted for by all variables in the model (including precollege variables). See appendix D for the differential contribution of precollege and college variables.

* Denotes a coefficient that is significantly larger ($p < .01$) for that gender.

scholarly self-confidence. This relationship likely reflects the impact of role modeling, as the presence of academically confident and successful female faculty may strengthen women's views of their own academic abilities. Another possibility is that the impact of the proportion of women faculty results from direct same-sex interactions between female students and their instructors. While these data do not permit us to explore the extent to which faculty interactions depend on the instructor's gender, other research does suggest that exposure to female faculty enhances women's academic confidence (Fassinger, 1995).

Connection to family also shapes this outcome for women, as attending college farther from home promotes scholarly confidence. Other research has also documented the importance of leaving home to attend college because it encourages a stronger sense of independence and emotional well-being for women (Sax, Bryant, & Gilmartin, 2004). The experience of leaving home provides female students with an opportunity to establish their academic identity in a new environment, thus enhancing their sense of scholarly self-confidence. Women who stay close to home often lose out on such opportunities. This has important implications for families because many parents think it is better for their daughters to remain close to home and attend local colleges. And women are in fact more likely than men to choose a college that allows them to be closer to their families, as described in chapter 2. Thus, campuses should consider ways to maximize on-campus engagement for female students who live at home or who have ongoing family responsibilities that require them to go home more frequently.

Scholar Personality: Factors Influencing Men Only

There are several experiences that uniquely contribute to men's scholarly personality. One is their choice of major; majoring in history or political science appears to enhance men's scholarly self-confidence, while majoring in math, physical science, or computer science fields has the opposite effect.[2] It is interesting to consider why scientific fields would inhibit the development of men's scholarly confidence. This may result from the high competition and stringent grading practices often found in the sciences. In addition, following along the lines of relative deprivation theory (Davis, 1966), it is possible that by comparing themselves with their peers, men in scientific fields view their own academic abilities in a less favorable light.

Men's scholarly self-confidence also is enhanced by aspects of the institutional peer group, including the student body's average partying tendencies. This finding is particularly puzzling because we would not expect a school with a strong partying culture to promote scholarly confidence. In fact, men at such campuses actually begin college with *lower* scholarly confidence than men at other institutions, yet over four years of college, their academic confidence grows. Could it be that a strong partying culture encourages men to view their own academic abilities as relatively stronger than that of their peers?

Working full-time as a student also promotes scholarly self-confidence among men only. At first, this may seem counterintuitive, given that full-time employment typically reduces the amount of time available for academic engagement. However, in this case, having a full-time job tends to enhance men's view of their academic abilities, perhaps via the skills and knowledge gained from the employment experience. This finding has implications for male college students who are concerned about needing to work full-time. Such men might benefit from knowing that full-time employment is an opportunity to hone their academic skills in a real-world setting.

Personality: Social Activist

College offers numerous opportunities for students to develop greater consciousness about the world around them and to consider their role in bringing about change. To understand how college contributes to students' concern for improving social conditions, a personality factor called the social activist was created. This factor represents students' commitment to four primary goals: helping others in difficulty, influencing social values, participating in community action programs, and influencing the political structure.[3] Women entering college score significantly higher than men on three of the four goals—helping others, influencing social values, and engaging in community action—and significantly lower than men on desire to influence the political structure. Each of these gender gaps remains steady over four years of college, though, as we'll see, the college experiences that relate to social activist goals are not always the same for women and men (see table 5.2).

Social Activist Personality: Aspects of College That Influence Both Genders

For the most part, extracurricular and academic engagement strengthen men's and women's social activist commitments. Performing volunteer work has the greatest impact on the development of men's and women's social activist orientation. Other influential aspects of engagement include attending religious services, joining campus clubs and groups, participating in organized demonstrations, and spending time studying or doing homework. Exposure to diversity also enhances students' commitment to social activism, as seen in the positive effects of attending racial/cultural awareness workshops and engaging in social interactions with individuals of a different race or ethnicity. These results suggest that campuses striving to produce graduates with a stronger commitment to social change ought to maximize opportunities for students to become engaged in campus life, especially in ways that expose them to community needs and issues about racial, ethnic, or cultural diversity.

Conversely, declines in activist orientations are apparent for those students who spend more time watching television. Indeed,

Table 5.2 Gender Differences in College-Level Predictors of Personality: Social Activist

	Women	Men	Variable type
Common predictors			
Public university	−	−	Institutional characteristics
Major: Engineering	−	−	Major
Major: History or political science	+	+	Major
Major: Physical sciences, math, statistics, or computer science	−	−	Major
Hours per week studying/ doing homework	+	+	Involvement in academics
Enrolled in women's studies course	+	+*	Involvement in academics
Challenged a professor's ideas in class	+	+*	Involvement with faculty
General faculty support	+	+	Involvement with faculty
Social diversity experiences	+	+*	Involvement with peers
Hours per week student clubs or groups	+	+*	Involvement with peers
Attended racial/cultural awareness workshop	+	+	Involvement with peers
Took part in demonstrations	+	+	Involvement with peers
Attended religious services	+	+*	Other involvement
Hours per week commuting	+	+	Other involvement
Hours per week household/ childcare duties	+	+	Other involvement
Hours per week watching television	−	−	Other involvement
Volunteering or community service	+	+	Other involvement
Unique predictors: Women			
Percentage of bachelor's degrees in science, math, and engineering	−		Peer group

(Continued)

Table 5.2 *(Continued)*

	Women	Men	Variable type
Living on campus	+		Residence
Major: Business	−		Major
Major: Social sciences	+		Major
Felt bored in class	−		Involvement in academics
Faculty did not take comments seriously	+		Involvement with faculty
Joined a fraternity or sorority	−		Involvement with peers
Had a part-time job off campus	+		Involvement in work
Hours per week reading for pleasure	+		Other involvement
Unique predictors: Men			
Number of full-time undergraduates		−	Institutional characteristics
Percentage of bachelor's degrees in education		+	Peer group
Peer mean: Gender role traditionalism		+	Peer group
Worked on an independent study project		+	Involvement in academics
Final R^2	38%	41%	

Notes: Direction of effect is noted only for variables that are significant at $p < .0001$.

R^2 represents the proportion of variance accounted for by all variables in the model (including precollege variables). See appendix D for the differential contribution of precollege and college variables.

* Denotes a coefficient that is significantly larger ($p < .01$) for that gender.

television has been linked to a decline in civic engagement and sense of social responsibility within the larger population as well (Putnam, 2000). The negative influence of television on students in college is a theme that appears numerous times throughout this book.

Faculty also play a role in promoting students' interest in social change. Specifically, students who feel supported by faculty and those who challenge professors' ideas in class have an enhanced social activist orientation. The latter finding may reflect a sense of empowerment experienced by students who take initiative in questioning a professor's ideas or perspectives. Clearly, faculty have an opportunity to empower students not only by providing them with academic and emotional support but also by creating opportunities for students to speak their minds in the classroom.

Interestingly, students who spend more time commuting and engaging in household/childcare responsibilities tend to experience an increased commitment to social activism. It is possible that these experiences provide more regular exposure to neighborhood or civic concerns, leading students to value community activism more. Further, students who are commuting or doing household chores may have greater daily exposure to the news via television, newspapers, or radio, thus enabling them to spend more time reflecting on larger societal issues.

Social Activist Personality: Factors Influencing Women Only

Majoring in the social sciences strengthens women's commitment to social activism, and majoring in business and attending colleges with larger science and engineering programs diminishes that commitment. These findings reflect the impact of disciplinary culture on students' values because social science fields—unlike the fields of business, science, or engineering—tend to reinforce social and community values, as demonstrated in the work of Smart, Feldman, and Ethington (2000). The negative influence of the science and engineering culture is particularly interesting since it shapes women's values regardless of whether the student herself majors in one of these fields.

Interestingly, thinking that faculty do not take their comments seriously strengthens commitment to social activism among women. This raises the question of whether feeling dismissed by faculty fuels women's desire to prove themselves in the noncollege context and motivates them to take action on behalf of others who have been mistreated or victimized. If so, this suggests an unantici-pated *positive* outcome of a chilly classroom climate for women.

Living on campus also helps build women's commitment to social activism. Gains here may be due to the nature of relation-ships formed in on-campus housing, as well as programming and services offered as part of residential life, especially those that expose students to diverse peer groups and new ideas.

Holding a part-time job off campus is another factor that fortifies women's commitment to social activism. This may be a reflection of spending more time immersed in the larger commu-nity, as working off campus puts these women in greater contact with the noncampus community and possibly makes them more aware of important issues facing society.

Surprisingly, membership in a sorority contributes to a decline in social activism, even given the emphasis on philan-thropy in college Panhellenic societies. Future research in the area of Greek life should question the nature and intensity of community service that is conducted as part of sorority member-ship to ensure that those experiences provide the same sort of benefits afforded to students who participate in community ser-vice organized via other campus units. Research should question whether the relatively homogenous makeup of sororities temper the value of the service experience.

Social Activist Personality: Factors Influencing Men Only

For men, commitment to social activism is strengthened at smaller institutions, ones that award a greater share of educa-tion degrees, and ones where the peer group is more strongly committed to traditional gender roles. It is not clear why an environment that values traditional or domestic roles for women would promote men's social activist goals, though it may be that this type of environment contributes to men's desire to promote family values, a conservative tenet that gained widespread atten-tion while these students attended college in the 1990s.[4]

Among measures of involvement, only one emerged as a significant predictor of social activism for men only: the positive effect of working on an independent study project. This suggests that for men, but not for women, working on independent research helps increase the commitment to influencing political and social change. Does this reflect gender differences in the topics explored or possibly the nature of the one-on-one interactions with faculty that often accompany independent study projects? Future research on the specific nature of the independent study experience would help answer these questions and could inform academic counselors on how to best advise women and men who seek independent study opportunities.

Personality: Artist

How does college affect women's and men's sense of their creative talents? Are artistic tendencies stimulated by some college experiences but stifled by others? Does this process differ for women and men? In this section, we'll explore the impact of college on the artist personality, as defined by students who place high priority on creating original artistic works and/or becoming accomplished in the performing arts.[5] At college entry, gender differences are evident on two of these characteristics, with men rating themselves more highly than women on artistic ability and creativity, a difference that remains significant over four years of college. As we'll see, aspects of college that contribute to the development of artistic orientations during college are fairly similar for women and men, with some exceptions (see table 5.3).

Artist Personality: Aspects of College That Influence Both Genders

Men's and women's artistic orientations are enhanced by aspects of college that relate directly to education in the arts—such as

Table 5.3 Gender Differences in College-Level Predictors of Personality: Artist

	Women	Men	Variable type
Common predictors			
Major: English or humanities	+	+*	Major
Major: Fine arts	+	+	Major
Challenged a professor's ideas in class	+	+	Involvement with faculty
Hours per week talking with faculty outside class	+	+*	Involvement with faculty
Took part in demonstrations	+	+*	Involvement with peers
Social diversity experiences	+	+	Involvement with peers
Hours per week household/ childcare duties	+	+*	Other involvement
Hours per week reading for pleasure	+	+	Other involvement
Hours per week watching television	−	−	Other involvement
Opposing predictors			
Hours per week using a personal computer	+	−	Involvement in academics
Unique predictors: Women			
Major: Education	+		Major
Worked on independent study project	+		Involvement in academics
Hours per week commuting	+		Other involvement
Hours per week exercising/ playing sports	+		Other involvement
Unique predictors: Men			
Number of full-time undergraduates		−	Institutional characteristics
Student-to-faculty ratio		−	Institutional characteristics
Percentage of bachelor's degrees in science, math, and engineering		−	Peer group
Aid: Grants and scholarships		−	Finances

Table 5.3 *(Continued)*

	Women	Men	Variable type
Major: Journalism or communications		+	Major
Major: Physical sciences, math, statistics, or computer science		−	Major
Major: Social sciences		−	Major
Attended racial/cultural awareness workshop		+	Involvement with peers
Final R^2	53%	54%	

Notes: Direction of effect is noted only for variables that are significant at $p < .0001$.

R^2 represents the proportion of variance accounted for by all variables in the model (including precollege variables). See appendix D for the differential contribution of precollege and college variables.

* Denotes a coefficient that is significantly larger ($p < .01$) for that gender.

majoring in the fine arts or humanities—or that may expand students' horizons in other ways, such as reading for pleasure, having diverse social interactions, and participating in organized demonstrations. Faculty also play an important role, as students' artistic inclinations grow stronger when they interact with professors outside the classroom and challenge them inside the classroom. Together, these findings highlight the role that exposure to new people, ideas, and conflict can play in developing artistic interests. Watching television, on the other hand, tends to suppress both men's and women's artistic orientations, a finding consistent with the generally negative effects of television on college students reported by Astin (1993c).

Artist Personality: Opposing Influences for Women and Men

Interestingly, time spent using a personal computer produces *opposite* effects for the two genders, with computer use associated with gains in artistic orientation for women and declines among men.

Because these data do not indicate the nature of the computer usage and because the Internet was a new phenomenon when these data were collected, the dynamics of these relationships are not clear. Recent research, however, sheds some light on this, observing that female college students are significantly more likely than males to use computers for intellectual and entertainment purposes, while males report a stronger technical interest in computers themselves, including installation, applications, and programming work (Rowell et al., 2003). Thus, understanding computers' role in promoting this and other college outcomes necessitates knowing more about how men and women use computers.

Artist Personality: Factors Influencing Women Only

Several aspects of involvement encourage the development of artistic orientations solely for women and include working on independent study projects, commuting, and exercising or playing sports. Although seemingly unrelated, these experiences all provide a mental space for women to explore creative ideas while disconnecting from formal academic pursuits.

Artist Personality: Factors Influencing Men Only

Scientifically oriented environments tend to suppress men's artistic orientations, as indicated by the negative effects of majoring in the physical sciences, attending colleges with a large undergraduate enrollment, and attending colleges with a large population of science majors. The dynamics behind this phenomenon are interesting to consider: How, and in what ways, do large scientific environments subtly or overtly discourage men's interest in the arts? Are men's artistic interests replaced by new avocations, perhaps those that are more aligned with a scientific culture?

Men's artistic interests also tend to diminish when they are the recipients of grants and scholarships. Since most grants and scholarships are awarded and retained based on academic achievement and potential, it may be that men who receive them have less time or freedom to explore their artistic interests.

Personality: Status Striver

To what extent do materialistic or status concerns motivate college men and women? How and why does this change over four years? The status striver outcome assesses students' goals in the following areas: being very well-off financially, obtaining recognition from colleagues, becoming an authority in one's field, being successful in one's own business, and having administrative responsibility for others' work.[6] This combination of items reflects an orientation not only toward earning money but also toward achieving professional status and recognition. At the start of college, gender differences are evident on three of these goals, with men expressing significantly higher commitments to financial well-being, business success, and professional recognition, with gender differentials on the latter two goals widening over time. Table 5.4 presents gender differences in the college student experiences that contribute to a status-striving orientation.

Status Striver Personality: Aspects of College That Influence Both Genders

For both women and men, status orientations are strengthened in environments where wealth and status are more highly valued, such as those found in business fields and on campuses where peers place greater emphasis on materialistic values. Interestingly, these environments promote status orientations more strongly for men than women, a finding consistent with other research (Astin & Kent, 1983). Why would a materialistic peer culture more strongly promote men's status-striving goals? Do such environments encourage men to adopt more traditional roles, such as that of the family breadwinner?

In addition to the peer climate, direct interactions with peers also influence students' status-striving tendencies. For example, increases in status orientation result from studying with other students, joining a fraternity or sorority, and partying behaviors. These findings are similar to those reported by Astin (1993c), who hypothesized that peer interactions

Table 5.4 Gender Differences in College-Level Predictors of Personality: Status Striver

	Women	Men	Variable type
Common predictors			
Peer mean: Materialism and social status	+	+*	Peer group
Major: Business	+	+*	Major
Hours per week using a personal computer	+*	+	Involvement in academics
Withdrew from school or took a leave of absence	−	−	Involvement in academics
Challenged a professor's ideas in class	+	+*	Involvement with faculty
General faculty support	+	+*	Involvement with faculty
Hours per week talking with faculty outside class	+	+*	Involvement with faculty
Joined a fraternity or sorority	+	+	Involvement with peers
Studied with other students	+	+*	Involvement with peers
Worked full-time while a student	+	+	Involvement in work
Hedonism (drinking, smoking, and partying)	+	+	Other involvement
Opposing predictors			
Public 4-year college	+	−	Institutional characteristics
Unique predictors: Women			
Other religious private 4-year college	−		Institutional characteristics
Peer mean: Hedonism	+		Peer group
Concern about financing college	−		Finances
Felt bored in class	−		Involvement in academics
Had a part-time job off campus	+		Involvement in work
Attended religious services	−		Other involvement
Hours per week watching television	+		Other involvement

Table 5.4 *(Continued)*

	Women	Men	Variable type
Unique predictors: Men			
Percentage of bachelor's degrees in social sciences		−	Peer group
Major: Education		−	Major
Major: Fine arts		+	Major
Hours per week socializing with friends		+	Involvement with peers
Hours per week reading for pleasure		−	Other involvement
Final R^2	31%	41%	

Notes: Direction of effect is noted only for variables that are significant at $p < .0001$.

R^2 represents the proportion of variance accounted for by all variables in the model (including precollege variables). See appendix D for the differential contribution of precollege and college variables.

* Denotes a coefficient that is significantly larger ($p < .01$) for that gender.

raise students' status orientations by transmitting materialistic values.

It is not just the peer group that raises students' status orientations; interactions with faculty, such as talking with professors outside class and challenging them in class, produce the same outcome. Given that the academic culture prioritizes professional recognition and status, it is not surprising that greater levels of faculty engagement indicate stronger interest in status-oriented goals. Interestingly, these particular relationships are stronger among men than women, suggesting a more direct influence of faculty on male students' values. This is a pattern that emerges throughout this book.

Status Striver Personality: Factors Influencing Women Only

Among aspects of college that uniquely relate to women's status-striving goals, two reflect the role of religious environments in reducing materialistic orientations: attending religious services while in college and enrolling in "other religious" (i.e., non-Catholic) private four-year colleges. Alternatively, a peer environment focused on hedonistic behaviors (i.e., drinking, smoking, and partying) increases women's orientation toward wealth and status, a finding in line with the effects of Greek membership noted for all students. The role of hedonistic environments is interesting since it remains significant even after considering the student's own partying behaviors. In other words, a partying culture, regardless of one's own behaviors, promotes materialistic values among women.

Status orientation also depends on how much time women spend watching television. While Astin (1993c) found television to be related to the development of materialistic values for all students, this study demonstrates the role that television plays uniquely for females. Perhaps these results reflect gender differences in television-viewing habits, as women have been shown to be more frequent viewers of soap operas, game shows, and other programming that emphasizes status and material wealth (Hooghe, 2002).

Another determinant of status orientations among women is having financial concerns, which relates to a decline in status-related values. This is curious because one might expect women who have significant concerns about their ability to pay for college to become *more* interested in financial well-being, not less so. Perhaps for these women, interest lies not in the long-term accumulation of wealth for materialistic or status purposes but in having enough money to reach their short-term goal of graduating from college.

Status Striver Personality: Factors Influencing Men Only

Several college experiences emerge as significant indicators of status orientation among men only. Consistent with the role of peer interactions in promoting materialistic values, noted earlier, socializing with friends relates to gains in men's status orientation, while reading for pleasure—a more solitary activity—is associated with declines in men's status-striving goals.

We also find that men's choice of major field affects their status orientation. Declines in status-striving goals are more likely among men who major in education or who attend institutions that award a greater share of bachelor's degrees in the social sciences. These relationships likely reflect an emphasis on noncompetitive, more humanitarian values within social disciplines, as suggested by the work of Holland (1973) and Smart et al. (2000).

On the other hand, majoring in the fine arts enhances men's status-striving goals. It is interesting to consider why the fine arts is associated with gains in status orientation for men but not women; this phenomenon raises the question of whether men are more likely than women to perceive the arts as a vehicle for attaining status, recognition, and notoriety.

Personality: Leader

It is clear from college mission statements that institutions desire to prepare students for leadership positions. Though conceptions of leadership vary from traditional, hierarchical leadership to more collaborative, consensus-building leadership, inherent in being a good leader is having the confidence to assume the role. Compared to women, men enter college with greater confidence in their leadership skills, a gender gap that grows over four years. This section explores what encourages students' sense of leadership confidence during college and how this differs for women and men. The leader personality is a composite of students' self-ratings on three characteristics: leadership ability, public-speaking ability, and social self-confidence.[7] As reported in table 5.5, the process of change on these dimensions of leadership is distinct for women and men.

Table 5.5 Gender Differences in College-Level Predictors of Personality: Leader

	Women	Men	Variable type
Common predictors			
Number of full-time undergraduates	−	−	Institutional characteristics
General faculty support	+	+	Involvement with faculty
Challenged a professor's ideas in class	+	+	Involvement with faculty
Hours per week student clubs or groups	+*	+	Involvement with peers
Took part in demonstrations	+	+	Involvement with peers
Leadership training	+	+	Involvement with peers
Student government	+	+	Involvement with peers
Studied with other students	+	+*	Involvement with peers
Joined a fraternity or sorority	+	+	Involvement with peers
Attended religious services	+	+	Other involvement
Hours per week watching television	−*	−	Other involvement
Major: Journalism or communications	+	+	Major
Unique predictors: Women			
Public 4-year college	+		Institutional characteristics
Distance from home	+		Residence
Major: Biological sciences	−		Major
Major: Business	+		Major
Enrolled in honors/advanced courses	+		Involvement in academics
Withdrew from school or took leave of absence	−		Involvement in academics
Attended racial/cultural awareness workshop	+		Involvement with peers
Hours per week socializing with friends	+		Involvement with peers
Unique predictors: Men			
Public university		−	Institutional characteristics

Table 5.5 *(Continued)*

	Women	Men	Variable type
Percentage of women faculty		+	Institutional characteristics
Peer mean: Hedonism		+	Peer group
Percentage of bachelor's degrees in education		+	Peer group
Living on campus		+	Residence
Major: Physical sciences, math, statistics, or computer science		−	Major
Worked full-time while a student		+	Involvement in work
Final R^2	53%	55%	

Notes: Direction of effect is noted only for variables that are significant at $p < .0001$.

R^2 represents the proportion of variance accounted for by all variables in the model (including precollege variables). See appendix D for the differential contribution of precollege and college variables.

* Denotes a coefficient that is significantly larger ($p < .01$) for that gender.

Leader Personality: Aspects of College That Influence Both Genders

For both women and men, the ability to develop leadership skills depends on having opportunities to do so. For example, gains in the leader personality are stronger for students who participate in extracurricular activities such as student government, leadership training, organized demonstrations, fraternities or sororities, and student clubs or groups. Leadership orientation also is enhanced by academic engagement, such as studying with other students, challenging professors in the classroom, and seeking out faculty for advice and support. These aspects of academic and extracurricular engagement reflect a certain degree of leadership initiative from the start because they are entirely voluntary. Yet even when accounting for the fairly high levels of self-confidence exhibited among students who choose to get involved in college, these forms of involvement *further* add to students' confidence in their leadership and social skills.

By contrast, experiences that can contribute to a sense of isolation relate to declines in leadership confidence. One of these is watching television, which takes time away from opportunities to develop leadership and interpersonal skills. Another is attending institutions with large undergraduate enrollments, a finding that may reflect the difficulty of assuming leadership positions and establishing social networks on more populous campuses. Larger institutions are thus challenged to create more opportunities for leadership; ideally, the number of students would provide greater, not fewer, opportunities to hone one's leadership abilities.

Leader Personality: Factors Influencing Women Only

An important aspect of leadership development specific to women is gaining distance from their parents. The farther from home a woman attends college, the more confidence she gains in her social, leadership, and public-speaking skills. This is similar to the benefits of leaving home on women's scholarly orientation, as discussed earlier. Once again, these findings have important implications for women and their parents when choosing a college. The challenge is to reconcile the desire of many women and their families to maintain proximity to one another with what is developmentally beneficial for the students.

Aspects of involvement—such as enrolling in honors courses, attending racial/cultural workshops, and socializing with friends— all promote women's leadership orientation. Conversely, withdrawing or taking a leave of absence—a clear indicator of noninvolvement in campus life—has a negative effect. Choice of major field also relates to women's leadership confidence, with higher-than-average gains noted for women majoring in business fields and lower-than-average gains found for women majoring in the biological sciences. The latter finding is consistent with previous research reporting that majoring in the biological sciences is associated with declines both in women's leadership self-confidence (Astin & Kent, 1983) and in their self-assessed ability to influence others (Kezar & Moriarty, 2000).

Leader Personality: Factors Influencing Men Only

The majority of factors that are unique to the development of men's leadership abilities reflect the role of the broader college environment. Particularly noteworthy is that men's leadership and social confidence benefit from attending colleges with greater proportions of women faculty. This is the first of several instances throughout this book where men are positively impacted by the presence of more female faculty. This finding raises a number of questions, such as whether gains in men's leadership and social self-confidence result directly from their interactions with female faculty, or whether such gains result from aspects of campus culture that exist at institutions with a greater female faculty presence. A similar question can be raised regarding another finding significant only for men: the decline in leadership abilities associated with majoring in physical science, computer science, math, or statistics. Do men pursuing these scientific fields have less time to engage in leadership opportunities in college, or does the scientific culture suppress men's confidence in their leadership and social skills?

Another noteworthy finding is the role of full-time employment in enhancing men's leadership confidence. Despite the many drawbacks resulting from full-time employment during college, such as lower retention rates and decreased satisfaction with college (Astin, 1993c), there's a silver lining: gains in men's social and leadership self-confidence. Why employment would not yield similar benefits for women is unclear and may relate to differences in the nature of women's and men's employment while in college, something future research will need to address.

Scientific Orientation

College affords many students the opportunity to cultivate or enhance their interest in science. Though scientific goals do not reign supreme for all students, an important question is whether college differentially shapes the scientific interests of women and men. Here we'll see how gender differences in college contribute to students' commitment to making a theoretical contribution to science. For both women and men, interest in this goal ranks near the bottom among the nineteen goals assessed on the Freshman Survey, and for the majority of women and men, interest in science declines further during college. Though interest in science is fairly low among the college population, the results of this research reveal a number of college experiences that can promote men's and women's scientific orientation (see table 5.6).

Scientific Orientation: Aspects of College That Influence Both Genders

Not surprisingly, choice of major field is a salient predictor of scientific orientation for both women and men, including the positive effects of majoring in the health professions, the physical sciences, and the biological sciences. Majoring in the biological sciences is in fact the strongest determinant of scientific interests for both genders, even more so for women than men. Majoring in business, on the other hand, diminishes students' interest in making scientific contributions. While it is certainly possible for business majors to contribute to science via management or sales positions in scientific industry, they are less likely to make *theoretical* advancements in science, as measured here.

Numerous forms of academic engagement positively influence men's and women's commitment to science, including spending time studying or doing homework, working on independent study projects, and working with faculty on research.

Table 5.6 Gender Differences in College-Level Predictors of Scientific Orientation

	Women	Men	Variable type
Common predictors			
Major: Biological sciences	+*	+	Major
Major: Health profession	+	+	Major
Major: Physical sciences, math, statistics, or computer science	+	+	Major
Major: Business	−	−	Major
Enrolled in honors/advanced courses	+	+*	Involvement in academics
Hours per week studying/ doing homework	+	+	Involvement in academics
Worked on independent study project	+	+	Involvement in academics
Faculty provided opportunity for research	+	+	Involvement with faculty
Hours per week talking with faculty outside class	+	+*	Involvement with faculty
Took part in demonstrations	+	+*	Involvement with peers
Joined a fraternity or sorority	−	−*	Involvement with peers
Unique predictors: Women			
Peer mean: Years of study in math and science	+		Peer group
Major: Fine arts	−		Major
Major: Psychology	+		Major
Studied with other students	+		Involvement with peers
Unique predictors: Men			
Percentage of women faculty		+	Institutional characteristics
Public university		−	Institutional characteristics
Peer mean: Intellectual self-esteem		−	Peer group
Major: Engineering		+	Major
Withdrew from school or took leave of absence		+	Involvement in academics

(Continued)

Table 5.6 *(Continued)*

	Women	Men	Variable type
Enrolled in ethnic studies course		−	Involvement in academics
Faculty did not take comments seriously		+	Involvement with faculty
Hours per week watching television		−	Other involvement
Hedonism (drinking, smoking, and partying)		+	Other involvement
Hours per week reading for pleasure		+	Other involvement
Final R^2	33%	33%	

Notes: Direction of effect is noted only for variables that are significant at $p < .0001$.

R^2 represents the proportion of variance accounted for by all variables in the model (including precollege variables). See appendix D for the differential contribution of precollege and college variables.

* Denotes a coefficient that is significantly larger ($p < .01$) for that gender.

Enrolling in honors courses and talking with faculty outside class, while an influence for both, was stronger for men. The latter result resonates with Colbeck, Cabrera, and Terenzini's (2001) finding that interacting with faculty is especially predictive of men's engineering orientation.

Scientific predisposition is also shaped by certain forms of nonacademic engagement with peers. First is the positive effect of participating in organized demonstrations, such as protests against military efforts, unfair labor practices, or tuition increases. The connection between scientific aspirations and campus activism is not clear; however, it may be that this finding reflects an orientation toward change, whether at the scientific or broader societal level.

Second is the negative effect of joining a fraternity or sorority. Perhaps the heightened status concerns of members of the Greek system, as noted earlier, dampen scientific interests. Indeed, other research indicates a declining interest in academic science among male students who place greater value on money and power (Sax, 2001). From a campus perspective, particular attention should be paid to science majors who choose to join the Greek system. They may benefit from the formation of study groups with other science majors (both Greek and non-Greek) to create a peer group that can mitigate this negative influence of the fraternity and sorority culture.

Scientific Orientation: Factors Influencing Women Only

The role of peer influence is particularly apparent when looking at the development of women's scientific orientation. In particular, attending institutions where the student body exhibits a stronger scientific orientation and spending more time studying with other students strengthen women's interest in science. The latter finding substantiates the work of Seymour and Hewitt (1997), who report that collaborating with other students enhances women's satisfaction and success in the sciences. Clearly, institutions interested in retaining women in the sciences should consider how to most effectively foster study groups for them. At the same time, researchers need to better understand the dynamics of study groups, especially for women in the sciences: To what extent do these groups function as social-emotional support versus a forum for reinforcing academic concepts? Further, how does this depend on the group's gender composition?

Scientific Orientation: Factors Influencing Men Only

The numerous forces shaping men's scientific orientation reflect a mix of both academic and nonacademic dimensions. The role of faculty members is particularly interesting because they act as both a positive and negative force in developing men's scientific commitment. For example, men's scientific orientation tends to grow stronger when there is a larger proportion of women faculty at the institution, reflecting yet another instance where men benefit from the presence of female faculty. Why this environment would benefit men but not women is unclear, especially since the proportion of female faculty promotes women's scholarly orientation, as noted earlier. These dynamics reflect a pattern found throughout this book that suggests the need for further research on the role played by female faculty.

In an unexpected finding, feeling that faculty did not take their comments seriously *enhances* men's scientific orientation. Perhaps having comments dismissed by faculty reinvigorates men's desire to make their *own* contributions to science, rather than rely on concepts transmitted by faculty whom they may disrespect or distrust. In other words, dismissive reactions from faculty may not discourage such men but instead may empower them to take initiative in their own quest for scientific knowledge.

Interestingly, withdrawing from school relates to gains in scientific orientation among men. Although the data do not reveal why some men left their institutions, or what they did during that time, it is possible that those who were anxious to make scientific contributions were able to pursue those interests through employment or other settings. This speculation certainly merits further investigation.

Men's choices regarding time allocation also affect their scientific orientation. First, men who spend more time reading for pleasure are likely to increase their scientific commitment during college. This finding likely underscores the role played by general intellectual curiosity, though it is also possible that many men select reading material that reflects—and thus reinforces—their preexisting scientific interests. Scientific interests also grow stronger among men who spend more time engaged in drinking, smoking, or partying behaviors, perhaps reflecting an orientation toward experimentation that is characteristic of scientific pursuits.

Next, time spent watching television is a negative force in developing men's scientific orientation. The effects of television raise several possibilities. Watching television certainly takes time away from academic engagement, which has already been described as an important determinant of scientific commitment. However, it is also worth considering how television portrayed science when these students attended college and whether we might expect different results with a more recent sample of students. For instance, the 1990s witnessed the growing popularity of science fiction programming, such as *The X-Files* and *Star Trek: The Next Generation;* the fantasy-oriented nature of these shows may not have piqued men's interest in pursuing science as a vocation. However, today's generation of college students is exposed to more reality-based scientific programming, such as *CSI: Crime Scene Investigation.* Such shows have been anecdotally credited with student interest in science-related careers and an increased enrollment in corresponding college majors, such as forensics (Catalani, 2006; Lemaine, 2004; Lovgren, 2004).

One of the more counterintuitive findings is the negative effect of highly intellectual peer groups on students' scientific orientation. Perhaps relative deprivation (Davis, 1966) is at play in this situation, and men exposed to highly intellectual peer groups begin to doubt their own potential to make scientific contributions. Another possibility is that highly intellectual peer groups encourage students to pursue a wider range of intellectual pursuits, thus causing some men to reconsider science as their primary interest.

Self-Rated Physical Health

College students face a variety of choices about how to live their lives—how much to study, socialize, eat, sleep, and exercise. The choices that they make have an impact not just on how well they perform but on how good they feel. The survey asks student to rate their physical health as compared to the average person their age, and responses reveal large differences between the genders, with men rating their physical health significantly higher than women's over the course of college, though the gender gap narrows slightly by senior year. Though students' interpretations of physical health are not known—do they define it in terms of physical fitness or medical wellness?—it is important to understand the ways in which college contributes to their perceptions of their physical health and whether this varies by gender. As shown in table 5.7, there are more differences than similarities in the experiences that contribute to men's and women's ratings of their physical health.

Physical Health: Aspects of College That Influence Both Genders

Only four college experiences contribute to both women's and men's conceptions of their physical health, three of which reflect engagement or nonengagement in physical activity. Specifically, participating in intercollegiate sports or otherwise regularly engaging in exercise or sports improves students' assessments of their physical health. Though this is not unexpected, what is more interesting is that these activities are far better predictors for men than women. In other words, time spent exercising and playing sports has a greater effect on men's perceptions of their physical health than it does on women's, suggesting that men view their physical health as more inextricably tied to sports and exercise, whereas women's sense of physical health may be shaped by other factors not measured in this study.[8]

While engaging in physical activity benefits students' confidence in their physical health, a measure of inactivity— watching television—relates to declines in students' sense of physical well-being. To some extent, such declines result from the passive and sedentary nature of watching television—and the increased consumption of food that tends to accompany it. In addition, the messages conveyed on television lead students to become more critical of their physical well-being, regardless of

Table 5.7 Gender Differences in College-Level Predictors of Self-Rated Physical Health

	Women	Men	Variable type
Common predictors			
Major: Psychology	−	−	Major
Participated in intercollegiate sports	+	+*	Involvement with peers
Hours per week exercising/ playing sports	+	+*	Other involvement
Hours per week watching television	−	−	Other involvement
Unique predictors: Women			
Living on campus	+		Residence
Faculty did not take comments seriously	−		Involvement with faculty
Faculty provided honest feedback about abilities	+		Involvement with faculty
Hours per week reading for pleasure	+		Other involvement
Unique predictors: Men			
Concern about financing college		−	Finances
Major: Social sciences		−	Major
Major: Education		+	Major
Enrolled in women's studies course		−	Involvement in academics
Took part in demonstrations		+	Involvement with peers
Had a part-time job off campus		+	Involvement in work
Final R^2	29%	43%	

Notes: Direction of effect is noted only for variables that are significant at $p < .0001$.

R^2 represents the proportion of variance accounted for by all variables in the model (including precollege variables). See appendix D for the differential contribution of precollege and college variables.

* Denotes a coefficient that is significantly larger ($p < .01$) for that gender.

their actual physical condition. Indeed, images in the media that emphasize a thin ideal body image, particularly in commercials, have been linked to distortions in both women's and men's perception of their bodies (Agliata & Tantleff-Dunn, 2004; Biocca & Myers, 1992).

Physical Health: Factors Influencing Women Only

The most noteworthy indicators of women's physical health are those that reflect engagement with faculty. Honest feedback from faculty about skills and abilities relates to gains in women's physical self-image, and feeling that faculty do not take their comments seriously tends to undercut physical confidence. Given that women's interactions with faculty are presumably centered around academic issues, it is worth considering why such interactions would impact their sense of *physical* well-being. It may be that feeling dismissed by faculty exacerbates women's feelings of intimidation and self-consciousness. The unique effects of faculty interactions on female students emerge several times in this book and signal the need to better understand the dynamics of such interactions, with particular attention on how these dynamics vary by the student's and faculty member's gender.

Physical Health: Factors Influencing Men Only

Among the more interesting predictors of men's physical health ratings are those that relate to their academic studies. Notably, majoring in the social sciences and enrolling in women's studies courses contribute to declines in men's sense of physical well-being. Similar findings have been reported in other studies, such as Kezar and Moriarty (2000), who found that women's studies classes were associated with declines in social self-confidence among men only, and Thomsen, Basu, and Reinitz (1995), who suggest that women's studies courses are "threatening" environments for male students. Though we do not have details on the classroom dynamics experienced by the students in this study, it is possible that the negative effects of women's studies on men's sense of physical well-being result from those men's status as a gender token. Indeed, in landmark research on tokenism by Kanter (1977), the experience of being a gender minority can lead to a heightened sense of visibility and self-consciousness. However, one finding that questions the tokenism theory is that men who major in another predominantly female field—education—are more likely to *gain* confidence in their physical health. Perhaps the salient factor is not the gender composition of the classroom but the climate in the classroom; in other words, the particular topics addressed in women's studies courses may raise questions of self-doubt for male students. Earlier work (Sax, 1996) supports the notion that curricular climate trumps gender composition in influencing students' self-confidence. Because of the connection between women's studies courses and men's sense of physical well-being, faculty teaching such courses should be attentive to potential changes in the well-being of male students in those classes.

Self-Rated Emotional Health

The emotional health of college students is a growing concern on college campuses, as indicated by the increasing number of students who seek out psychological counseling to deal with a variety of issues, including anxiety, stress, eating disorders, and suicidal tendencies. Further, women enter college with significantly lower ratings on emotional health than do men, a gap that only grows wider over the course of college. Colleges have an opportunity to respond to students' emotional health concerns, but outside of counseling centers, what can colleges do to positively impact students' sense of emotional well-being? Are there strategies that may be particularly useful for female students? As shown in table 5.8, while there are some commonalities in the factors affecting students' sense of emotional well-being, there also are numerous interesting differences.

Table 5.8 Gender Differences in College-Level Predictors of Self-Rated Emotional Health

	Women	Men	Variable type
Common predictors			
Withdrew from school or took a leave of absence	−	−	Involvement in academics
Faculty provided honest feedback about abilities	+	+	Involvement with faculty
General faculty support	+	+	Involvement with faculty
Hours per week socializing with friends	+	+	Involvement with peers
Attended religious services	+	+*	Other involvement
Hours per week exercising/playing sports	+	+	Other involvement
Hedonism (drinking, smoking, and partying)	−	−	Other involvement
Unique predictors: Women			
Peer mean: Living on campus	+		Peer group
Distance from home	+		Residence
Aid: Work	+		Finances
Joined a fraternity or sorority	+		Involvement with peers
Hours per week commuting	−		Other involvement
Hours per week watching television	−		Other involvement
Unique predictors: Men			
Percentage of women faculty		+	Institutional characteristics
Living on campus		+	Residence
Aid: Loans		−	Finances
Major: Physical sciences, math, statistics, or computer science		−	Major
Participated in intercollegiate sports		+	Involvement with peers
Final R^2	25%	27%	

Notes: Direction of effect is noted only for variables that are significant at $p < .0001$.

R^2 represents the proportion of variance accounted for by all variables in the model (including precollege variables). See appendix D for the differential contribution of precollege and college variables.

* Denotes a coefficient that is significantly larger ($p < .01$) for that gender.

Emotional Health: Aspects of College That Influence Both Genders

For both genders, involvement is key to developing positive emotional self-concept. Activities such as exercise, sports, socializing with peers, and attending religious services help women and men to feel more emotionally healthy relative to their peers. In fact, religious service attendance is the strongest college-level determinant of emotional well-being for male students.

Interactions with faculty also play a role in students' feelings of emotional well-being, with self-ratings higher among women and men who feel academically and emotionally supported by faculty and who receive honest feedback from faculty about their skills and abilities. By contrast, disconnecting from the academic environment relates negatively to students' emotional well-being, and there are declines among women and men who withdraw from school or take a leave of absence. However, one aspect of involvement—the hedonistic activities of drinking, smoking, and partying—relates to a weaker sense of emotional health among students. This finding is significant because, for many college students, partying behaviors often involve a high degree of peer socializing, a factor just noted as enhancing emotional well-being. So it appears that while the social aspect of partying may benefit students' psychological health, drinking and smoking behaviors per se are associated with declines in students' self-reported emotional well-being. Or perhaps the reverse is true: women engage in partying behaviors as a result of declines in their sense of emotional well-being. Future research should address the causality of these relationships by examining the timing of drinking and smoking behaviors vis-à-vis changes in emotional health.

Emotional Health: Factors Influencing Women Only

Two themes emerge when examining the unique predictors of emotional health self-ratings for women. The first relates to the importance of establishing independence from one's family. Women's sense of emotional well-being benefits from their attending college farther from home but tends to suffer as a result of frequent commuting—an activity more common among students living with their families. These results resonate with findings reported earlier, and they speak once again to the importance of women gaining independence from their family. Financial independence may also be critical to women's emotional well-being; this study shows that paying for college with money saved from employment is significant in promoting women's self-rated emotional health.

The second theme relates to the importance of engaging with the campus community. Joining a sorority or attending a campus with a strong residential component enhances women's sense of their emotional well-being, results consistent with Astin's (1993c) finding that a stronger student community related to gains in emotional well-being for all students. Given the growing numbers of college women struggling with emotional health concerns, it is important for campuses to maximize women's exposure to supportive campus communities, especially for those women who are more isolated from residence halls, sororities, or other group living situations. Indeed, women who engage in a more isolating behavior—that is, watching television—tend to report greater-than-average declines in their emotional health. As discussed earlier with respect to physical health, further research is needed to uncover the extent to which the negative effects of watching television are attributable to the isolated and inactive nature of the activity or to the images that are conveyed by this medium about "ideal" health and lifestyles. The more we can learn about which aspects of television contribute to which detrimental outcomes, the better equipped campus practitioners will be to help students use their time more productively and to provide alternative programming to counteract television's negative influence.

Emotional Health: Factors Influencing Men Only

Like women, men's emotional well-being also is enhanced by measures of campus engagement, such as living on campus and participating in intercollegiate sports. In addition, aspects of climate also affect men's emotional health. For example, men's emotional health tends to grow stronger at campuses with greater numbers of female faculty. It is particularly remarkable that the presence of female faculty is *not* a predictor of emotional health for women students, especially given research showing that both male and female students view female faculty as more supportive, approachable, and sensitive than male faculty (Fassinger, 1995). It is not known from these data whether gains in men's sense of emotional well-being result from interacting more with female faculty or from being in a more supportive climate that is created by greater numbers of female faculty. Indeed, national data on college faculty show women faculty to be significantly more committed to promoting students' emotional development than their male counterparts (Lindholm, Szelenyi, Hurtado, & Korn, 2005).

Another aspect of the environment is the student's major field, and here we find that majoring in the physical sciences relates to declines in men's emotional health assessments. As with the effect of faculty gender composition, it is curious that majoring in the physical sciences influences men's emotional health but not women's, especially given women's underrepresentation in those fields and the numerous reports of a chilly climate for women in the sciences. However, other research supports the notion that men's emotional well-being is more sensitive to the dynamics of the college scientific culture than is the case for women. Specifically, a major ethnography of undergraduate science education found that the sciences' competitive culture undermined men's morale more than women's, especially because men tend to approach their science education as a solo endeavor (Seymour & Hewitt, 1997). Women in that study, on the other hand, were more likely to explore coping strategies, such as working collaboratively with other students and seeking help from the institution. Because of this, campuses should do more than just focus on recruiting and retaining more women in the sciences; they also should give more attention to their male students' psychological needs.

Feeling Overwhelmed

One of the greatest challenges facing students as they transition to college is effectively managing their time. Feeling "overwhelmed by all I have to do" is a common concern among both genders, but it is a more significant source of stress for female students. This is likely due to the range of responsibilities that women undertake—volunteering, participating in student clubs, fulfilling household commitments, studying—more frequently than do men. As shown in table 5.9, changes in feeling overwhelmed during college reveal interesting information about what contributes to student stress during college and how that differs by gender.

Feeling Overwhelmed: Aspects of College That Influence Both Genders

Engaging in leisure-time activities, such as socializing or reading for pleasure, tends to alleviate stress for both genders. In fact, reading for pleasure is the most potent predictor of stress reduction for college women. Yet these findings do raise questions about causality: do socializing and pleasure reading reduce stress levels, or do students engage in these behaviors more frequently as a result of actually feeling less burdened by their responsibilities?

Studying, on the other hand, relates to gains in feeling overwhelmed for both women and men. As is the case for socializing and reading for pleasure, it is not clear whether time

Table 5.9 Gender Differences in College-Level Predictors of Feeling Overwhelmed

	Women	Men	Variable type
Common predictors			
Felt bored in class	+*	+	Involvement in academics
Hours per week studying/ doing homework	+	+	Involvement in academics
Faculty did not take comments seriously	+	+	Involvement with faculty
Studied with other students	+	+	Involvement with peers
Hours per week socializing with friends	−	−*	Involvement with peers
Hours per week reading for pleasure	−*	−	Other involvement
Opposing predictors			
Challenged a professor's ideas in class	+	−	Involvement with faculty
Unique predictors: Women			
Percentage of nonwhite students	+		Institutional characteristics
Peer mean: Materialism and social status	−		Peer group
Major: Engineering	+		Major
Major: Physical sciences, math, statistics, or computer science	+		Major
Major: Social sciences	+		Major
Enrolled in women's studies course	+		Involvement in academics
Worked on independent study project	+		Involvement in academics
Student government	−		Involvement with peers
Hedonism (drinking, smoking, and partying)	+		Other involvement
Hours per week exercising/ playing sports	−		Other involvement

(Continued)

Table 5.9 (Continued)

	Women	Men	Variable type
Unique predictors: Men			
Percentage of women faculty		−	Institutional characteristics
Major: Business		−	Major
Attended racial/cultural awareness workshop		+	Involvement with peers
Hours per week commuting		+	Other involvement
Hours per week watching television		−	Other involvement
Final R^2	18%	18%	

Notes: Direction of effect is noted only for variables that are significant at $p < .0001$.

R^2 represents the proportion of variance accounted for by all variables in the model (including precollege variables). See appendix D for the differential contribution of precollege and college variables.

* Denotes a coefficient that is significantly larger ($p < .01$) for that gender.

spent studying leads to higher stress levels or whether feeling overwhelmed leads students to spend extra time studying. Future research will need to address that question. In either case, one thing is clear: the more time students spend trying to meet academic demands does not reduce the pressure they feel to meet those commitments.

Experiences in the classroom also contribute to feelings of stress for both genders. First is feeling bored in class, which portends higher levels of stress, especially among women. It is possible that in-class boredom is a function of feeling disengaged or lost during class time and that difficulties comprehending course material raise students' anxiety levels. The other course-related contributor to stress is students' feeling that faculty did not take their comments seriously. This finding is similar to the impact of feeling dismissed on women's sense of physical health and suggests that faculty can have an unintended negative effect on their students. It is important for campuses to reflect on how students and faculty perceive their interactions with one another.

To what extent is there a disconnect between faculty intentions and student reactions? What is the best way to educate faculty about the possibly harmful effects of their classroom behaviors?

Feeling Overwhelmed: Opposing Influences for Women and Men

Faculty's potentially negative effect on students, and women in particular, is also revealed in one of this book's more fascinating findings: challenging professors' ideas in class relates to increases in stress among women but declines in stress among men. This raises the question of how women and men interpret their classroom interactions with professors. Might challenging professors in the classroom release stress for men while promoting anxiety among women? Evidence of the latter is provided by Salter and Persaud (2003), who report discomfort and anxiety among women who spoke out in classes, especially when the professor was perceived as discouraging. It is also possible that the judgment of peers heightens women's anxiety in this situation. Future research should probe more deeply into the conditions that allow women to feel safe in challenging faculty or other students. Faculty should create spaces for women to feel comfortable expressing their views, perhaps by encouraging smaller group activities.

Feeling Overwhelmed: Factors Influencing Women Only

For women, a combination of academic and extracurricular experiences affect feelings of stress. Majoring in the physical sciences, engineering, and even the social sciences contributes to gains in stress for women students only. This raises the question about whether it is the climate in these fields, or the intensity of the academic demands, that heightens women's feelings of stress, though it is likely a combination of both.

Interestingly, women's studies courses—which presumably offer a welcoming climate for women—also relate to increases in stress. One possibility is that these courses raise women's consciousness and sense of obligation to advocate for gender equity, which even further raises their sense of feeling overwhelmed by all that they have to do. Other research on the impact of women's studies courses supports that proposition (Bargad & Hyde, 1991; Stake & Hoffman, 2001; Thomsen et al., 1995).

We also find more pronounced gains in stress among women who undertake independent study opportunities. Given that independent study is typically not required of students, this finding highlights the potential downside of assuming this additional academic responsibility, at least for women.

Women's stress levels also stem from their involvement in extracurricular activities. Exercise, sports, and participation in student government tend to alleviate stress among college women. Though these behaviors do involve a time commitment that might otherwise contribute to stress, these particular forms of involvement—like socializing and reading for pleasure, noted earlier—provide women with a healthy release from purely academic pressures.

Alternatively, more hedonistic forms of release—such as drinking, smoking, and other partying behaviors—are associated with increases in stress among women. Here the direction of effect is not clear. On the one hand, gains in stress may precede partying behaviors, as stress-motivated drinking among college students has been shown to be more prevalent among women than men (Perkins, 1999; Wechsler & Rohman, 1981). On the other hand, the emotional consequences of partying behaviors may be greater for women than men, especially as they relate to outcomes such as relationship problems, academic problems, or unwanted sexual activity.

Finally, and quite interestingly, the peer group's concern with materialism and status contributes to lower stress levels among women. This finding is counterintuitive because we might imagine that a materialistic peer culture would add to students' own stress, especially among students who have fewer resources. One interpretation is that by placing greater emphasis on status, power, and wealth, the value system in a highly materialistic peer environment de-emphasizes academics, thereby reducing women's own concern about meeting their academic and other responsibilities.

Feeling Overwhelmed: Factors Influencing Men Only

An interesting range of experiences relate to stress levels among men. Some are unsurprising, such as the fact that commuting to campus contributes to stress and that watching television helps alleviate stress. In fact, television viewing is the college experience most strongly associated with stress reduction in men.

More surprising is the effect of attending a racial or cultural awareness workshop, which relates to increases in men's feelings of being overwhelmed. As suggested by the work of Tatum (1992), this finding may reflect how exposure to race-related content heightens some students' sense of anxiety or guilt. In fact, these workshops may contribute to stress by raising men's expectations to *do* something about racial inequities, a possibility supported by the positive effect of these workshops on social activist goals, reported earlier. Though it is unclear why this phenomenon would be detected only among men, other research suggests that awareness of one's own group privilege has a greater impact on psychological well-being for men than women (Branscombe, 1998).

Finally, men are less likely to develop stress if they are enrolled at campuses with greater proportions of women faculty. This once again demonstrates the unique benefits accrued by men in institutions with more female faculty, as reported earlier in this chapter with respect to leadership orientation, scientific orientation, and emotional health. This emerging pattern is peculiar because it is not clear why men would benefit more from the presence of female faculty than do women. As was the case with the discussion earlier, more information is needed to understand whether women faculty directly attend to men's developmental needs or whether there is a positive climate shift for men when more women are on the faculty.

Self-Change: Cultural Awareness

In a time of heightened international tensions and a global economy, the need to raise students' consciousness about the world around them is more important than ever. This section addresses the extent to which students believe they have strengthened their cultural awareness, as defined by their understanding of local community problems, understanding of national social problems, knowledge of people of other races or cultures, and ability to get along with people of other races or cultures. The majority of students do report gains in these areas during college, with practically no gender difference in the perception of these gains. Shown in table 5.10 are aspects of college that enhance or detract from the development of women's and men's cultural awareness.

Cultural Awareness: Aspects of College That Influence Both Genders

Among aspects of college related to gains in cultural awareness, the majority are significant for both women and men. This finding is consistent with Pascarella and Terenzini's (2005) conclusion that despite women's higher scores on measures of social and cultural awareness, the impact of college on this and related outcomes is generally similar for women and men. This point is further supported by the fact that nearly every predictor of cultural awareness in this study was also identified by Astin (1993c) using combined samples of men and women. The present study,

Table 5.10 Gender Differences in College-Level Predictors of Self-Change: Cultural Awareness

	Women	Men	Variable type
Common predictors			
Percentage of women faculty	+	+*	Institutional characteristics
Percentage of bachelor's degrees in science, math, and engineering	−	−	Peer group
Living on campus	+	+	Residence
Major: Social sciences	+	+	Major
Enrolled in ethnic studies course	+	+	Involvement in academics
Enrolled in women's studies course	+	+*	Involvement in academics
General faculty support	+	+*	Involvement with faculty
Attended racial/cultural awareness workshop	+	+	Involvement with peers
Hours per week student clubs or groups	+	+	Involvement with peers
Leadership training	+	+*	Involvement with peers
Social diversity experiences	+	+*	Involvement with peers
Studied with other students	+	+*	Involvement with peers
Took part in demonstrations	+*	+	Involvement with peers
Hours per week reading for pleasure	+	+	Other involvement
Volunteering or community service	+*	+	Other involvement
Unique predictors: Women			
Major: Physical sciences, math, statistics, or computer science	−		Major
Unique predictors: Men			
Percentage of bachelor's degrees in education		+	Peer group
Percentage of women undergraduates		+	Peer group

(Continued)

Table 5.10 *(Continued)*

	Women	Men	Variable type
Major: Business		−	Major
Major: Engineering		−	Major
Hours per week studying/ doing homework		+	Involvement in academics
Felt bored in class		−	Involvement in academics
Hours per week talking with faculty outside class		+	Involvement with faculty
Attended religious services		+	Other involvement
Final R^2	23%	27%	

Notes: Direction of effect is noted only for variables that are significant at $p < .0001$.

R^2 represents the proportion of variance accounted for by all variables in the model (including precollege variables). See appendix D for the differential contribution of precollege and college variables.

* Denotes a coefficient that is significantly larger ($p < .01$) for that gender.

however, identifies whether the effects of these factors were stronger for one gender or the other.

Growth in cultural awareness is most strongly enhanced by experiences that expose students to a broad range of people and viewpoints, such as attending racial/cultural awareness workshops, enrolling in ethnic studies courses, enrolling in women's studies courses, participating in social diversity experiences, participating in organized demonstrations, volunteering, living on campus, being involved in student clubs and groups, studying with other students, participating in leadership training, and even reading for pleasure. Faculty also play a role in promoting cultural awareness, as indicated by the positive effects of general faculty support and of attending colleges with greater percentages of women faculty. It is interesting to note that the only variable to relate negatively to cultural awareness for students of both genders is the percentage of bachelor's degrees awarded in science and engineering fields. This finding resonates with the negative effect of scientific culture on female students' desire to effect social or cultural change, as noted earlier in this chapter.

Cultural Awareness: Factors Influencing Women Only

Only one aspect of college uniquely relates to cultural awareness among women: majoring in mathematics or physical sciences. In this case, the relationship is negative, suggesting that math and physical science fields discourage women's interest in larger social issues. This is similar to the effect of the physical sciences on women's social activist orientations, as noted earlier. In fact, other work has shown that women drop out of academic science due to a perceived lack of connection between science and issues of societal or cultural importance (Sax, 1994d, 2001). Such women often opt for careers as physicians or teachers because they perceive that these occupations will enable them to have a direct impact on others' well-being. However, those women represent a loss to the scientific research community, which could benefit from the perspectives and talents of a more diverse pool of students.

Cultural Awareness: Factors Influencing Men Only

For men, attending institutions with greater proportions of female students encourages gains in cultural awareness. Related to that is the fact that men's cultural awareness is positively influenced by attending institutions that award a greater percentage of degrees in education (a traditionally female field) and is negatively influenced by majoring in business or engineering (traditionally male fields). The role played by a strong female presence is also demonstrated in several studies showing the positive effects of women's colleges on students' cultural awareness and acceptance of diversity (Astin, 1993c; Kim, 2001; Smith, 1990). However, the contribution of the present study is an examination of women's representation as it affects *men* at *coeducational* institutions. These results underscore findings reported in Sax (1996), which highlighted the connection between predominantly female campus environments and progressive outlooks on issues of race and gender.

Self-Change: Religious Beliefs and Convictions

Do students' religious beliefs and convictions become stronger or weaker during college? Evidence from this study suggests that, for both women and men, religious commitments grow marginally stronger during college. However, this is the area of *least* growth for students, who report much larger gains in other attributes, such as overall knowledge, cognitive abilities, and interpersonal and leadership skills. Gains in religious commitment are slightly larger among women, with 40 percent of women and 35 percent of men reporting that their religious beliefs and convictions became "stronger" or "much stronger" during college. Table 5.11 provides aspects of the college experience that contribute to the strength of women's and men's religious convictions.

Religious Convictions: Aspects of College That Influence Both Genders

Several aspects of involvement portend a strengthening of religious commitments among both women and men, such as attending religious services and participating in student clubs and groups, some of which have a religious affiliation. However, isolating or hedonistic activities—such as watching television and drinking, smoking, and partying—tend to signify a weakening of religious convictions during college.

The institution's characteristics, such as size and type, are also especially salient forces in developing both gender's religious convictions. Specifically, religious beliefs and convictions are strengthened at smaller institutions, most notably private, religiously affiliated four-year colleges. The role of the peer group is particularly significant, in that religious convictions tend to be suppressed at colleges where the student body exhibits liberal, materialistic, or scientific orientations. It may be that many students find their traditional religious beliefs to be at

Table 5.11 Gender Differences in College-Level Predictors of Self-Change: Religious Beliefs and Convictions

	Women	Men	Variable type
Common predictors			
Other religious private 4-year college	+	+	Institutional characteristics
Number of full-time undergraduates	–	–	Institutional characteristics
Peer mean: Expectation to get a job in college	+	+	Peer group
Peer mean: Materialism and social status	–	–	Peer group
Peer mean: Political views	–	–	Peer group
Peer mean: Years of study in math and science	–	–	Peer group
Hours per week student clubs or groups	+	+	Involvement with peers
Attended religious services	+	+*	Other involvement
Hedonism (drinking, smoking, and partying)	–	–	Other involvement
Hours per week watching television	–	–	Other involvement
Opposing predictors			
Enrolled in women's studies course	–	+	Involvement in academics
Participated in intercollegiate sports	–	+	Involvement with peers
Unique predictors: Women			
Private nonsectarian 4-year college	+		Institutional characteristics
Public 4-year college	–		Institutional characteristics
Felt bored in class	–		Involvement in academics
Hours per week reading for pleasure	+		Other involvement

(Continued)

Table 5.11 *(Continued)*

	Women	Men	Variable type
Unique predictors: Men			
Major: Psychology		−	Major
Social diversity experiences		+	Involvement with peers
Final R^2	28%	32%	

Notes: Direction of effect is noted only for variables that are significant at $p < .0001$.

R^2 represents the proportion of variance accounted for by all variables in the model (including precollege variables). See appendix D for the differential contribution of precollege and college variables.

* Denotes a coefficient that is significantly larger ($p < .01$) for that gender.

odds with these student cultures, making it difficult to hold on to their religious commitments during college.

Religious Convictions: Opposing Influences for Women and Men

Two aspects of student involvement produce opposite effects on religious convictions for the two genders. First is enrolling in women's studies courses, which relates to a strengthening of religious beliefs for men but a weakening religious commitment among women. Enrolling in women's studies may lead women to question the traditional gender role values of their own religion. In fact, women's studies courses have been associated with increased awareness of and sensitivity to gender issues among female students (Bargad & Hyde, 1991; Stake & Hoffman, 2001; Stake, Roades, Rose, Ellis, & West, 1994).

There are at least two possible explanations for gains in religious convictions among men enrolling in women's studies courses. One is that the knowledge and perspectives provided in those courses may strengthen men's commitment to compassion and justice, values inherent in many religious doctrines. Another, and more controversial, possibility is that awareness of gender inequities presented in women's studies courses may reaffirm the religious convictions of men who already espouse traditional gender role orientations.

The other college experience yielding opposite effects on the strength of women's and men's religious convictions is participation in intercollegiate athletics. Here involvement in team sports is associated with greater religious commitment among men but a weaker commitment among women. These dynamics, like those related to women's studies courses, are fascinating to explore. Consider the frequently televised images of male college football and basketball players engaged in locker-room or sideline prayer, and it is not hard to imagine intercollegiate sports as reinforcing men's religious convictions. Participating in intercollegiate sports, however, represents a less traditional activity for women. Given many religions' emphasis on traditional gender roles, participating in competitive sports may weaken a sense of religious conviction among some female athletes.

Religious Convictions: Factors Influencing Women Only

Intellectual stimulation appears to be particularly important in strengthening women's religious commitments, as evidenced by two aspects of involvement. The first is feeling bored in class, which detracts from women's religious commitment, and the second is reading for pleasure, which promotes stronger religious convictions. This suggests that, for women, feeling intellectually engaged both inside and outside the classroom strengthens religious beliefs. Though we do not know specifically what types of reading materials strengthen women's religious convictions, it is possible that religious texts are included in their definition of pleasure reading. Future research should identify what men and women constitute as pleasure reading and probe more deeply into how different forms of writing—including novels, poetry, magazines, newspapers, and Web sites—contribute differentially to aspects of student development.

Religious Convictions: Factors Influencing Men Only

Only two aspects of college relate to changes in religious beliefs and convictions for men only: majoring in psychology, which contributes to declines in religious commitments, and social diversity experiences, which predicts a strengthening of convictions. Recall that social diversity experiences also promoted gains in cultural awareness, especially for men; these findings emphasize the potential for diverse interactions to foster both spiritual and cultural awareness among men.

Summary

College women and men view themselves quite differently from each other, as evidenced by gender differences across numerous self-ratings and measures of value orientation. Men, for example, exhibit greater self-confidence than women when it comes to their intellectual abilities, leadership potential, artistic talents, and physical and psychological well-being. They also express a stronger orientation toward science and place greater personal importance on attaining positions of status or power. Women, on the other hand, have a stronger community orientation; they identify helping others, improving communities, and learning about people from different racial/ethnic backgrounds as important endeavors. Women are also more likely than men to report a strengthening of religious convictions during college.

This chapter set out to reveal whether the impact of college on these traits would differ for women and men. An examination of the several hundred significant relationships identified for women and men reveals that gender differences do exist in the factors contributing to these outcomes. Each of these conditional effects raises new questions for research and offers new insights for campus practitioners. To better appreciate the relevance of such a complex set of findings, it's worth taking another look at the gender-based patterns of influence that have emerged across multiple outcomes.

We have learned that when students and faculty interact with one another—whether in a classroom, faculty office, or laboratory—the result of such exchanges is often different for male and female students. Though faculty may think that they are treating women and men the same—and, in fact, they might actually be doing so—women and men tend to *react* differently to these encounters. For example, when women take the initiative to challenge their professors in the classroom, it often results in heightened stress. For men, the opposite is true: facing up to faculty appears to alleviate stress. The consequences of feeling undervalued may be especially severe for female students, whose sense of physical well-being is sensitive to treatment by their professors.

These results have important implications for faculty, who need to be mindful of the possible unintended consequences of their interactions with female students in and out of the classroom. Faculty should be better educated about how to create an open exchange of ideas in a way that leaves all students feeling that their perspectives were heard and valued. Counselors and academic advisers who want to best serve the needs of their stressed-out female students ought to probe more deeply about women's interactions with their professors and their perceived treatment in the classroom. Also, campuses should use orientation and first-year seminars as an opportunity to better educate students about what to expect from faculty, so students know that critical feedback or tough questions from professors do not necessarily indicate that the faculty are second-guessing them, but instead are pushing them for all the right reasons. Certainly, we need to look toward future research as a way of identifying effective strategies for promoting healthier student-faculty interactions as well as an inclusive and nonthreatening classroom climate for students of both genders.

One of the important questions for future research is how all these dynamics relate to the faculty member's gender. Do the behaviors of women faculty have the same effect on male and female students? Though the data in this study do not provide answers to this question, we do find, somewhat surprisingly, that campuses with higher proportions of female faculty tend to provide uniquely positive environments for male students. As women compose a greater share of faculty ranks, male students develop more confidence in their leadership skills and a healthier sense of psychological well-being. They also become more interested in science and develop greater consciousness about the world around them. Though female students also benefit from greater numbers of women faculty, especially in terms of their academic confidence, the advantages appear to be more salient for men. This can also be viewed in another way: campuses dominated by male faculty tend to inhibit aspects of men's development. How and why does this happen? Once again, it is incumbent on future research to help us better understand how the gender composition of the faculty shapes campus culture.

Through workshops, courses, and residential-life programming, campuses provide a variety of opportunities for students to learn about the history and experiences of people from different racial, ethnic, and cultural backgrounds. Students also create their own opportunities to learn about one another by forming personal relationships with students from different backgrounds. But exposure to diversity also yields differential effects on women and men. Developing friendships or romantic relationships with individuals of different racial/ethnic backgrounds tends to impact men's sense of cultural awareness more strongly than women's. Taking women's studies courses also enhances men's broader cultural interests more strongly than women's. And participating in campus-based diversity workshops encourages a more creative and artistic orientation among men. Thus, we might view diverse interactions and learning experiences as particularly eye-opening experiences for male students.

The evidence certainly points to the value of encouraging students, and especially men, to expand their social and academic horizons by engaging with topics and people that reflect a range of backgrounds and perspectives. Yet enlightenment also has its challenges, as evidenced by heightened stress levels among men who participate in diversity workshops and a weakening of self-rated physical health among men enrolling in women's studies courses. Though it can be anxiety provoking to engage in self-reflection and question long-standing beliefs, it is also an important part of students' developmental processes. Thus, as campuses continue to introduce and expand diversity programming, it may be useful to assess the extent to which such programming closes the loop by addressing the developmental repercussions that arise, especially for men who may be experiencing greater internal struggle following these learning opportunities.

Religious involvement also plays a more salient role in the lives of college men than it does for women. Attending religious services, presumably in a formal setting such as a church or synagogue, leads men to develop a stronger commitment to learning about the world around them and contributing to social change. It also encourages men to feel a greater sense of emotional health and religious conviction. This does not suggest that college women are not developing their religious or spiritual identities—in fact, women report greater gains in their religious convictions during college than do men—but instead that the impact of religious *involvement* tends to be stronger for men. Here future research can be informative by identifying which specific forms of religious involvement are more influential for which students. Do women and men benefit equally from Bible or Torah study? What impact do spiritual meditation groups or religiously based online social networking have on men's and women's identity development? The answers to these questions may help campus practitioners most effectively advise students who seek to make religious or spiritual connections during college.

Another theme that has emerged in this chapter is that gaining distance from one's family is particularly important for female students. Parents—especially those who discourage their daughters from going away to college—may be interested in knowing that leaving home enables women to develop a stronger sense of confidence in their academic abilities and in their potential to be effective leaders. Going away to college also promotes women's psychological well-being, whereas those staying close to home tend to feel more emotionally stunted. For men, on the other hand, whether they attend college close to home or three thousand miles away seems to make no practical difference on these aspects of identity development.

While students and their parents might use this information to help guide their decisions in the college admissions process, campuses may benefit from knowing that they should pay special attention to the needs of female students who remain strongly connected to their families during college. Indeed, for many women, especially the growing numbers of low-income women attending college, moving far away from home is simply not an option. Efforts should thus be made to involve these women as much as possible in campus life, so that they can reap some of the benefits accrued by women who are able to attend college farther from home. Further, more research is needed to uncover why women benefit more than men from gaining distance from their families. What sorts of ongoing student-parent interactions are most or least beneficial for women and men? Might the results of the present study differ for a more current sample of students who are able to use technology to remain connected to their families regardless of the distance between them?

Several of these themes reemerge in the following chapters, which examine the influence of college on men's and women's political and social values as well as on their academic and career goals. Chapter 8 revisits these and other themes and discusses more fully the practical implications of these results for college planning, programming, and research.

Notes

1. This factor is similar, though not identical, to Astin's (1993b, 1993c) scholar typology; however, his factor also included mathematical ability and degree aspirations, which the present study examines as separate outcome measures.

2. The negative effect of scientific fields is inconsistent with previous research revealing gains in scholarly/academic self-confidence among scientific/technical majors overall (Astin, 1993c) and men in particular (Pascarella, Smart, Ethington, & Nettles, 1987). However, both Astin (1993c) and Pascarella et al. (1987) include mathematical ability in their indicators of academic self-confidence, such that we would expect greater confidence among students majoring in scientific fields. The present study analyzes math ability as a stand-alone college outcome in chapter 7.

3. The social activist factor is identical to that used by Astin (1993b, 1993c).

4. This possibility is supported by the fact that the item with the highest loading in the social activist factor is "influencing social values."

5. The artist factor is nearly identical to that used by Astin (1993b, 1993c), though his did not include a measure of creativity.

6. The status striver factor is identical to that used by Astin (1993b, 1993c).

7. The leader factor is similar to the leader typology used by Astin (1993b, 1993c) and the social self-concept factor identified by Pascarella et al. (1987), although those versions also included self-rated popularity.

8. This is supported by the fact that variables included in the model are better predictors of men's physical health ratings than women's, as indicated by the R^2 listed at the bottom of table 5.7.

6

POLITICAL AND SOCIAL VALUES

Decades of research provide clear evidence that college plays a role in developing students' values and attitudes. Changes in students' value orientations are primarily viewed as a function of interactions with peers and faculty both in and out of the classroom. However, unlike some outcomes of college where there is agreement about what constitutes positive change—such as with academic self-confidence, physical health, and psychological well-being—there is generally no consensus in higher education about what are considered desirable changes in students' values and attitudes. Consequently, information about how college affects changes in this domain may not provide clear direction for changes in practice.

Nevertheless, understanding the ways in which students' college experiences shape their beliefs and value orientations is important because it enables campus practitioners to consider additional consequences of student engagement with programs, services, practitioners, and student peers. In addition, knowing whether college differentially influences women's and men's values further enhances our understanding of these dynamics, especially since some of the largest gender differences among incoming students relate to value orientation. In this chapter, gender differences in the impact of college are assessed across the following domains: political engagement, political orientation, attitudes on a wide range of political and social issues, and values in the realms of racial understanding, family, and self.

Political Engagement

Given the fairly low levels of political engagement reported among students entering college, especially among women, it is useful to examine what colleges can do to encourage students' interest and involvement in the political arena. And it is especially important since developing political interest during college can serve as the foundation for students' longer-term awareness of political issues and current events. This section considers political engagement as both behavioral and attitudinal, as indicated by a composite of two survey questions: how frequently students discuss politics and how much they value keeping up to date on political affairs. As shown in table 6.1, the college years do provide numerous opportunities for students to become more politically engaged, most often as a result of their interactions with peers, faculty, and the curriculum.

Political Engagement: Aspects of College That Influence Both Genders

For both women and men, heightened interest in politics stems from engaging in cocurricular campus leadership opportunities, such as involvement in campus government, membership in student clubs and groups, and participation in organized demonstrations. These findings reinforce the value of providing students with a wide range of leadership opportunities that allow them to see firsthand the connection between issues and action, whether at the campus, community, or broader societal level.

Political interest also is enhanced by academic involvement, such as with faculty and the curriculum. Faculty, for example, contribute to gains in students' political engagement by interacting with them outside class, creating an atmosphere where students can challenge them, and being supportive of students, both academically and personally. It is difficult to know from these results whether faculty intentionally encourage students to

**Table 6.1 Gender Differences in College-Level Predictors
of Political Engagement**

	Women	Men	Variable type
Common predictors			
Major: History or political science	+	+	Major
Major: Health profession	–	–	Major
Enrolled in ethnic studies course	+	+*	Involvement in academics
Enrolled in women's studies course	+	+*	Involvement in academics
Hours per week using a personal computer	+	+	Involvement in academics
Challenged a professor's ideas in class	+	+	Involvement with faculty
General faculty support	+	+*	Involvement with faculty
Hours per week talking with faculty outside class	+	+	Involvement with faculty
Hours per week student clubs or groups	+	+*	Involvement with peers
Student government	+	+*	Involvement with peers
Took part in demonstrations	+	+	Involvement with peers
Tutored another student	+	+*	Involvement with peers
Hours per week reading for pleasure	+	+	Other involvement
Opposing predictors			
Peer mean: Living on campus	+	–	Peer group
Unique predictors: Women			
Peer mean: Intellectual self-esteem	+		Peer group
Peer mean: Socioeconomic status	+		Peer group
Major: Journalism or communications	+		Major
Major: Engineering	–		Major

(Continued)

Table 6.1 *(Continued)*

	Women	Men	Variable type
Hedonism (drinking, smoking, and partying)	+		Other involvement
Hours per week household/ childcare duties	+		Other involvement
Unique predictors: Men			
Number of full-time undergraduates		−	Institutional characteristics
Living on campus		+	Residence
Major: Physical sciences, math, statistics, or computer science		−	Major
Major: Psychology		−	Major
Hours per week studying/doing homework		+	Involvement in academics
Final R^2	37%	41%	

Notes: Direction of effect is noted only for variables that are significant at $p < .0001$.

R^2 represents the proportion of variance accounted for by all variables in the model (including precollege variables). See appendix D for the differential contribution of precollege and college variables.

* Denotes a coefficient that is significantly larger ($p < .01$) for that gender.

become more politically engaged, or whether intellectually stimulating and positive faculty interactions raise students' awareness of political and social issues, thus providing a springboard for greater interest in political affairs. Future research should probe more deeply into the nature of topics that students and faculty address outside the formal classroom setting.

The influence of becoming aware also is evident in the role played by the curriculum. Specifically, students majoring in history or political science and those taking ethnic and/or women's studies courses tend to engage more politically. These academic environments generally provide students with an opportunity to learn about and reflect on current political and social issues, such as the economy, national security, affirmative action, and gender equity. Surprisingly, however, majoring in the health professions predicts declines in political engagement for women and men. It is unclear why undergraduates in majors such as nursing, pharmacology, and physical therapy would become less politically engaged relative to their peers in other fields, especially given that health care is a major national issue. Perhaps for some of these students, frustration with the status of health care and related insurance issues converts to pessimism and disinterest in political affairs. For others, perhaps the time-intensive nature of health science majors precludes them from engaging in political issues.

Finally, political engagement is seen in both women and men who spend time using computers and reading for pleasure. In each of these cases, the direction of effect is not immediately clear. It is possible that pleasure reading and computer use, particularly time on the Internet, expose students to a variety of political issues, thus raising their awareness and interest in these areas. It is equally possible that gains in political interest may *lead* students to spend more time using computers or reading books, newspapers, and magazines to learn more about specific political issues and current events. Future research should identify what students are reading, both online and offline, and how that influences their interest in political issues. Such information may point campus political groups to ways they can reach particular student populations, creating a kind of synergy for political activism.

Political Engagement: Opposing Influences for Women and Men

Interestingly, attending a more residential campus affects men's and women's political engagement in *opposite* ways. For women, interest in politics is strengthened at campuses where more students live on campus, perhaps reflecting heightened opportunities for extracurricular involvement or informal interactions with faculty, which have already been shown to promote political engagement. For men, however, attending residential colleges relates to declines in political engagement. In other words, interest in politics grows stronger for men at campuses with a larger commuter population. Without additional information on the nature of men's interactions with residential or commuter populations, this finding is difficult to interpret. Future research could tell us, for example, whether exposure to a commuter population raises men's awareness of larger political issues and events, regardless of whether the student himself lives on or off campus.

Political Engagement: Factors Influencing Women Only

Though we have already seen ways in which a major field contributes to political engagement for both genders, we now see that some disciplines influence political interest uniquely for each gender. Majoring in engineering, for example, is associated with a weakening interest in politics for female students. In fact, as shown in other research, the perceived lack of connection between science and engineering fields and broader political and social issues deters women's persistence in these fields during college (Sax, 2001). Yet women who major in journalism or communication fields grow more interested in politics during the course of their college career. This is surely a function of the attention that these fields devote to political issues, especially relative to what is addressed in other majors, with the exception of history and political science, as noted earlier.

Characteristics of the student peer group also shape women's attention to politics, with wealthier and more intellectually self-confident student bodies raising women's interest in politics. It's worth noting that partying behaviors—another aspect of peer group interaction—also relate to gains in women's interest in politics. It is not clear why the effect of partying would be observed for women only, though it is possible that it reflects the influence of women partying with men, a group exhibiting relatively greater political interest overall.

Political Engagement: Factors Influencing Men Only

The influence of the curriculum is again revealed as men majoring in psychology or the physical sciences become less interested in politics during college. Perhaps these fields narrow the scope of men's attention to issues more germane to these particular disciplines, rather than open them to broader political and social issues. We also find that, uniquely for men, time spent studying or doing homework enhances political engagement. This finding is consistent with the role of exposure to content knowledge, as reflected earlier in the effects of taking women's studies or ethnic studies courses, reading for pleasure, and using computers. Simply put, the more time devoted to learning, the greater men's concern with political issues.

Political Orientation

Women begin college with more liberal political orientations than do men, a gender gap that remains steady over four years. However, political leanings do change over the course of college, with both genders becoming increasingly more liberal over time. Though the liberalizing effect of college is well documented in higher education research, we lack an understanding of whether the influence of college on students' political orientation differs for women and men. This section describes aspects of college that contribute to changes in students' political orientation—either in becoming more liberal or more conservative—and explores whether these factors differentiate by gender. The nature of change is indeed different for women and men, such that the majority of the influences on students' political orientation are unique to one gender or the other. In table 6.2, positive relationships indicate improvement in a liberal direction, while negative relationships point to shifts in a conservative direction.

Table 6.2 Gender Differences in College-Level Predictors of Political Orientation

	Women	Men	Variable type
Common predictors			
Peer mean: Political views	+	+	Peer group
Enrolled in ethnic studies course	+	+*	Involvement in academics
Attended racial/cultural awareness workshop	+	+	Involvement with peers
Took part in demonstrations	+	+	Involvement with peers
Attended religious services	−*	−	Other involvement
Unique predictors: Women			
Peer mean: Understanding of others	−		Peer group
Major: Social sciences	+		Major
Major: Business	−		Major
Major: Journalism or communications	−		Major
Enrolled in women's studies course	+		Involvement in academics
Student government	−		Involvement with peers
Joined a fraternity or sorority	−		Involvement with peers
Worked part-time on campus	+		Involvement in work
Hedonism (drinking, smoking, and partying)	+		Other involvement
Unique predictors: Men			
Public university		−	Institutional characteristics
Concern about financing college		+	Finances
Major: English or humanities		+	Major
Hours per week talking with faculty outside class		+	Involvement with faculty
Participated in intercollegiate sports		+	Involvement with peers
Hours per week watching television		−	Other involvement
Final R^2	43%	40%	

Notes: Direction of effect is noted only for variables that are significant at $p < .0001$.

R^2 represents the proportion of variance accounted for by all variables in the model (including precollege variables). See appendix D for the differential contribution of precollege and college variables.

* Denotes a coefficient that is significantly larger ($p < .01$) for that gender.

Political Orientation: Aspects of College That Influence Both Genders

Student peer groups play an influential role in contributing to liberal political orientations for both women and men. Specifically, those students who are exposed to more liberal peer groups—such as through enrolling in ethnic studies courses, attending racial cultural awareness workshops, or taking part in organized demonstrations—tend to develop more liberal political orientations over the course of college. By contrast, religious service attendance is associated with shifts in a more politically conservative direction, especially among women. These findings are in line with numerous studies documenting the impact of these peer environments on political orientations of all students, regardless of gender (Astin, 1993c; Dey, 1996, 1997a; Pascarella & Terenzini, 2005).

Political Orientation: Factors Influencing Women Only

Peer group influence is again evident when we look at the forces shaping political orientation exclusively for women. In particular, two campus subcultures—student government and the Greek system—are associated with the development of more conservative viewpoints among women students. The effects of these experiences likely owe to the relatively more conservative peer groups found in student government, fraternities, and sororities, as other research on this topic suggests (Astin, 1993c; Astin & Denson, 2006). Yet drinking, smoking, and general partying contribute to more liberal orientations among women. Astin (1993c) also found that partying behaviors contribute to the development of students' liberal orientations, though his study did not differentiate by gender.

Women's political orientations also are shaped by their choice of major field, with those majoring in the social sciences and taking women's studies courses experiencing higher-than-expected gains in liberalism during college. Increases in conservative identification, on the other hand, are observed among women majoring in business or journalism/communications, which is indeed unusual, given that the media is often assailed today for its supposed liberal bias. These results perhaps reflect the more conservative values found among both students and faculty in "enterprising" disciplines, as discussed in Smart, Feldman, and Ethington (2000).

Political Orientation: Factors Influencing Men Only

Among the college experiences that influence men's political orientation, the most interesting is interacting with faculty, which is associated with developing a more liberal ideology. This finding is noteworthy given some political conservatives' concerns that colleges are rife with faculty who indoctrinate students in their liberal philosophies. As with the other effects of faculty interaction, the dynamics behind this relationship are not known. Are gains in liberalism the result of specific politically oriented discussions? Or does exposure to faculty encourage men to be generally more accepting of a wide range of viewpoints and therefore less conservative in their own opinions? A study by Astin and Denson (2006) suggests that faculty's influence on students' political views is not nearly as strong as the role played by student peers, a finding also observed in the present study. It's clear that whatever role faculty play in influencing students' stated political ideology, that influence is more salient for men than women.

Another factor that contributes to men's political orientation is their television-viewing habits; in fact, watching more television tends to promote more conservative ideologies. Television viewing is influential in a variety of ways, as revealed throughout this book. In each case, it sparks several questions: What are students watching? How do men's and women's viewing habits differ? And how do those differences influence the development of students' political orientation? Though it is not colleges' responsibility to control their students' television viewing or other interactions with media, knowing how media influences students' values can help campus practitioners better understand changes they may witness among their students.

Classic Liberalism

While we previously examined how college affects students' identification with ideological labels, let's now take a look at students' views on specific political issues. Attitudes on six issues—the environment, health care, taxation, gun control, energy consumption, and consumer advocacy—were combined together to gauge classic liberalism, which generally indicates support for governmental action or regulation on these topics. In each of these areas (with the exception of taxation), women begin college with more liberal views than men, revealing gender gaps that remain significant over four years of college. Aspects of college that shape student attitudes on the role of government are largely similar for women and men, though there are some differences (see table 6.3).

Classic Liberalism: Aspects of College That Influence Both Genders

Institutional culture is a consistent force shaping students' beliefs regarding appropriate levels of governmental regulation. More classically liberal viewpoints are observed among students attending campuses with a greater percentage of women students and faculty members and those where the student body espouses more liberal political ideologies. Conversely, exposure to typically more conservative environments—such as with a business major or in peer groups oriented toward science or

**Table 6.3 Gender Differences in College-Level Predictors
of Classic Liberalism**

	Women	Men	Variable type
Common predictors			
Percentage of women faculty	+	+*	Institutional characteristics
Public 4-year college	+	+*	Institutional characteristics
Public university	−	−*	Institutional characteristics
Peer mean: Political views	+	+*	Peer group
Percentage of women undergraduates	+	+*	Peer group
Peer mean: Scientific orientation	−	−*	Peer group
Peer mean: Gender role traditionalism	−	−*	Peer group
Major: Business	−	−*	Major
Enrolled in ethnic studies course	+	+*	Involvement in academics
Enrolled in women's studies course	+	+*	Involvement in academics
General faculty support	+	+*	Involvement with faculty
Social diversity experiences	+	+*	Involvement with peers
Took part in demonstrations	+	+*	Involvement with peers
Attended religious services	−	−*	Other involvement
Unique predictors: Women			
Hours per week using a personal computer	−		Involvement in academics
Hours per week talking with faculty outside class	+		Involvement with faculty
Joined a fraternity or sorority	−		Involvement with peers
Leadership training	−		Involvement with peers
Unique predictors: Men			
Student-to-faculty ratio		−	Institutional characteristics
Peer mean: Understanding of others		+	Peer group
Major: English or humanities		+	Major

Table 6.3 *(Continued)*

	Women	Men	Variable type
Withdrew from school or took a leave of absence		—	Involvement in academics
Final R^2	37%	45%	

Notes: Direction of effect is noted only for variables that are significant at $p < .0001$.

R^2 represents the proportion of variance accounted for by all variables in the model (including precollege variables). See appendix D for the differential contribution of precollege and college variables.

* Denotes a coefficient that is significantly larger ($p < .01$) for that gender.

traditional gender roles—encourages more conservative views about the federal government's role.

Support for an increasingly active government role also results from aspects of student involvement, some of which reflect interactions with faculty and several of which represent activities that expose students to a diverse range of people, issues, and perspectives: feeling supported by faculty, taking ethnic studies or women's studies courses, engaging in social diversity experiences, and taking part in organized demonstrations. The role of diversity activities in promoting more liberal viewpoints is also documented by Astin (1993c). The only student behavior that fosters more conservative views on government's role for both women and men is attending religious services, which was also noted earlier as a predictor of more conservative political labels. As suggested earlier, this may reflect both the influence of religiously based values as well as the effect of peer group socialization in religious settings.

Classic Liberalism: Factors Influencing Women Only

Interaction with faculty outside the classroom contributes to liberal-leaning points of view in women students. As noted earlier, further research into the nature of student-faculty interactions is necessary to uncover the dynamics behind such shifts in students' values. In what ways do faculty directly and indirectly encourage students to adopt more liberal attitudes about political issues? Do faculty intentionally transmit their values to students, or do they expose students to issues and perspectives that encourage those students to reconsider previously held values and beliefs?

Earlier we saw that sorority membership and student leadership contribute to conservative shifts in women's political ideology. These college experiences also account for more conservative views regarding the role of the federal government. While these influences are presumably due to the effect of more conservative peer groups in these settings, it could also be that assuming leadership positions strengthens women's belief in individual agency, a perspective that may run counter to supporting an expanded governmental role. Simply put, women who have assumed leadership roles in college may be more inclined to believe that individual initiative, rather than governmental oversight, best addresses issues such as the environment and energy consumption.

Classic Liberalism: Factors Influencing Men Only

A factor that contributes to men's liberal views is attending colleges with smaller student-faculty ratios and those where the student body exhibits a greater degree of "understanding of others." These results suggest that smaller, more compassionate collegiate peer groups encourage men to believe that problems such as the environment, health care, and energy consumption require strong governmental oversight. Conversely, withdrawing temporarily from school—an act that removes the student from the influence of college faculty and peers—relates to more conservative views regarding the government's role.

Gender Role Traditionalism

How does college affect students' attitudes regarding gender roles? Does college foster more liberal or conservative views regarding women's place in society? Approximately one in six women and one in four men enter college endorsing a 1950s norm that "the activities of married women are best confined to the home and family." Over four years of college, support for traditional gender roles subsides for both groups, more so among the men, resulting in a narrowing of the gender gap over time.

Looking at table 6.4, we see the factors affecting men's and women's gender role attitudes, with positive relationships indicating more traditional viewpoints and negative relationships indicating more progressive or egalitarian viewpoints. Interestingly, the vast majority of college environments and experiences affecting gender role attitudes are unique to each gender, suggesting that changes in beliefs about gender roles result from markedly different sets of experiences for the two sexes. This is a prime example of the benefits of examining college impact separately by gender because considering women and men as one group may overlook college influences that are unique for either sex.

Gender Role Traditionalism: Aspects of College That Influence Both Genders

For both women and men, experiencing diversity in their social lives—such as dating or dining with students from different racial/ethnic backgrounds—promotes more progressive gender role attitudes. It may be that socializing with people of different racial/ethnic groups encourages students to be more accepting of nontraditional roles and more critical of stereotyped expectations. Indeed, we've already seen that diversity activities predict more liberal attitudes among students. Diverse social interactions also may raise students' awareness of the variety of familial situations, many of which necessitate two working parents and thus deviate from the 1950s white middle-class norm of father as breadwinner and mother as homemaker.

Support for egalitarian gender roles also results from receiving honest feedback from faculty. Though the reason for this

Table 6.4 Gender Differences in College-Level Predictors of Gender Role Traditionalism

	Women	Men	Variable type
Common predictors			
Faculty provided honest feedback about abilities	−	−	Involvement with faculty
Social diversity experiences	−	−	Involvement with peers
Opposing predictors			
Percentage of bachelor's degrees in education	+	−	Peer group
Faculty provided opportunity for research	+	−	Involvement with faculty
Unique predictors: Women			
Peer mean: Living on campus	−		Peer group
Aid: Work	+		Finances
Aid: Family or self	−		Finances
Concern about financing college	−		Finances
Major: Biological sciences	+		Major
Major: Education	+		Major
Enrolled in honors/advanced courses	−		Involvement in academics
Hours per week talking with faculty outside class	+		Involvement with faculty
Challenged a professor's ideas in class	−		Involvement with faculty
Took part in demonstrations	+		Involvement with peers
Hedonism (drinking, smoking, and partying)	−		Other involvement
Unique predictors: Men			
Public university		−	Institutional characteristics
Peer mean: Gender role traditionalism		+	Peer group
Living on campus		−	Residence
Major: Fine arts		+	Major

Table 6.4 *(Continued)*

	Women	Men	Variable type
Major: Physical sciences, math, statistics, or computer science		+	Major
Major: English or humanities		−	Major
Withdrew from school or took a leave of absence		+	Involvement in academics
Enrolled in ethnic studies course		−	Involvement in academics
General faculty support		−	Involvement with faculty
Attended racial/cultural awareness workshop		−	Involvement with peers
Joined a fraternity or sorority		+	Involvement with peers
Final R^2	17%	25%	

Notes: Direction of effect is noted only for variables that are significant at $p < .0001$.

R^2 represents the proportion of variance accounted for by all variables in the model (including precollege variables). See appendix D for the differential contribution of precollege and college variables.

relationship is not immediately clear, interactions with faculty often influence either men's or women's gender role attitudes, producing a curious pattern of effects that is evident throughout this section.

Gender Role Traditionalism: Opposing Influences for Women and Men

Two aspects of college significantly predict students' gender role attitudes, but they do so in opposite ways for women and men. One is working with faculty on research, which relates to the development of more egalitarian gender role attitudes among men but more conservative views among women. These findings are in line with results reported by Bryant (2003), who found that interaction with faculty relates to progressive attitudes among men and more traditional gender role attitudes among women. Without additional information on the nature of student-faculty interactions in the context of research or the gender of the faculty with whom they work, it is difficult to determine what accounts for these discrepant results. However, one interpretation is that working with faculty on research exposes women to the long hours and heavy workload often necessary to gain professional success, at least in academia, causing some to question how they themselves would be able to balance a professional career with raising a family. Additional research into the nature of students' research experiences is necessary to test this hypothesis.

Another aspect of college yielding contradictory influences on women's and men's gender role expectations is the proportion of education bachelor's degrees awarded by the college. For women, colleges granting a larger share of education degrees produce female graduates with more traditional gender role attitudes. This is perhaps not surprising given that teaching is a historically traditional career path for women. Thus, being surrounded by greater percentages of women pursuing a traditionally female occupation may make women's gender role attitudes more conservative. For men, on the other hand, attending institutions awarding a greater share of education degrees relates to developing more egalitarian gender role attitudes. This finding resonates with results reported earlier regarding gains in men's cultural awareness and commitment to social activism in colleges with more education majors. We can interpret this to mean that an institutional emphasis on teacher training encourages men to expand their horizons in numerous ways, including becoming more open-minded about what constitutes appropriate roles for married women.

Gender Role Traditionalism: Factors Influencing Women Only

In one of the more intriguing findings in this research, we find that the more time that women spend talking with faculty outside class, the more traditional their gender role attitudes become. Taken together with a finding reported earlier—that working with faculty on research relates to more conservative gender role attitudes—this finding raises questions about *how* faculty influence women's beliefs about gender. Do some faculty discourage women from pursuing careers, especially those that may be demanding or presumably incompatible with raising a family? Do faculty occasionally depict traditional gender roles as the ideal? This seems unlikely given that college faculties generally have a liberal orientation. In fact, women's interactions with faculty do not always promote conservative views about gender roles because results also show that challenging a professor's ideas in the classroom relates to developing more progressive gender role attitudes.

These examples reveal the complexity of student-faculty interactions and the difficulty of interpreting their meaning without additional information. The nature of causality is particularly unclear; perhaps the initiative required to challenge professors in the classroom—especially when those professors are likely to be men—is a *function* of women having already developed a stronger commitment to gender equity during college. Once again, these findings raise numerous questions for future research on the nature of women's interactions with faculty, how that depends on the instructor's gender, and the extent to which faculty transmit overt or subtle messages about appropriate gender roles.

We also find that majoring in education gives rise to more traditional gender role attitudes in female students, a result consistent with an institutional emphasis on the education field noted earlier. Perhaps women choose teaching as a career because they think that it will be compatible with raising children or allow them to take a temporary or permanent leave to raise their families.

Women's financial situations also influence their attitude regarding gender roles, though not in entirely consistent ways.

First, monetary concerns and reliance on family financial support cultivate more progressive gender role attitudes among female students. One interpretation of this finding is that women who are concerned about their ability to pay for college and those who depend on family money are more conscious of the importance of achieving financial independence and therefore more strongly endorse women's employment outside the home. On the other hand, women who expect to work during college to pay for their education become more traditional in their gender role attitudes. It is possible that for many of these women, the experience of working while attending school, and the associated challenges of balancing employment with academic demands, leads them to question whether they themselves would be able to balance having a career with raising children. Clearly, these speculations merit further study of how college women's financial standing shapes their outlook on jobs, marriage, and motherhood.

Gender Role Traditionalism: Factors Influencing Men Only

Several of the unique predictors of men's gender role attitudes reflect the influence of student peer groups. For example, men's belief that married women should be confined to domestic roles can be seen at campuses where other students hold more traditional views regarding gender. Similarly, men who join fraternities become more strongly committed to the notion that married women should assume traditional family roles. Other work (Astin, 1993c; Sanday, 1990) has documented the negative effects of fraternity membership vis-à-vis feminist ideals; however, it is worth mentioning that in this study, sorority membership had no effect on women's gender role attitudes.

A counterpoint to fraternities may be found in liberal environments such as ethnic studies courses and racial/cultural awareness workshops, which cultivate a more progressive outlook among men regarding the social roles of married women. Similarly, Bryant (2003) found that men who participated in diversity activities became more supportive of feminist ideals.

Faculty's role in influencing both women's and men's gender role attitudes is evident in a variety of ways. We have already seen that more egalitarian attitudes are observed among men who work with faculty on research and who receive constructive faculty feedback. We also find that men who have received support, advice, and encouragement from faculty develop more progressive attitudes regarding gender roles. Taken together, these findings suggest that positive experiences with faculty encourage men to adopt more progressive views regarding the appropriate societal roles for married women. Repeating a question raised earlier with respect to political orientation, do faculty directly influence students' attitudes by intentionally transmitting values, or do they indirectly broaden students' perspectives, thus contributing to a more liberal or progressive shift in attitudes? Further, how does this depend on the instructor's gender? Once again, these are important questions to consider in future research.

Permissiveness

The college years often are considered a time of exploration, especially in terms of students' behaviors in the realm of sex and drugs. Though historically students are thought to become more permissive during college, is this equally true for women and men? Further, are there gender differences in college experiences that lead students to change their outlook on what they consider acceptable behaviors? Here we'll examine the impact of college on students' attitudes regarding issues of personal freedom, as reflected in their agreement with the following four propositions: abortion should be legal, marijuana should be legal, casual sex is permissible, and homosexual relationships should not be prohibited.

When students enter college, there are significant gender differences for three of these items, with women reporting more liberal attitudes than men on the topic of homosexuality but more conservative viewpoints on casual sex and the legalization of marijuana. Gender differences on these attitudes diminish over four years of college, though in each case, a significant gender gap remains.

Table 6.5 reveals the college environments and experiences that relate to developing a more permissive stance about sex, sexuality, drugs, and reproductive rights. For both women and men, a wide range of experiences, many of which reflect the nature and extent of students' interactions with campus peer groups, influence attitudes on these issues. The pattern of effects, however, is distinct for the two genders.

Permissiveness: Aspects of College That Influence Both Genders

A combination of individual behaviors and peer influences shape both women's and men's permissive orientations. This is evident in the influence of attending religious services, which relates to declines in permissiveness and hedonistic behaviors—such as drinking, smoking, and partying—that encourage students to develop more open attitudes. These findings indicate ways in which attitudes regarding sex, drugs, abortion, and homosexuality may be influenced not just by students' behaviors but also by the more liberal or conservative orientations of the peers with whom they engage in these activities. The peer group's influence is clearly demonstrated by the third-strongest predictor of permissiveness: the political orientation of the students enrolled at the institution. In this case, the more liberal the student peer group, the more likely students are to adopt permissive orientations. The influence of peers is a recurring theme throughout this

Table 6.5 Gender Differences in College-Level Predictors of Permissiveness

	Women	Men	Variable type
Common predictors			
Other private 4-year college	−*	−	Institutional characteristics
Peer mean: Political views	+	+	Peer group
Peer mean: Years of study in math and science	+	+	Peer group
Percentage of bachelor's degrees in history, political science, and social sciences	+	+	Peer group
Hedonism (drinking, smoking, and partying)	+*	+	Other involvement
Attended religious services	−	−	Other involvement
Opposing predictors			
Major: Education	−	+	Major
Unique predictors: Women			
Percentage of bachelor's degrees in science, math, and engineering	+		Peer group
Major: Social sciences	+		Major
Major: Business	−		Major
Felt bored in class	+		Involvement in academics
Enrolled in ethnic studies course	+		Involvement in academics
Faculty provided honest feedback about abilities	+		Involvement with faculty
Hours per week student clubs or groups	+		Involvement with peers
Social diversity experiences	+		Involvement with peers
Studied with other students	+		Involvement with peers
Took part in demonstrations	+		Involvement with peers
Hours per week exercising/ playing sports	−		Other involvement

(Continued)

Table 6.5 *(Continued)*

	Women	Men	Variable type
Unique predictors: Men			
Peer mean: Understanding of others		+	Peer group
Faculty did not take comments seriously		+	Involvement with faculty
Worked full-time while a student		+	Involvement in work
Worked part-time off campus		+	Involvement in work
Hours per week reading for pleasure		+	Other involvement
Final R^2	65%	66%	

Notes: Direction of effect is noted only for variables that are significant at $p < .0001$.

R^2 represents the proportion of variance accounted for by all variables in the model (including precollege variables). See appendix D for the differential contribution of precollege and college variables.

* Denotes a coefficient that is significantly larger ($p < .01$) for that gender.

book, though we will soon see examples of how peer group interactions shape permissive values in different ways for the two sexes.

Permissiveness: Opposing Influences for Women and Men

Majoring in education yields opposite effects on women and men, as was the case when we examined the contrasting effects of the education field on men's and women's gender role orientations. An education major is associated with more liberal attitudes regarding abortion, drugs, and sexuality among men but more conservative attitudes on these issues for women. Further inspection of the data reveals an interesting fact: education majors are more popular among men with liberal orientations but more popular among women with conservative leanings.

Thus, an education major may reinforce students' initial predispositions. Further, this result bolsters the notion that we cannot generalize about the influence of a college experience or a specific major, since it may depend on the student's gender and/or any other characteristic.

Permissiveness: Factors Influencing Women Only

For women, changes in attitudes about sex, drugs, abortion, and homosexuality are largely influenced by their interactions with other students. They tend to become more liberal regarding these topics when they engage in group-based peer interactions—such as study groups, clubs, and organizations—and participate in protests or demonstrations.

More permissive values are also observed among women who engage in diversity-related activities, such as taking ethnic studies courses and socializing with students of different racial/ethnic backgrounds. These sorts of activities expose women to a range of viewpoints, which may enable them to become more open-minded on issues related to sexuality and drugs.

However, another aspect of involvement—exercising and playing sports—contributes to more restrictive attitudes among women. Perhaps women concerned with maintaining a physically active lifestyle become less inclined to use drugs or engage in casual sex and thus may develop more conservative views on those topics, or perhaps they are influenced by health-conscious and empowered female peers whom they meet while engaged in sports and exercise. Further investigation is necessary to understand how sports and exercise influence women's attitudes, especially regarding casual sex and drug use.

Aspects of academic life also affect women's permissive orientations; those who major in the social sciences tend to develop more liberal attitudes regarding sex, drugs, and abortion, while women majoring in business become more conservative on these issues. We have already seen how majoring in business encourages more conservative political views among women; the present finding reflects the influence of this major on their social views.

Finally, we witness that women who are frequently bored in the college classroom develop more permissive social views. Cause and effect is particularly difficult to untangle in this situation, as boredom inside the classroom may encourage women to seek satisfaction and stimulation through permissive behaviors outside class. Alternatively, women who engage in a more permissive lifestyle outside class—especially with respect to sexual behaviors and the use of alcohol and drugs—may view their in-class experiences as relatively dull.

Permissiveness: Factors Influencing Men Only

Among aspects of college relating uniquely to the development of men's permissive attitudes, two reflect the role of employment, with full- or part-time jobs giving rise to more permissive values. This raises the question of how men's workplaces shape their values. Do they encounter more or less permissive behaviors with their coworkers than with their student peers? This issue is not well addressed in the research on college impact, which typically examines how the time devoted to a job affects students, without probing how specific values and workplace cultures affect them. Consequently, these findings suggest a potentially interesting area for future research.

We also find that, for men only, a culture of empathy—as reflected in the peer group's "understanding of others"—contributes to the development of more liberal attitudes regarding sex and drugs. This finding is similar to the effect of more empathic peer groups noted earlier with respect to classic liberalism. Together, these findings suggest that more compassionate environments encourage men to become more accepting, tolerant, and liberal in their viewpoints.

Raising a Family

For most students, the college years represent a transitional phase in their lives between childhood and adulthood. Though parenthood is usually several years off, this period of transition may cause students to reevaluate the importance they place on raising a family. Among the nearly two dozen long-term goals included on the Freshman Survey—such as making money, achieving authority, and making a difference in the world—students entering college consistently rank "raising a family" as their number-one personal goal. Family orientation is equally strong among women and men entering college, though women's interest in raising a family grows more so than men's over four years.

In what ways does college encourage or discourage students' family orientation? To what extent does this differ for women and men? As shown in table 6.6, aspects of college that contribute to women's and men's interest in raising a family are quite different.

Raising a Family: Aspects of College That Influence Both Genders

Only three aspects of college yield similar effects on family orientation for women and men, and each reflects the influence of group-based values. Specifically, interest in raising a family grows notably stronger among men and women who are members of the Greek system and who more frequently attend religious services. The influence of these settings on family orientation may reflect the emphasis on traditional family values prevalent in many major religions and often observed in fraternities and sororities. In addition, students who spend more time socializing with friends—though not necessarily in an organized group setting—develop stronger commitments to raising a family.

Table 6.6 Gender Differences in College-Level Predictors of Goal: Raising a Family

	Women	Men	Variable type
Common predictors			
Hours per week socializing with friends	+	+	Involvement with peers
Joined a fraternity or sorority	+	+	Involvement with peers
Attended religious services	+	+*	Other involvement
Opposing predictors			
Tutored another student	−	+	Involvement with peers
Unique predictors: Women			
Percentage of women faculty	−		Institutional characteristics
Percentage of nonwhite students	+		Peer group
Aid: Grants and scholarships	−		Finances
Concern about financing college	−		Finances
Major: Business	+		Major
Major: Psychology	−		Major
Hours per week household/ childcare duties	+		Other involvement
Hours per week watching television	+		Other involvement
Unique predictors: Men			
Public 4-year college		−	Institutional characteristics
Peer mean: Socioeconomic status		+	Peer group
Living on campus		+	Residence
Major: Journalism or communications		+	Major
General faculty support		+	Involvement with faculty
Hours per week student clubs or groups		+	Involvement with peers
Final R^2	28%	32%	

Notes: Direction of effect is noted only for variables that are significant at $p < .0001$.

R^2 represents the proportion of variance accounted for by all variables in the model (including precollege variables). See appendix D for the differential contribution of precollege and college variables.

* Denotes a coefficient that is significantly larger ($p < .01$) for that gender.

Raising a Family: Opposing Influence for Women and Men

Tutoring other students relates to gains in family orientation among men but declines among women. This is an especially puzzling finding because one might expect tutoring experiences, especially positive ones, to exemplify one of the rewards of raising a family: teaching and empowering others. Although men who tutor others realize this gain, tutoring experiences appear to weaken women's desire to have a family. Is it possible that tutoring enlightens women about ways to nurture or educate others that can be accomplished without necessarily having children themselves? Though research on tutoring often centers on its cognitive benefits, these findings demonstrate that more needs to be understood about tutoring's effect on student values, especially in ways that may differ for the two genders.

Raising a Family: Factors Influencing Women Only

College influences on women's family orientation reveal several curious findings. First, there's a fairly provocative result: female students become less likely to consider raising a family as an important personal goal at campuses employing more women faculty. Although an explanation for this finding is not immediately clear, perhaps it reflects the influence of role modeling, since female faculty report less interest in raising families and tend to have fewer children than male faculty (Lindholm, Szelenyi, Hurtado, & Korn, 2005). Such an environment also exposes female students to large numbers of women who are pursuing challenging and fulfilling careers; this alone may cause some women to reconsider family as their primary goal.

Finances also play a role in women's perspectives on family. Reliance on grants or scholarships, as well as concern about their ability to pay for college, tends to weaken women's family orientations. Given the costs associated with having and caring for children, perhaps facing financial insecurity in college causes women to reconsider raising a family as their top priority. This is likely to become an even more salient issue over time, since the numbers of women experiencing financial strain in college is growing, as reported earlier.

Women's commitment to raising a family also is influenced by their choice of two academic majors: business and psychology. Majoring in business leads to increases in family orientation, perhaps due to a perception that business careers will provide women with financial resources, flexibility, and/or day care that will enable them to balance their professional lives with raising a family. Majoring in the field of psychology, on the other hand, weakens women's family orientation. It is conceivable that studying psychology heightens women's consciousness about the problems that emanate from family life, including marital problems and child-rearing challenges, thus causing them to question their personal interest in having children.

Women's commitment to family also stems from the amount of time they spend watching television in college, with more television contributing to stronger family orientations. In part, this finding may owe to the frequently idealized images of motherhood presented in television programming that's more popular among women, such as situation comedies and soap operas (Ex, Janssens, & Korzilius, 2002). Time spent on household or child-care duties during college also enhances women's family orientation. Though it is not known whether these activities include caring for family members or nonfamily members, it may be encouraging that greater exposure to the realities and rewards of family life reinforces women's interest in having and raising children themselves.

Raising a Family: Factors Influencing Men Only

Looking at the college experiences that predict family orientation among men, we find several aspects of engagement with faculty and students. For example, men who receive support and encouragement from faculty are more likely to increase their long-term commitment to raising a family. It may be that having a supportive faculty mentor piques men's interest in ultimately mentoring or advising their own children, a correlation similar to the rewards of tutoring, discussed earlier. Interaction with students also promotes men's family orientations, as seen in the effects of living on campus and participating in student clubs and groups. Clearly, achieving a sense of connectedness while in college—whether with faculty or students—enhances men's desire to reap similar benefits through family life.

Developing a Meaningful Philosophy of Life

The college years often offer students the opportunity to develop a sense of meaning and purpose in their lives. Indeed, research conducted by the Higher Education Research Institute (2006) shows that students' quest for meaning and purpose is central to their college experience and that students expect colleges to encourage their development in this regard. However, when compared to other goals, such as raising a family and being well-off financially, interest in developing a meaningful philosophy of life is far less important to today's college students. Gender differences in this goal are small, with first-year men reporting slightly greater philosophical orientations than women, a difference that disappears over four years.

Here we'll look at the various ways in which college affects students' long-term commitment to developing a meaningful philosophy of life, as well as examine the extent to which this differs for women and men. Table 6.7 reveals that involvement is central to both women's and men's development of this goal, with some noteworthy gender differences.

Developing a Meaningful Philosophy: Aspects of College That Influence Both Genders

For both genders, feeling supported by faculty represents the strongest collegiate influence on the commitment to developing a meaningful philosophy of life. Here students who receive

Table 6.7 Gender Differences in College-Level Predictors of Goal: Developing a Meaningful Philosophy of Life

	Women	Men	Variable type
Common predictors			
Challenged professor's ideas in class	+	+	Involvement with faculty
General faculty support	+	+*	Involvement with faculty
Attended racial/cultural awareness workshop	+	+	Involvement with peers
Joined a fraternity or sorority	−	−	Involvement with peers
Social diversity experiences	+	+*	Involvement with peers
Hours per week reading for pleasure	+	+*	Other involvement
Hours per week exercising/ playing sports	+	+	Other involvement
Volunteering or community service	+	+	Other involvement
Hours per week watching television	−	−	Other involvement
Unique predictors: Women			
Other religious private 4-year college	+		Institutional characteristics
Major: Physical sciences, math, statistics, or computer science	−		Major
Faculty provided honest feedback about abilities	+		Involvement with faculty
Hours per week commuting	+		Other involvement
Unique predictors: Men			
Public university		−	Institutional characteristics
Percentage of bachelor's degrees in education		+	Peer group
Aid: Work		+	Finances
Aid: Loans		−	Finances
Major: Engineering		−	Major

Table 6.7 (Continued)

	Women	Men	Variable type
Major: Social sciences		−	Major
Final R^2	24%	29%	

Notes: Direction of effect is noted only for variables that are significant at $p < .0001$.

R^2 represents the proportion of variance accounted for by all variables in the model (including precollege variables). See appendix D for the differential contribution of precollege and college variables.

* Denotes a coefficient that is significantly larger ($p < .01$) for that gender.

intellectual and personal support and guidance from their professors become more strongly committed to finding meaning and purpose in their own lives. This finding has powerful implications for campus practice, as it demonstrates that the benefits of student-faculty relationships extend well beyond the academic realm. Clearly, campuses aiming to inspire greater introspection and search for meaning among their students can do so by encouraging their faculty to spend more one-on-one time with students, especially in ways that are caring and validating.

Also important in fostering philosophical orientations among both women and men is encouraging them to expand beyond their comfort zone and gain exposure to diverse environments and viewpoints, including attending racial/cultural awareness workshops, having social diversity experiences, performing volunteer work, and challenging professors' ideas in class. Conversely, joining the Greek system and watching television, activities noted earlier as enhancing status orientations among one or both genders, weakens students' philosophical orientation.

Interest in developing a meaningful philosophy of life also is indicated by leisure-time activities, such as reading for pleasure and playing sports or exercising. These activities offer a release from academic pursuits that can inspire deeper thinking about the meaning of students' lives and their place in the world; further, these activities also predict declines in stress for one or both genders, as noted in chapter 5. Campuses aiming to encourage a philosophical or contemplative orientation among their students would do well to promote opportunities for sports and exercise and to inspire students to continue reading beyond their class assignments.

Developing a Meaningful Philosophy: Factors Influencing Women Only

The importance of faculty in fostering self-exploration was discussed earlier with respect to both genders, but it is especially vital to women, with those who receive honest feedback from faculty becoming significantly more interested in developing a meaningful philosophy of life. This once again underscores the importance of receiving individualized attention from instructors.

We also find that an interest in developing meaning and purpose in life is enhanced by the time that women spend commuting. One of the benefits of traveling to or from school via car, bus, or other transportation may be the opportunity to reflect on the meaning of life and to consider one's longer-term goals.

Finally, majoring in the physical sciences appears to suppress women's commitment to developing a meaningful life philosophy. This finding may reflect the culture of many physical science fields, which emphasize concrete facts and testable hypotheses as opposed to more esoteric concepts, like the meaning of life. However, this result may also stem from the typically heavy workload in the physical sciences; indeed, as noted in chapter 5, majoring in the physical sciences relates to women's unique development of time-related stress.

Developing a Meaningful Philosophy: Factors Influencing Men Only

The role of academic major also is evident for men, whose philosophical interests are weakened in engineering and social science fields. Again, we witness a negative relationship between majoring in scientific fields and the search for meaning in students' own lives.

Men's financial situations also influence their philosophical orientation. In particular, paying for college expenses with money *earned* (via employment during college) predicts a higher commitment to developing a philosophy of life, a finding that could be used as a selling point for work-study programs. Conversely, paying for college with money *borrowed* (via loans) relates to declines in a philosophical orientation. It is possible that men who incur significant debt during college think that they need to focus their energies on seemingly more practical pursuits, such as getting a good job, rather than on finding meaning and purpose in their lives.

Promoting Racial Understanding

As college campuses have become more racially and ethnically diverse, institutions have implemented numerous academic and cocurricular programs designed to educate students about the variety of backgrounds and perspectives represented on their campus and in society. One important goal of such efforts is to instill in students a sense of appreciation for existing differences across racial, ethnic, economic, or other forces that can often divide students. The longitudinal sample used in this book includes students who attended college in the late 1990s, when issues such as affirmative action and immigration were gaining more attention in the United States. Students completing the Freshman Survey were asked to indicate how important it was for them to be involved in efforts to promote racial understanding. Only one-third of all first-year students considered this to be an important personal goal, with women reporting a stronger commitment to promoting racial understanding than men, a gender gap that widened over the course of college.

This section describes the college experiences and environments that contribute to changes in men's and women's interest in promoting racial understanding. For the most part, aspects of involvement have similar effects for women and men, with effects of the major field more common among women and the influence of the campuswide peer group more salient for men. (See table 6.8.)

Promoting Racial Understanding: Aspects of College That Influence Both Genders

Regardless of gender, commitment to promoting racial understanding is strengthened by academic and extracurricular experiences involving exposure to a diverse range of people and perspectives: enrolling in ethnic studies courses, performing volunteer work, participating in demonstrations, attending racial/cultural awareness workshops, and interacting socially with people from different racial/ethnic backgrounds. Social diversity experiences are in fact the strongest determinant of this outcome for both genders. As underscored by Pascarella and Terenzini (2005), "The weight of evidence is reasonably clear and consistent in suggesting that, across racial-ethnic groups, having friends of another race and being a member of an interracial friendship group has significant and positive net effects on racial-ethnic attitudes and values" (p. 311). Conversely, membership in a fraternity or sorority—a social environment often lacking in racial diversity—discourages interest in improving race relations. Similar effects of Greek membership on students' "openness to diversity" are reported in Pascarella, Edison, Nora, Hagedorn, and Terenzini (1996).

Interest in improving race relations also stems from meaningful and supportive interactions with faculty. Notably, faculty support is more influential for men's commitment to racial understanding than for women's. Faculty support also yielded stronger effects on men's egalitarian gender role attitudes (as reported earlier in this

Table 6.8 Gender Differences in College-Level Predictors of Goal: Promoting Racial Understanding

	Women	Men	Variable type
Common predictors			
Public university	−	−	Institutional characteristics
Major: Engineering	−	−	Major
Enrolled in ethnic studies course	+	+	Involvement in academics
Felt bored in class	−	−	Involvement in academics
General faculty support	+	+*	Involvement with faculty
Attended racial/cultural awareness workshop	+	+*	Involvement with peers
Social diversity experiences	+	+*	Involvement with peers
Took part in demonstrations	+	+	Involvement with peers
Joined a fraternity or sorority	−	−	Involvement with peers
Volunteering or community service	+	+	Other involvement
Unique predictors: Women			
Major: English or humanities	+		Major
Major: Social sciences	+		Major
Major: Business	−		Major
Major: Physical sciences, math, statistics, or computer science	−		Major
Hours per week reading for pleasure	+		Other involvement
Unique predictors: Men			
Number of full-time undergraduates		−	Institutional characteristics
Percentage of women undergraduates		+	Peer group
Percentage of nonwhite students		−	Peer group
College selectivity		−	Peer group

(Continued)

Table 6.8 *(Continued)*

	Women	Men	Variable type
Faculty provided honest feedback about abilities		+	Involvement with faculty
Hours per week talking with faculty outside class		+	Involvement with faculty
Hours per week watching television		−	Other involvement
Final R^2	35%	36%	

Notes: Direction of effect is noted only for variables that are significant at $p < .0001$.

R^2 represents the proportion of variance accounted for by all variables in the model (including precollege variables). See appendix D for the differential contribution of precollege and college variables.

* Denotes a coefficient that is significantly larger ($p < .01$) for that gender.

chapter), suggesting that faculty play a pivotal role in raising men's awareness of racial *and* gender equity issues.

Commitment to promoting racial understanding also is affected by feeling bored in class, attending public universities, and majoring in engineering, each of which inhibits interest in actively improving race relations. It is worth noting that these same variables also negatively predict students' commitment to social activism (as reported in chapter 5), thereby further reinforcing the role played by these behavioral and environmental contexts in inhibiting students' broader concern for society.

Promoting Racial Understanding: Factors Influencing Women Only

Interestingly, major fields represent four of the five college environments that shape women's commitment to racial understanding. Specifically, gains in women's commitment to these efforts are associated with majoring in the social sciences or humanities, while relative declines are observed among women majoring in business and the physical sciences. These findings reflect differences in the nature of disciplinary values regarding concern for others' welfare, as described by Smart et al. (2000). If campuses aim to encourage students' development of race-related compassion, they should give serious attention to how to reach students—especially women—who major in business and scientific fields.

Promoting Racial Understanding: Factors Influencing Men Only

Whereas disciplinary culture appears to be particularly critical in shaping women's interest in improving race relations, institutional and peer environments are uniquely relevant for men. For example, attending institutions with a greater percentage of women undergraduates enhances men's interest in improving racial understanding, but attending larger and more selective institutions, as well as colleges enrolling a greater percentage of nonwhite students, produces the opposite effect. The latter finding is surprising because it reveals that men's interest in improving race relations declines as the number of nonwhite students at the college increases. Could it be that men at colleges with significant nonwhite populations view conditions for racial/ethnic minorities as acceptable in their present form, rather than something in need of improvement? Or do men at those institutions develop a resistance to improving race relations? As discussed by Gurin, Dey, Hurtado, and Gurin (2002), the sheer percentage of nonwhite students on a campus does not guarantee a more hospitable racial climate. Of greater importance, the authors note, are the nature and quality of students' encounters with diversity. Indeed, as shown in this study, *engagement* with diversity is the most potent influence on men's and women's commitment to improving racial understanding.

We also find that spending more time interacting with and receiving honest feedback from faculty strengthens men's commitment to promoting racial understanding. These results underscore faculty's pivotal role in promoting greater sensitivity to race issues among male students, as discussed earlier.

Finally, time spent watching television is the only behavioral measure to negatively predict concerns about race among men only. Though we do not have information on the specific viewing habits for the men in this study, perhaps this finding reflects the popularity of sports programming among male college students. In fact, research has consistently demonstrated persistent racial biases among commentators for televised intercollegiate basketball and football games (Rada & Wulfemeyer, 2005; Rainville & McCormick, 1977). If television encourages men to view racial minorities in stereotypical and/or negative ways, it may also reduce their motivation to help improve race relations.

Summary

Echoing findings from decades of research, the impact of college on students' political and social values is clearly a function of broad environmental influences as well as individual interactions with members of the campus community. However, as revealed in this chapter, the nature of these influences is often quite different for women and men. Three areas of gender difference in the impact of college stand out from among the numerous findings reported in this chapter: the influence of student-faculty interactions, diversity activities, and leadership opportunities.

In a theme that continues from chapter 5, women's and men's interactions with their professors relate somewhat differently to their political and social values. For both genders, spending time with professors and receiving quality mentoring appear to promote political interest and more liberal political orientations, though these relationships are often stronger for male students. In fact, the more time that men spend talking with professors outside class, the more likely they will place themselves at the liberal end of the ideological continuum. Faculty also appear to have a liberalizing effect on men's gender role attitudes, as those men who work with faculty on research or who otherwise receive guidance and mentorship from faculty become less supportive of traditional domestic roles for married women. Ironically, women who participate in faculty research actually become *more* likely to support traditional gender roles.

As discussed earlier, such findings beg for future research that can focus more closely on the dynamics of student-faculty interaction. We need to develop a better understanding of how working with or otherwise getting to know faculty influences students' value orientations. To what extent are political and social issues the centerpiece of such conversations? To what degree do faculty divulge their own personal viewpoints? And how do such dynamics vary across different combinations of student and faculty gender? Is it possible that the more powerful liberalizing effect of faculty on male students is due to the current predominance of men among the faculty? Would the same results be revealed for men who interact with female professors? This is an area ripe for investigation; past research has too often focused on the *quantity* rather than the *quality* of student-faculty interactions.

Another theme that continues from the prior chapter is the more powerful role of diversity activities in shaping men's values and orientations. Being exposed to diversity in the curriculum—such as with ethnic studies or women's studies courses—contributes to gains in liberalism and political engagement, especially among male students. Diversity in the cocurriculum, as in the form of multicultural awareness workshops, also encourages liberal viewpoints and a commitment to working on race relations more frequently among male students.

Why would diversity programming more strongly influence men's political interest and values? As discussed in chapter 5, diversity activities may be particularly eye-opening for men. They appear to alter men's worldviews more dramatically than women's, causing men to question themselves and their role in the larger world. More liberal viewpoints and a commitment to improving race relations are a result of this new enlightenment.

What needs to be better understood is the process by which these changes take place. What particular aspects of diversity-related programming contribute to the different aspects of development for women and men? The answer to this question is critical for campus practitioners, who should be more informed on how their programs and courses affect students, especially because such effects may vary by gender, race, or other important student characteristics.

This chapter has also revealed how different forms of engagement on campus shape women's political attitudes and social values. In particular, engaging in certain student organizations and leadership opportunities—such as student government, leadership training, and the Greek system—is associated with a shift toward more conservative political viewpoints exclusively among women. As discussed earlier, it is likely that these forms of involvement expose women to more conservative peer groups that, intentionally or not, encourage them to become more conservative in their own political views. On the other hand, exposure to a more liberal group of peers—those who spend more time drinking, smoking, and partying—encourages more liberal, progressive, and permissive views among female students. Taken together with the liberalizing influence of diversity courses for men, these findings raise questions about which student peer groups are more or less influential for one gender or the other. Why would diversity education have a greater impact on men's political views and student government and Greek membership demonstrate a stronger influence on women's attitudes? Research has long demonstrated the role of peer groups in shaping students' attitudes and values, but it is clear from this study that more needs to be understood about how gender shapes these dynamics.

7

ACADEMIC OUTCOMES

The connection between gender and academic achievement is complex. On the one hand, women can be viewed as an educational success story because they outpace men in terms of college enrollment, persistence, performance, and engagement. They have also made great strides in a number of traditionally male-dominated fields, such as medicine, law, and business. On the other hand, women reveal comparatively low levels of confidence in their intellectual capabilities; they demonstrate a reluctance to believe, or perhaps to admit, that they are as competent as their performance would suggest. Even more troubling is that the gender gap in academic confidence tends to grow wider over the course of college. This chapter considers which college experiences enhance students' academic performance, self-perceptions, and aspirations and whether those results differ by gender. Due to the nature of the Cooperative Institutional Research Program questionnaires, the academic outcomes examined here are limited primarily to aspirations and subjective self-assessments.[1] Only one outcome—college GPA—directly reflects students' academic performance. As the following pages will show, curricular and cocurricular engagement enhances *both* women's and men's academic outcomes, with notable gender differences as a result of student-faculty interactions.

College GPA

The grades that students receive in college are an important indicator of academic success, and if those grades are good, they also point the way to opportunities like fellowships, awards, and

**Table 7.1 Gender Differences in College-Level Predictors
of College GPA**

	Women	Men	Variable type
Common predictors			
Percentage of women faculty	+	+*	Institutional characteristics
Number of full-time undergraduates	−	−	Institutional characteristics
Public university	−	−*	Institutional characteristics
Percentage of women undergraduates	+	+	Peer group
Peer mean: Intellectual self-esteem	−	−	Peer group
Major: Education	+	+	Major
Major: Fine arts	+	+	Major
Major: Business	−	−	Major
Enrolled in honors/advanced courses	+	+	Involvement in academics
Hours per week studying/doing homework	+	+*	Involvement in academics
Worked on independent study project	+	+	Involvement in academics
Felt bored in class	−	−*	Involvement in academics
Withdrew from school or took a leave of absence	−	−	Involvement in academics
Faculty provided honest feedback about abilities	+*	+	Involvement with faculty
General faculty support	+	+*	Involvement with faculty
Hours per week talking with faculty outside class	+	+*	Involvement with faculty
Hours per week student clubs or groups	+	+	Involvement with peers
Tutored another student	+	+*	Involvement with peers
Joined a fraternity or sorority	−	−	Involvement with peers
Hedonism (drinking, smoking, and partying)	−	−*	Other involvement
Hours per week household/ childcare duties	−	−	Other involvement

Table 7.1 *(Continued)*

	Women	Men	Variable type
Opposing predictors			
Hours per week exercising/ playing sports	+	−	Other involvement
Unique predictors: Women			
Concern about financing college	+		Finances
Major: Engineering	−		Major
Social diversity experiences	−		Involvement with peers
Unique predictors: Men			
Public 4-year college		+	Institutional characteristics
Peer mean: Gender role traditionalism		+	Peer group
Peer mean: Artistic interests		−	Peer group
Major: Journalism or communications		−	Major
Leadership training		+	Involvement with peers
Worked part-time off campus		−	Involvement in work
Hours per week reading for pleasure		−	Other involvement
Final R^2	47%	48%	

Notes: Direction of effect is noted only for variables that are significant at $p < .0001$.

R^2 represents the proportion of variance accounted for by all variables in the model (including precollege variables). See appendix D for the differential contribution of precollege and college variables.

* Denotes a coefficient that is significantly larger ($p < .01$) for that gender.

admission to graduate school. While grades distinguish between higher-performing and lower-performing students, we also find that they distinguish between the genders, with women earning significantly better grades than men in both high school and college. Although we can partially attribute women's higher grades to the fact that they spend more time studying and doing homework, other factors also contribute to their superior academic performance. In looking at table 7.1, we see that students' grades are the product of a broad range of both proximal and distal sources of influence in college; these are generally consistent with the body of research on college's impact on academic performance as reported in Astin (1993c) and Pascarella and Terenzini (2005). Further, the vast majority of these predictors are important for both genders.

College GPA: Aspects of College That Influence Both Genders

For women as well as men, academic engagement is central to receiving high marks in college. The influence of engagement is generally more salient for men, as studying, tutoring other students, conducting independent study, taking honors courses, and spending quality time with faculty are each indicative of good grades for male students. Clearly, one way of addressing the gender gap in academic performance is to connect more male students to individualized teaching and learning opportunities with faculty and peers. Conversely, becoming disengaged from academics brings about lower overall GPAs for both genders, as evidenced by the negative influence of withdrawing from school, feeling bored in class, partying, and fulfilling household/childcare commitments.

Men's and women's GPA also is a function of their major field and the broader campus environment. Most notable is the fact that students are more likely to underperform at large, public universities and colleges with highly intellectual peer groups. This may reflect the influence of competitive grading practices, whereby high-caliber students may get lower grades than they are accustomed to receiving.

Higher-than-expected grades, on the other hand, are found at campuses with greater proportions of female students and faculty. This finding raises numerous questions about the type of academic environment that having more women on campus creates. Are women professors more lenient in their grading than male professors? Do female students exert a positive influence on the academic habits of both genders? Given the role of gender composition, as identified numerous times in this book, it is important for future research to probe more deeply into the seemingly positive climate created when a campus is composed of greater numbers of women students and faculty. This question is particularly important given the increase in female students and faculty at colleges nationwide.

College GPA: Opposing Influences on Women and Men

One of the most fascinating influences on GPA is the amount of time that students spend exercising or playing sports, which contributes to higher college grades among women but lower grades among men. These results bear some similarity to those reported by Umbach, Palmer, Kuh, and Hannah (2006), who found that participating in intercollegiate athletics predicted lower grades for male students. The implications of this finding depend on how it is interpreted. Perhaps women involved in sports develop more effective time management strategies that allow them to balance exercise with academics. Or perhaps their involvement in sports exposes them to the influence of female peer groups who also prioritize academics. On the other hand, sports and exercise further expose men to the influence of male peer groups, whose academic achievement levels tend to be lower than women's. In addition, some male athletes may de-emphasize academics because they think, no matter how unrealistically, that they may have a future career in professional sports, an option less frequently available to women. Clearly, this intriguing finding merits further research and attention at the campus level. For example—as suggested by Simons, Van Rheenen, and Covington (1999)—campuses can better integrate athletes into the academic community by offering athletes academic resources that also expose them to non-athletes, educating coaches about athletes' academic needs, and facilitating more positive interactions between athletic departments and faculty.

College GPA: Factors Influencing Women Only

Each of the unique influences on women's GPA reveals interesting information about how women's outlook and experiences shape their academic performance. Interestingly, at a time when more low-income women are enrolling in college, having significant financial concerns relates to better-than-expected college grades. This may reflect an underlying commitment to education among the women who attend college despite financial challenges.

Engineering is the only major field to predict college grades solely for women. Here we find that women majoring in engineering tend to receive lower grades than expected based on the relatively high grades they earned in high school. Perhaps this is a function of the heightened stress levels experienced by female engineering majors, as reported in chapter 5, combined with the traditionally competitive grading practices in engineering courses. Another possibility is that the stress experienced by female engineering majors results in part from the lower-than-expected grades they receive. Future research on the climate for women in engineering should untangle this issue of causality so that academic advisers and other campus personnel can better assist women engineering majors who may be struggling academically.

Finally, social diversity experiences—such as dating, dining with, or studying with somebody of a different race or ethnicity—relate to lower grades for women. This is the only instance in this study where social diversity experiences trigger a negative outcome for students; its influence on other outcomes is uniformly positive. Though an explanation is not immediately clear, it is possible that these effects are attributable not to the diverse nature of the interactions but to the time women invest in these social activities.

College GPA: Factors Influencing Men Only

For men, institutional culture plays a key role in either promoting or inhibiting academic success. Interestingly, a campus peer group that supports traditional gender roles relates to higher

GPAs among men. This curious result resonates with a finding reported by Whitt, Pascarella, Nesheim, Marth, and Pierson (2003), who show that an unsupportive or chilly campus climate for women predicted higher scores for men on a measure of cognitive development (specifically, reading comprehension). This raises the question of *why* campuses with traditional gender role orientations boost men's grades and whether such institutions either subtly or intentionally place greater value on men's educational achievement. Men's grades are also influenced by another aspect of the peer culture—orientation toward the arts. In this case, campuses where students place greater emphasis on artistic creativity tend to weaken men's academic performance. These two findings point out ways in which the values of the college environment may shape men's orientation toward academics. Thus, colleges that are concerned about the academic performance of their male students should consider their student body's values and beliefs and ways they can mitigate the potentially negative effects of student peer culture.

In addition to the numerous aspects of academic engagement aiding in both genders' success, certain experiences relate specifically to men's grades. Leadership training, for example, is a positive force in men's academic achievement. However, activities that remove men from the formal academic environment—such as working off campus and reading for pleasure—tend to suppress men's grades. Overall, given men's relatively lower grades compared to women, it is especially important for campuses to recognize the importance of on-campus engagement for male students.

Self-Rated Mathematical Ability

One of the most consistent and significant gender gaps among entering college students is their level of mathematical self-confidence. Regardless of ability, women time and again rate themselves lower than men on their mathematical skills, a gender gap that becomes larger during college. In what ways does college contribute to women's and men's confidence in their mathematical abilities? Are there ways in which institutions can stem the decline in mathematical confidence that occurs with both genders during college?

In the following pages, we will examine aspects of college that affect students' beliefs about their mathematical abilities and whether different strategies might be employed for male and female students. Mathematical self-confidence is indicated by students' self-ratings of their mathematical ability on a 5-point scale ranging from "lowest 10 percent" to "highest 10 percent" relative to other people their age. While research often combines mathematical self-ratings together with other academic self-ratings, earlier work has demonstrated important gender differences in the factors influencing the development of math confidence during college (Sax, 1994b, 1994c)—differences that do not emerge when examining broader indicators of academic self-concept, such as the scholar personality presented in chapter 5. Table 7.2 presents the college environments and experiences related to the development of men's and women's mathematical self-confidence.

Mathematical Ability: Aspects of College That Influence Both Genders

Not surprisingly, major field is an important determinant of mathematical self-confidence during college. Majoring in math-intensive fields—such as engineering, physical sciences, mathematics, statistics, and business—strengthens men's and women's belief in their mathematical aptitude. Notably, the influence of these majors is stronger for women than men, suggesting that continued exposure to mathematics is particularly important for female students. Conversely, fields that tend not to emphasize quantitative skills—such as English, the humanities, ethnic studies, and psychology—appear to suppress men's and women's

Table 7.2 Gender Differences in College-Level Predictors of Self-Rated Mathematical Ability

	Women	Men	Variable type
Common predictors			
Peer mean: Socioeconomic status	−	−	Peer group
Major: Business	+*	+	Major
Major: Engineering	+*	+	Major
Major: Physical sciences, math, statistics, or computer science	+*	+	Major
Major: English or humanities	−	−*	Major
Major: Psychology	−	−	Major
Hours per week using a personal computer	+	+	Involvement in academics
Enrolled in ethnic studies course	−	−	Involvement in academics
Studied with other students	+*	+	Involvement with peers
Tutored another student	+	+	Involvement with peers
Hours per week household/childcare duties	+	+	Other involvement
Unique predictors: Women			
Student-to-faculty ratio	+		Institutional characteristics
Percentage of bachelor's degrees in science, math, and engineering	+		Peer group
Major: Education	+		Major
Faculty did not take comments seriously	−		Involvement with faculty
Unique predictors: Men			
Percentage of women faculty		+	Institutional characteristics
Peer mean: Artistic interests		−	Peer group
Major: History or political science		−	Major
Major: Journalism or communications		−	Major

(Continued)

Table 7.2 (Continued)

	Women	Men	Variable type
Hours per week studying/doing homework		+	Involvement in academics
Faculty provided opportunity for research		+	Involvement with faculty
General faculty support		+	Involvement with faculty
Hours per week commuting		+	Other involvement
Hours per week reading for pleasure		+	Other involvement
Final R^2	53%	56%	

Notes: Direction of effect is noted only for variables that are significant at $p < .0001$.

R^2 represents the proportion of variance accounted for by all variables in the model (including precollege variables). See appendix D for the differential contribution of precollege and college variables.

* Denotes a coefficient that is significantly larger ($p < .01$) for that gender.

mathematical self-confidence. These results underscore a key factor in the widening gender gap in mathematical confidence during college: women's and men's differential major field choices. Though colleges are not in a position to mandate that more women major in math-related fields, they can consider ways to foster math confidence among women across all disciplines.

One way is to promote the formation of study groups, given that studying with other students encourages a sense of math confidence, especially among women. In fact, the effects of study groups are evident regardless of students' major, thus presenting one way for campuses to foster greater mathematical confidence for students across all academic disciplines. However, since the specific dynamics of study groups are not known from these data, future research should examine how study groups' gender composition and the nature of interactions among group members affect women and men. An important question is whether perceived gains in math ability result from the *teaching* or the *learning* that occurs in a group setting. The importance of teaching others also is revealed in the effects of tutoring other students, which relates to gains in mathematical self-confidence for both women and men.

Mathematical Ability: Factors Influencing Women Only

Only four aspects of college relate to changes in math confidence solely for women, two of which are institutional characteristics. In particular, larger institutions—especially those enrolling greater numbers of students majoring in science, math, and engineering—promote women's sense of confidence in their math skills. Majoring in education also strengthens math self-ratings for women and may reflect the content of education courses designed to prepare students to become math or science teachers or to teach those concepts through general studies.

Women's mathematical confidence also grows because of interactions with faculty. Specifically, regardless of major field, women who feel that faculty did not take their comments seriously report greater-than-average declines in their mathematical self-confidence. Other research has revealed a weakening of math confidence among women who spend more time interacting with faculty (Sax, 1994b). Further, as discussed in chapter 5, feeling dismissed by faculty relates to declines in women's self-rated physical health. Clearly, greater attention needs to be paid—through both research and practice—to student-faculty interactions and their oftentimes negative consequences. We must ask ourselves: What are the situations in which women feel that faculty do not take their comments seriously? How do faculty view those same interactions, and in what ways do they expect female students to respond? Are dismissive comments made more often by female or male faculty, and in what context? The more light that can be shed on this issue, the better equipped institutions will be to advise faculty on effective ways of interacting with students and to provide resources for women who experience self-doubt as a result of their interactions with professors.

Mathematical Ability: Factors Influencing Men Only

The influence of faculty is again apparent among college experiences related to men's mathematical self-confidence. Here improved math confidence is observed among men who work with faculty on research and who feel personally and academically supported by their professors. In addition, just as we have seen the positive influence of a female faculty presence on other outcomes for men—such as their scientific orientation, emotional well-being, and leadership confidence—the percentage of women faculty at the institution contributes to heightened math confidence for men only. This pattern of effects suggests that greater numbers of female faculty contribute to an environment that is particularly supportive for male students, though some benefits have been documented for women as well.

Time spent studying, doing homework, and reading for pleasure also boost men's mathematical self-confidence. The influence of reading for pleasure is similar to its role in promoting scientific orientation solely for men and may reflect choices of reading material, with men historically reading more scientific and technical books and magazines than women, who tend to prefer reading fiction. Thus, men's and women's different reading preferences during college serve to reinforce gender gaps in math confidence.

Men's math confidence also depends on their choice of major field, with greater-than-average declines observed among men majoring in fields that do not emphasize mathematical concepts in the curriculum, such as history, political science, journalism, and communications.

Self-Rated Drive to Achieve

Colleges seek to admit students who possess a motivation to succeed because these students are considered a good investment of resources and are likely to reflect well on the institution when they graduate. Students who lack such motivation are often weeded out during the admissions process, and if they are not, they may be at risk of low grades or even dropping out. Despite the fact that women demonstrate higher levels of academic achievement than men coming into college, their drive to achieve is fairly similar to men's. In fact, drive to achieve is the only self-rating measure that does not produce significant gender differences either at college entry or four years later. However, there are differences in the factors associated with *changes* in drive to achieve during college, as shown in table 7.3.

Drive to Achieve: Aspects of College That Influence Both Genders

For both women and men, participating in a variety of academic and extracurricular activities strengthens achievement orientation. Particularly powerful are measures of academic engagement, such as enrolling in honors/advanced courses, working on independent study projects, tutoring other students, studying, and doing homework. Aspects of involvement with faculty also promote students' self-assessed drive to achieve, including the positive influence of being supported by faculty, challenging professors' ideas in class, and receiving honest feedback from instructors. Aspects of extracurricular engagement also boost achievement motivation and include participating in student clubs and groups, spending time exercising or playing sports, having diverse social interactions, and participating in organized demonstrations. Conversely, aspects of *disengagement* detract from students' sense of achievement motivation, including watching television, feeling bored in class, withdrawing from school, and taking a leave of absence. Clearly, these

Table 7.3 Gender Differences in College-Level Predictors of Self-Rated Drive to Achieve

	Women	Men	Variable type
Common predictors			
Number of full-time undergraduates	−	−	Institutional characteristics
Enrolled in honors/advanced courses	+	+	Involvement in academics
Hours per week studying/ doing homework	+	+*	Involvement in academics
Worked on independent study project	+	+	Involvement in academics
Felt bored in class	−*	−	Involvement in academics
Withdrew from school or took a leave of absence	−	−*	Involvement in academics
Challenged a professor's ideas in class	+	+*	Involvement with faculty
Faculty provided honest feedback about abilities	+*	+	Involvement with faculty
General faculty support	+	+	Involvement with faculty
Hours per week student clubs or groups	+	+	Involvement with peers
Social diversity experiences	+	+*	Involvement with peers
Took part in demonstrations	+	+	Involvement with peers
Tutored another student	+	+	Involvement with peers
Hours per week exercising/ playing sports	+	+	Other involvement
Hours per week watching television	−	−	Other involvement
Opposing predictors			
Percentage of bachelor's degrees in history, political science, and social sciences	+	−	Peer group
Unique predictors: Women			
Percentage of women faculty	+		Institutional characteristics
Public 4-year college	+		Institutional characteristics

Table 7.3 (Continued)

	Women	Men	Variable type
Peer mean: Socioeconomic status	−		Peer group
Major: Biological sciences	+		Major
Unique predictors: Men			
Peer mean: Materialism and social status		+	Peer group
Peer mean: Understanding of others		−	Peer group
Living on campus		+	Residence
Concern about financing college		−	Finances
Major: Fine arts		+	Major
Major: Psychology		−	Major
Major: Social sciences		−	Major
Hours per week socializing with friends		−	Involvement with peers
Final R^2	31%	41%	

Notes: Direction of effect is noted only for variables that are significant at $p < .0001$.

R^2 represents the proportion of variance accounted for by all variables in the model (including precollege variables). See appendix D for the differential contribution of precollege and college variables.

* Denotes a coefficient that is significantly larger ($p < .01$) for that gender.

results underscore the importance of student engagement in activities that will better integrate them into the academic and social campus communities.

Drive to Achieve: Opposing Influences for Women and Men

Only one aspect of college relates in *opposite* ways to men's and women's drive to achieve: the percentage of bachelor's degrees awarded in the social sciences. A greater emphasis on social science accounts for an increased drive to achieve among women but declines among men. Though the meaning of these opposing effects is not immediately clear, additional findings reported later in this section suggest other ways in which the social sciences appear to subvert men's drive to achieve. As we will see later on, these results may reflect differences in how women and men define achievement.

Drive to Achieve: Factors Influencing Women Only

Among aspects of college that promote women's drive to achieve, perhaps the most interesting is the proportion of female faculty at the institution. Such an environment has been shown to be a positive force for numerous aspects of men's development, but for women, it thus far relates only to scholarly self-confidence and drive to achieve. This perhaps reflects the impact of role modeling by female academics who, by virtue of their profession, are likely to be achievement oriented themselves.

Women's drive to achieve also is influenced by the socioeconomic status of the peer group. Here we find that women attending colleges with students from wealthier families become less likely to view themselves as driven to achieve. This finding may reflect the influential role of peer groups in shaping—and sometimes suppressing—women's achievement orientation, as described by Komarovsky (1985) and Holland and Eisenhart (1990). Colleges with wealthier student bodies should thus take stock of the peer group's commitment to achievement and the potential influence of campus culture on women's motivation.

Drive to Achieve: Factors Influencing Men Only

A combination of major field and peer group influences shapes men's drive to achieve. With respect to major, achievement motivation becomes stronger among men majoring in the fine arts and weaker among those majoring in psychology or the social sciences. Consistent with results reported earlier, we see once again social sciences' negative influence exclusively on men's achievement motivation. Additional results may shed light on this phenomenon because men's drive to achieve is hindered by time spent socializing with friends and by a peer group demonstrating higher "understanding of others," while it is strengthened by a peer group focused more on materialism and social status.

It is interesting to consider why social interactions, empathic and non-status-oriented peer groups, and disciplines that promote awareness of social dynamics would lead men to rate themselves lower on drive to achieve. One possibility is that men view achievement in more individualistic terms than women, but that when exposed to environments with high levels of social interaction and empathy, men begin to value community goals over individual goals. Conversely, environments with little social interaction and low levels of empathy may reinforce men's individualistic tendencies, thus enhancing their drive to achieve. This hypothesis merits further investigation, especially since one environment that is typically social in nature—living on campus—strengthens men's drive to achieve.

We also find that men's financial situation affects their drive to achieve, as worrying about whether they will have enough funds to complete college contributes to declines in achievement motivation. This finding suggests that campuses should pay special attention to changes in motivation among male students who are struggling financially.

Self-Rated Competitiveness

The largest gender difference among all outcomes examined in this book is in the area of self-rated competitiveness, with men much more likely than women to rate themselves highly on this trait over the course of college. However, it is important to acknowledge that students' definitions of competitiveness likely vary and may vary further by gender. First, there may be discrepancies in how favorably students view this term because it connotes both positive (e.g., competitive as "talented") and negative (e.g., competitive as "aggressive") traits. Second, the item does not specify the domain of competitiveness, so students may view it through an academic, social, athletic, or other lens. Looking at table 7.4, we see numerous gender differences in the college environments and experiences that relate to students' self-rated competitiveness. Given that being competitive connotes both positive and negative images, it is difficult to suggest how campuses should respond to these findings. Yet practitioners may still find it useful to understand how such orientations change as a result of students' college experiences.

Competitiveness: Aspects of College That Influence Both Genders

For both women and men, a key factor in developing competitive self-confidence during college is taking initiative to seek out opportunities for learning and leadership. This is evidenced by the positive effect of such experiences as taking honors courses, working with faculty on research, meeting with faculty outside class, and getting involved in student government or other forms of leadership. To the extent that students must compete with each other for these opportunities, those who are successful might naturally view themselves as more competitive than their peers.

Time spent exercising or playing sports also promotes students', especially women's, sense of competitiveness. Though women engage in sports and exercise less frequently than men, this finding reveals that women who devote time to sports and exercise are more comfortable describing themselves as competitive individuals.

Table 7.4 Gender Differences in College-Level Predictors of Self-Rated Competitiveness

	Women	Men	Variable type
Common predictors			
Enrolled in honors/advanced courses	+*	+	Involvement in academics
Hours per week using a personal computer	+	+	Involvement in academics
Challenged a professor's ideas in class	+*	+	Involvement with faculty
Faculty provided opportunity for research	+	+	Involvement with faculty
General faculty support	+	+	Involvement with faculty
Hours per week talking with faculty outside class	+	+*	Involvement with faculty
Student government	+	+	Involvement with peers
Leadership training	+	+	Involvement with peers
Hours per week exercising/ playing sports	+*	+	Other involvement
Unique predictors: Women			
Public 4-year college	+		Institutional characteristics
Peer mean: Socioeconomic status	−		Peer group
Percentage of bachelor's degrees in history, political science, and social sciences	+		Peer group
College selectivity	−		Peer group
Aid: Family or self	−		Finances
Major: Health profession	−		Major
Felt bored in class	−		Involvement in academics
Hours per week commuting	−		Other involvement
Unique predictors: Men			
Percentage of women faculty		+	Institutional characteristics
Peer mean: Materialism and social status		+	Peer group

(Continued)

Table 7.4 *(Continued)*

	Women	Men	*Variable type*
Aid: Grants and scholarships		+	Finances
Major: Business		+	Major
Major: Fine arts		+	Major
Major: Journalism or communications		+	Major
Faculty did not take comments seriously		−	Involvement with faculty
Joined a fraternity or sorority		+	Involvement with peers
Worked part-time on campus		−	Involvement in work
Hedonism (drinking, smoking, and partying)		−	Other involvement
Hours per week reading for pleasure		−	Other involvement
Final R^2	35%	43%	

Notes: Direction of effect is noted only for variables that are significant at $p < .0001$.

R^2 represents the proportion of variance accounted for by all variables in the model (including precollege variables). See appendix D for the differential contribution of precollege and college variables.

* Denotes a coefficient that is significantly larger ($p < .01$) for that gender.

Competitiveness: Factors Influencing Women Only

The majority of factors uniquely related to women's competitive orientations reflect the role of campuswide or disciplinary environments. Here we find that public four-year colleges and institutions awarding a greater share of degrees in social science fields tend to strengthen women's ratings on competitiveness. Alternatively, campuses that are more academically selective and that enroll students from higher socioeconomic backgrounds tend to suppress women's competitive orientation. This phenomenon may be something akin to relative deprivation (Davis, 1966), as higher-achieving and wealthier peer groups tend to have above-average self-confidence; thus, women may view themselves in a relatively less competitive light.

Certain college experiences also weaken women's sense of competitiveness, including feeling bored in class and time spent commuting. Each of these represents a form of disengagement from campus life, suggesting that competitiveness is enhanced among women who are more inspired academically and more frequently present on campus.

Competitiveness: Factors Influencing Men Only

Several findings reveal ways in which peers' values influence men's competitive self-ratings. In particular, more materialistic campus subcultures promote a sense of competitiveness among men, including joining a fraternity, majoring in business, and attending campuses where students place greater emphasis on wealth and social status.

Other experiences—such as reading for pleasure, drinking, and smoking—inhibit the development of men's competitive orientations. Perhaps these behaviors reflect activities that do not require students to compete for participation, unlike honors courses, faculty research projects, and student government, which, as noted earlier, enhance students' competitive nature.

Results also point to faculty's influence on men's competitive orientations. Feeling that faculty did not take their comments seriously in class leads to declines in men's sense of competitiveness. However, attending colleges with greater proportions of female faculty promotes more competitive orientations. This is similar to the effects of female faculty on men's self-ratings as reported thus far with respect to math confidence, leadership ability, and emotional well-being. In each of these cases, the presence of women faculty reinforces initial gender differences in self-perceptions.

Self-Change: Critical Thinking and Knowledge

Chief among any institution's goals is developing students' intellectual capacities. Colleges design their programs and services in ways that maximize students' cognitive growth and acquisition of new knowledge. After four years of college, to what extent do students believe they have grown in these ways, and does this differ for women and men? The follow-up survey assesses how much change students think they have experienced across six domains: the ability to think critically, analytical and problem-solving skills, general knowledge, writing skills, knowledge of a particular field or discipline, and reading speed and comprehension. Gender differences in these six areas are practically nonexistent, showing that women and men are equally likely to believe that they have improved across a range of cognitive abilities. Table 7.5 reveals numerous commonalities—and some gender differences—in the aspects of college that influence students' beliefs about their cognitive gains.

Critical Thinking and Knowledge: Aspects of College That Influence Both Genders

Consistent with conclusions drawn by Astin (1993c) and Pascarella and Terenzini (2005), academic engagement is critical to the development of students' cognitive abilities. By far the strongest determinant of this outcome for women and men is feeling supported, both personally and academically, by faculty. Other student-faculty interactions also are important to contributing to gains in this area, including time spent talking with faculty outside class and challenging professors' ideas in class. Clearly, the opportunity to nurture connections with faculty directly links to the knowledge and skills students feel they have developed during college.

Engagement is also central to the belief that one's knowledge and skills have improved over the course of college. Students

Table 7.5 Gender Differences in College-Level Predictors of Self-Change: Critical Thinking and Knowledge

	Women	Men	Variable type
Common predictors			
Number of full-time undergraduates	−	−	Institutional characteristics
Percentage of women faculty	+	+	Institutional characteristics
Percentage of bachelor's degrees in science, math, and engineering	−	−	Peer group
Peer mean: Competitiveness	−	−	Peer group
Enrolled in ethnic studies course	+	+	Involvement in academics
Withdrew from school or took a leave of absence	−	−	Involvement in academics
Hours per week studying/ doing homework	+	+*	Involvement in academics
Hours per week using a personal computer	+	+	Involvement in academics
Felt bored in class	−	−*	Involvement in academics
Challenged a professor's ideas in class	+*	+	Involvement with faculty
General faculty support	+	+*	Involvement with faculty
Hours per week talking with faculty outside class	+	+	Involvement with faculty
Hours per week student clubs or groups	+	+	Involvement with peers
Social diversity experiences	+	+*	Involvement with peers
Unique predictors: Women			
Private nonsectarian 4-year college	+		Institutional characteristics
Public university	−		Institutional characteristics
Peer mean: Living on campus	+		Peer group
Major: Education	−		Major
Major: English or humanities	+		Major
Took part in demonstrations	+		Involvement with peers

(Continued)

Table 7.5 *(Continued)*

	Women	Men	Variable type
Unique predictors: Men			
Percentage of bachelor's degrees in education		+	Peer group
Living on campus		+	Residence
Major: History or political science		+	Major
Major: Journalism or communications		−	Major
Enrolled in honors/advanced courses		+	Involvement in academics
Hours per week reading for pleasure		+	Other involvement
Final R^2	23%	33%	

Notes: Direction of effect is noted only for variables that are significant at $p < .0001$.

R^2 represents the proportion of variance accounted for by all variables in the model (including precollege variables). See appendix D for the differential contribution of precollege and college variables.

* Denotes a coefficient that is significantly larger ($p < .01$) for that gender.

who devote more time to their studies or who participate in student groups report greater gains in knowledge and cognitive skills, while those who are bored in class, withdraw temporarily from school, or exhibit other forms of academic disengagement reveal smaller gains in this area.

It's important to note that students who seek out diversity in their personal and academic lives also report cognitive gains. Specifically, enrolling in ethnic studies and socializing with students of another racial/ethnic group help strengthen students' beliefs about their intellectual capacities. Thus, while diversity activities have already been shown to enhance students' concern for others' welfare and commitment to improving race relations, they apparently yield broad cognitive benefits as well.

The campus environment also influences students' self-perceived gains in knowledge and critical-thinking skills. Students attending campuses with more female faculty are more likely to report cognitive gains, once again reflecting the benefit of recruiting more women faculty to an institution. Conversely, students attending large, competitive, and scientifically oriented institutions are less likely to believe that they have made improvements in their cognitive skills during college. Though the climate at such institutions may be difficult to change, practitioners would be wise to consider how to maximize those engagement opportunities within their purview. Given findings presented earlier in this section, this means fostering greater opportunities for students to connect with faculty and to be exposed to diversity in the curriculum and in social settings.

Critical Thinking and Knowledge: Factors Influencing Women Only

Institutional environment also influences self-assessed cognitive growth uniquely for women. Attending a private four-year, residential college helps strengthen critical-thinking skills and knowledge, whereas attending public universities produces the opposite effect. Once again, these findings remind us of the importance of maximizing students' opportunities to get involved, something that is more easily achieved at smaller, residential campuses.

Choice of major field also relates to students' conceptions of their cognitive growth. Students majoring in English and the humanities are particularly likely to believe that their knowledge and intellectual abilities have improved since entering college. In a more troubling finding, those majoring in education report fewer gains in the areas of critical thinking, problem solving, and content knowledge. Could it be that those who study these intellectual domains become more self-critical? Considering the number of future teachers who enroll in the education major as undergraduates, campuses and researchers must examine this issue more carefully.

Critical Thinking and Knowledge: Factors Influencing Men Only

Men's cognitive development benefits from several aspects of intellectual engagement, such as taking honors/advanced courses and reading for pleasure. The effect of reading has been noted elsewhere in this book as a positive force in developing scientific orientation and mathematical self-confidence and as a negative influence on college grades. Clearly, men reap intellectual rewards from reading books, magazines, or other materials, even if the time they devote to nonclass reading detracts from the formal grades that they receive.

Interestingly, while majoring in education minimizes women's reports of cognitive gains, attending campuses that award a higher percentage of degrees in education leads to larger gains in this area for men, regardless of their own major. This finding is consistent with the beneficial role of large education programs as it relates to other areas of growth among male students: cultural awareness and commitment to social activism. Further research should examine in greater depth whether and how academic programs in education shape an institution's culture and values.

Degree Aspirations

The vast majority of male and female students entering four-year colleges and universities plan to earn a bachelor's degree, and growing numbers also expect to earn a master's, doctoral, or professional degree at some point in their lives. Although the women and men in this study held fairly similar degree aspirations when they began college, a gender gap emerged over four years, mostly due to increases in the proportion of women planning to earn a master's degree. In this section, we will examine whether college exerts different effects on women's and men's degree goals. Table 7.6 shows that for the most part, the college environmental and experiential factors that predict degree aspirations are largely consistent for the two genders, though some differences are apparent.

Degree Aspirations: Aspects of College That Influence Both Genders

Men's and women's degree aspirations benefit from opportunities to engage with peers and faculty in academic and other learning environments. Feeling supported by faculty, participating in student clubs and groups, performing volunteer work, and even being employed on campus are just some of the many aspects of involvement that raise students' aspirations for postbaccalaureate degrees. Conversely, fewer opportunities to engage in the campus community, such as at larger institutions or when students take a temporary leave of absence, tend to suppress degree aspirations.

Another factor worth considering is that students enrolling in institutions with a greater percentage of women students and faculty experience higher degree aspirations. This result echoes the numerous positive effects of female representation revealed throughout this book, a phenomenon that is discussed further in chapter 8.

Degree Aspirations: Factors Influencing Women Only

When it comes to women's aspirations for advanced degrees, the role of campus peer groups is evident. In particular, student bodies characterized by strong math and science preparation or a high degree of interest in altruism and social activism promote women's interest in obtaining advanced degrees. These relationships likely reflect the influence of students in those peer cultures who

Table 7.6 Gender Differences in College-Level Predictors of Degree Aspirations

	Women	Men	Variable type
Common predictors			
Percentage of women faculty	+	+	Institutional characteristics
Private Catholic 4-year college	+	+	Institutional characteristics
Number of full-time undergraduates	−	−*	Institutional characteristics
Student-to-faculty ratio	−	−	Institutional characteristics
Percentage of women undergraduates	+	+	Peer group
Major: Education	+	+	Major
Major: History or political science	+	+	Major
Major: Business	−	−	Major
Major: Engineering	−	−	Major
Hours per week studying/ doing homework	+	+	Involvement in academics
Worked on independent study project	+	+*	Involvement in academics
Felt bored in class	−	−*	Involvement in academics
Withdrew from school or took a leave of absence	−*	−	Involvement in academics
Challenged a professor's ideas in class	+	+	Involvement with faculty
General faculty support	+	+	Involvement with faculty
Hours per week student clubs or groups	+	+	Involvement with peers
Took part in demonstrations	+	+	Involvement with peers
Tutored another student	+	+	Involvement with peers
Worked part-time on campus	+	+	Involvement in work
Volunteering or community service	+	+	Other involvement
Unique predictors: Women			
Peer mean: Altruism and social activism	+		Peer group

Table 7.6 (Continued)

	Women	Men	Variable type
Peer mean: Years of study in math and science	+		Peer group
Major: Psychology	+		Major
Faculty did not take comments seriously	−		Involvement with faculty
Attended racial/cultural awareness workshop	+		Involvement with peers
Worked part-time off campus	+		Involvement in work
Hours per week exercising/ playing sports	+		Other involvement
Hours per week household/ childcare duties	−		Other involvement
Unique predictors: Men			
Major: Biological sciences		+	Major
Final R^2	29%	32%	

Notes: Direction of effect is noted only for variables that are significant at $p < .0001$.

R^2 represents the proportion of variance accounted for by all variables in the model (including precollege variables). See appendix D for the differential contribution of precollege and college variables.

* Denotes a coefficient that is significantly larger ($p < .01$) for that gender.

tend to have higher aspirations and more ambition. Higher degree aspirations also are evident for women who attend racial awareness workshops and those who spend more time on sports and exercise.

A key negative force in developing graduate degree aspirations is the nature of women's interactions with faculty. Women reporting that faculty did not take their comments seriously became discouraged and developed comparatively less interest in graduate school than other women. Although the specific dynamics of student-faculty interactions are not known from these data, this finding shows that faculty who are dismissive of women's opinions or perspectives can stifle those students' aspirations. In fact, we have already seen that for women only, feeling dismissed by faculty relates to declines in self-rated mathematical ability and physical health. Clearly, this calls for an examination of how faculty treat students both inside and outside the classroom, how students perceive this treatment, and how these results vary by the sex of the student and the sex of the instructor.

Degree Aspirations: Factors Influencing Men Only

Only one variable indicates degree aspirations solely for men: the positive effects of majoring in the biological sciences. This finding may reflect the fact that men who major in biological science often plan to earn advanced degrees in medicine. In fact, other research has shown that men who are biological science majors are significantly more likely than their female counterparts to enroll in medical school within five years of graduation (Sax, 2001).

Career Sex-Atypicality

Despite the progress that women have made in pursuing fields that were once considered nontraditional for their gender, such as law and medicine, students' occupational orientations remain highly dependent on whether they are male or female. Indeed, as discussed in chapter 2, historical patterns of gender difference persist in several fields, including education, nursing, engineering, business, and computer programming.[2]

Though influences on students' career orientation are largely determined before college, we must consider whether and how the college years further shape the gender-based traditionalism of career choices. In the following pages, we will examine career sex-atypicality as a reflection of the proportion of first-year students aspiring toward a particular career. For students to be considered sex-atypical in their career goals, the percentage of the opposite sex aspiring to a particular career must be at least double the percentage from among their own gender. For women, sex-atypical careers include working as an engineer, military service worker, law enforcement official, architect, business owner, computer programmer, farmer/rancher, skilled trade worker, clergy member, or conservationist. Sex-atypical careers for men include aspiring to be an interior decorator, nurse, social worker, elementary school teacher, homemaker, dietician, interpreter, business clerk, psychologist, school counselor, veterinarian, lab technician, or therapist.

The nature of this college outcome requires a unique presentation of the results. Specifically, the *meaning* of career sex-atypicality is inherently different for each sex. What is considered atypical for women is considered typical for men. Thus, the presentation of the results does not focus on direct comparisons of predictors; instead, results are presented separately for women and men (see tables 7.7 and 7.8).

Table 7.7 College-Level Predictors of Women's Career Sex-Atypicality

	Direction of effect	*Variable type*
Student-to-faculty ratio	+	Institutional characteristics
Peer mean: Years of study in math and science	+	Peer group
Peer mean: Understanding of others	−	Peer group
Aid: Family or self	−	Finances
Took honors/advanced courses	−	Involvement in academics
Tutored another student	+	Involvement in academics
Hours per week using a personal computer	+	Involvement in academics
Studied with other students	+	Involvement in academics
Enrolled in ethnic studies course	+	Involvement in academics
Had a part-time job off campus	−	Involvement in work

Note: Direction of effect is noted only for variables that are significant at $p < .0001$.

Table 7.8 College-Level Predictors of Men's Career Sex-Atypicality

	Direction of effect	Variable type
Hours per week using a personal computer	−	Involvement in academics
Enrolled in women's studies course	+	Involvement in academics
General faculty support	+	Involvement with faculty
Hours per week talking with faculty outside class	−	Involvement with faculty
Hedonism (drinking, smoking, and partying)	−	Other involvement
Hours per week watching television	+	Other involvement

Note: Direction of effect is noted only for variables that are significant at $p < .0001$.

Career Sex-Atypicality: Aspects of College That Influence Both Genders

Using a personal computer in college predicts shifts toward traditionally male careers for both men and women. Although this finding reflects the fact that traditionally male fields such as computer science and engineering demand advanced computer training, we are reminded that computers, despite their use by students of both sexes, continue to be perceived as a male domain (Margolis & Fisher, 2002).

Curricular diversity also influences both men's and women's career choice. For women, the likelihood of shifting toward more sex-atypical careers is higher when they enroll in an ethnic studies course in college. For men, taking a women's studies course is associated with higher rates of nontraditional career aspirations. These results are in line with Lease (2003), who suggests that college experiences that are "designed to broaden students' experiences and expose them to new cultures, ideas, and perspectives might affect their interest in nontraditional occupations" (p. 245). Thus, campus diversity programming is one way to encourage students to be open minded in their career interests.

Career Sex-Atypicality: Factors Influencing Women Only

Women are more likely to select nontraditional careers when they attend colleges that are larger and that enroll students with greater scientific preparation. Conversely, a student body with empathic tendencies often promotes women's selection of traditional careers, as suggested by the higher rate of traditional career choice among women attending institutions where the peer group had higher scores on "understanding of others." It is possible that these supportive environments validate women's tendencies to pursue fields that require more empathic and nurturing skills, such as nursing, education, and counseling.

Women's financial situations also influence their likelihood of aspiring to traditionally masculine versus feminine careers. Specifically, women who receive more money from family or personal savings and who are employed part-time off campus have more interest in traditionally female careers. These financial indicators reflect an initiative among women to secure extra funding for college; it is possible that women who are concerned about financial stability become more practical or, in this case, traditional in their career outlook, despite the fact that female-dominated fields tend to be less financially lucrative. Male-dominated fields may simply be perceived as offering too many challenges or too few opportunities for women. Future research should examine more closely how a dependency on financial aid and employment affect women's career aspirations.

Academic experiences in college also influence female students' career choices. Taking honors courses is related to selecting traditionally female careers, while studying with and tutoring other students are related to sex-atypical career choices. In the case of tutoring, though it may be that women majoring in math and science fields are more likely to become tutors (given the number of students seeking tutoring in those fields), findings could also signal the benefits of tutoring on women's confidence to pursue nontraditional careers.

Career Sex-Atypicality: Factors Influencing Men Only

Men's interactions with faculty produce a pair of contrasting results. Whereas time spent talking with college faculty outside class is associated with a shift toward traditionally masculine career choices, perceiving high levels of support from faculty—in the form of advice, respect, or encouragement—encourages men to consider sex-atypical careers. This result reflects a tension between quantity and quality in student-faculty interactions, such that sheer frequency of interaction relates to more traditional career interests—perhaps due to the necessity of greater out-of-class student-faculty interaction in the traditionally male sciences—whereas receiving support and encouragement from faculty may give male students freedom to consider nontraditional fields. Again, as mentioned throughout this book, information on the gender of the instructor is vital to gain a better understanding of these dynamics.

Two additional college behaviors predict changes in career decisions for men only. The first is that more traditional career choices grow out of hedonism, as defined by drinking, smoking, or other partying behaviors. This raises the question of whether a partying culture reinforces traditional gender role expectations among men; indeed, as shown earlier, joining a fraternity promotes more traditional gender expectations among male students.

Finally, the time men spend watching television shapes their career aspirations. Men who spend more time in front of the television become more receptive to pursuing traditionally feminine fields, such as teaching, social work, and psychology. Perhaps men are attracted to the ways in which these fields are portrayed on television. Future research that identifies what kinds of television programming college-age men and women watch would help us further understand these results.

Summary

Gender differences in the academic realm present somewhat of a paradox: while men report relatively higher levels of confidence in their intellectual, mathematical, and competitive abilities, it is the women who actually demonstrate higher levels of academic achievement. In fact, women earn better grades than men even when we account for the fact that they devote more time to their coursework.

When looking at how college affects students' academic achievement, aspirations, and self-confidence, one thing stands out for both genders: the importance of academic engagement. Studying, taking honors courses, pursuing independent study courses, and generally feeling interested in learning contribute to gains for women and men across a number of academic outcomes. Thus, efforts in higher education to promote student engagement are vital to both genders.

Yet there are some ways in which a different set of factors drive academic outcomes for women and men. These themes are not as readily apparent as they were for personality and identity (chapter 5) and political and social values (chapter 6). However, certain experiences and environmental forces produce noteworthy differences in their effects on women and men.

Probably the most consistent theme to emerge from this chapter is the way in which women and men react differently to their interactions with faculty. Though both genders benefit in numerous ways from the time they spend with faculty—both in and out of the classroom—negative experiences appear to be particularly detrimental for women. For example, feeling that faculty do not take their comments seriously relates to lower grades, less interest in graduate school, and a decline in math confidence. Feeling dismissed by their professors may lead women to question their own understanding of a subject and the conclusions they draw; ultimately, this can heighten feelings of self-doubt and diminish longer-term interest in the subject. On the other hand, men seem to be particular beneficiaries of positive relations with faculty; in fact, those who report more positive or collaborative relations—such as feeling supported by faculty or working with faculty on research—tend to earn higher grades, develop greater confidence in their math abilities, and become more open minded in their career choices. Men also appear to derive benefits—such as better grades and greater math confidence—from attending colleges with greater numbers of women faculty.

Thus, echoing a conclusion drawn in chapter 5, it is imperative to develop a clearer understanding of the nature of women's and men's interactions with their professors. Under what conditions does a student feel that a faculty member is not taking her seriously? To what extent are faculty aware that their actions are interpreted as dismissive or that they incite a negative reaction in female students? Faculty and other campus practitioners—especially those involved in counseling and advising—ought to discuss this topic and explore what can be done to promote healthier student-faculty dynamics. Clearly, positive and encouraging interactions hold the promise of improving the college experience for both genders.

This chapter also highlights the influence of the campuswide peer culture on students' academic orientations. For example, we find that a scientifically oriented student culture encourages women to have confidence in their mathematical abilities, to consider nontraditional careers, and to aim for higher academic degrees. On the other hand, attending an academically selective college tends to diminish women's achievement orientation and sense of competitiveness. Aspects of the peer culture also influence men, as in the finding that a materialistic campus culture promotes a sense of competitiveness among men only.

Though practitioners have a limited influence on the broader campus culture, they can use this knowledge of peer group influences to anticipate aspects of development for their male and female students. To be more relevant to campus practice, perhaps future research should focus less on the characteristics of the broad campus environment and pay more attention to how the characteristics, attitudes, and values of more proximal sources of peer group influence, such as particular student groups and campus organizations, affect women and men. Other research has shown these microenvironments to be more potent predictors of student outcomes, although from a methodological standpoint, quantitative research has found it difficult to generate sufficient data on the nature of peer groups that are defined by campus subenvironments.

Though many other interesting findings are revealed in this chapter—such as the opposite effects of sports and exercise on women's and men's GPAs—they do not form a clear pattern of differential impact. However, as will be reported in chapter 8, larger patterns are observed when such data are examined along with findings from across the entire study.

Notes

1. Academic traits are also reflected in the scholar personality, which was presented in chapter 5.
2. Portions of the career sex-atypicality section appear in Sax and Bryant (2006).

8

WHERE SHOULD WE GO FROM HERE?

Implications of the Gender Gap for Campus Practice and Future Research

At a time of women's great progress in higher education, and corresponding concerns about men's educational attainment, this book has raised a number of questions and used a variety of approaches to take a closer look at the gender gap among college students. It aims to add context to what have become oversimplified but popular messages—that gender equity has been achieved, that women are an academic success story, and that men are experiencing an educational crisis. There is some truth to each of these messages, but they tend to convey the status of women and men as a zero-sum game: if one gender is succeeding, the other must be failing. The reality is that both genders face obstacles and challenges in their pursuit of higher education, and it is incumbent on the higher education community to gain a deeper understanding of the nuances and implications of the gender gap in college.

As we have seen throughout this book, gender shapes not just the characteristics of women and men entering college but also the way in which women and men *experience* college. In various ways and to varying extents, gender influences how women's and men's interactions with people, programs, and services on campus ultimately contribute to their academic success, their beliefs about themselves, and their outlook on life. This is not to suggest that college predicts wholly different gender-based patterns of development. To be sure, broad-sweeping notions of "how college affects women" or "how college affects men" are not evident here. Instead, this book uncovers literally hundreds of conditional effects, or ways in which women and men react differently to their experiences in college. Each of these has the potential to alter campus practice and to suggest important directions for future research.

In some ways, these results are not surprising. After all, gender differences—though typically small—are exceptionally well documented, not just in education, but across practically all social contexts. Further, the notion that women and men develop in somewhat different ways during the college years is supported by highly regarded theories from a range of disciplines. And yet, in the vast body of empirical research on how college affects students, there has been fairly limited evidence that college impacts the two genders differently. Instead, our collective thinking about how college affects students has been shaped by a body of research that too often considers men and women in the aggregate. We have understood how students in general react to their experiences in college, but we have lacked an in-depth understanding of how gender or other defining characteristics—such as race, ethnicity, social class, or sexual orientation—shape the influence of college. As a result, practitioners' ability to design programming that attends to the unique needs of different student populations has been limited.

What we have learned through this project propels our understanding of how the dynamics of college impact depend on students' gender. It builds on the work of higher education scholars who have also uncovered gender differences in the influence of college, but it extends their work by including a wider range of college environments and student outcomes. It also sheds light on the applicability of feminist developmental theories to the study of college impact by revealing ways in which interpersonal relations shape the college experience of *both* genders. What follows are highlights of this project's major contributions to our thinking about educational practice, to higher education research, and to our theoretical notions about women's and men's development.

Implications for Campus Practice and Future Research

Those of us working in higher education will have a range of viewpoints about how the findings in this book apply to practice. Evidence of gender differences in student characteristics or in the nature of college impact causes us to reflect on our own experiences: Do these gender differences reflect what we see on our own campuses? Do they suggest the need to change our programs and services? In my own experience sharing the results of this study with campus practitioners across the country, I have learned that the results resonate deeply with their observations about college campuses but that conversations about what to do rarely occur. Part of the problem is that the responsibility to address gender differences does not reside with one campus department or unit, such as a gender studies department or a women's resource center. Rather, gender gaps and gender-based college influences have implications across a range of programs, services, and units—including residential life, academic advising, counseling, recreation, and the provost's office, to name a few. The ability to improve the college experience for both sexes depends on fostering greater communication about gender both within and between these various campus units.

To jump-start this conversation, this chapter presents some of the major findings and implications emanating from this study. Campus practitioners are encouraged to consider the relevance of these suggestions for their program or unit and to develop additional strategies for raising consciousness about these and other gender issues among faculty, administrators, staff, and students.

Financial Circumstances

An important trend in higher education is the emergence of an economic gender gap. As more women from lower socioeconomic classes attend college, female college students' average income has fallen further behind men's. In fact, while family incomes were equivalent for women and men in the 1960s, since then, median family incomes for male students have risen by approximately 42 percent, relative to a 16 percent increase among women. Consequently, first-year college women are substantially more concerned than their male counterparts about whether they will have enough money to complete college. To be sure, financial concerns weigh heavily on *both* genders, but the emerging economic gender gap is noteworthy, especially since women are now more likely than men to seek employment while in college.

Implications for Practice. The growing number of women who need to work during college naturally raises concerns about whether employment will compromise their academic success. And yet this book demonstrates ways in which women *benefit* from their employment experiences, such as becoming more committed to social activism and more interested in attending graduate school. Thus, colleges should evaluate whether they allocate student aid and work-study opportunities fairly to women and men, including whether both genders have equal access to employment that pays well, offers good working conditions, and is relevant to students' academic and career interests. Further, campus personnel need to keep in mind that the rising enrollment of women—though evidence of women's academic success—also signifies a population of students with growing economic concerns.

Directions for Future Research. Though numerous studies have examined the impact of students' work experiences—and present conflicting evidence of whether or not employment is beneficial to the student—we don't know how different types of jobs relate to different aspects of student development. Research has primarily focused on the amount of time that students spend working, rather than their specific type of employment. This question will become more important to answer as more students, and especially women, seek employment in college. We should know, for example, whether having a job in the campus bookstore relates to a different set of outcomes than working in the admissions office, in the recreation center, or at the local coffeehouse or retail store. Ultimately, we should know which types of work experiences are most beneficial and the extent to which women and men have equal access to the most desirable positions.

Connection to Family

Research has long demonstrated the advantages of going away to college, and it has largely been assumed that leaving home is equally important for both genders. However, we have seen here that leaving home may be especially beneficial for female students. These benefits include the development of greater scholarly confidence, stronger leadership skills, and a healthy sense of emotional well-being. For men, whether they live close to home or thousands of miles away is less relevant to their development in college. This supports other research suggesting that men are not as dependent on or closely tied to their families as are women (Kenny & Donaldson, 1991); thus, gaining distance from family is simply not as critical for men.

Implications for Practice. Though the present study suggests that it is better for women to maintain distance from their families when they attend college, our notion of distance has changed dramatically in the decade since the data for this study were collected. Today, students and parents stay in frequent contact with one another via cell phones, text messaging, and e-mail. In fact, the role of families in students' lives is an area of concern in higher education given the growing number of parents—sometimes referred to as helicopter parents—who are involved in the daily lives and academic affairs of their college-age children. The challenge facing colleges and universities is how to encourage women to develop a healthy sense of independence in light of their ongoing connection to their parents. This goal does not mean that women should sever ties with their families; that is neither realistic nor desirable. In fact, autonomy and connection need not be mutually exclusive. Echoing a conclusion drawn by Josselson (1987), college women face the challenge of "becoming different and maintaining connection at the same time" (p. 171).

Directions for Future Research. As just mentioned, changes in technology make it easier for students to stay connected with their parents. There is already evidence that women use cell phones and e-mail to stay in more frequent contact with their parents than do men (Wolf, Harper, & Sax, 2007). However, we know very little about the *consequences* of women's ongoing connection to their parents. One study reveals that women who stay in more frequent contact with their parents—through any form of communication—are less satisfied with their social experiences in college and that parental involvement in academic decision making correlates with lower self-assessed cognitive development among women (Harper, Wolf, & Sax, 2007). In these examples, however, causal relationships cannot be established. Thus, we are left to wonder whether women *turn* to their families as a result of academic or social difficulties or whether ongoing dependence on their family inhibits their personal and academic development. As parents and students stay increasingly connected—regardless of how far apart they are—future research will need to address how the type and frequency of student-parent communications relate to students' personal, academic, and social development during college. We may find that what is considered excessive communication in some families could, in other families, represent an important source of academic and social support. Further, the extent to which this varies by gender, race, and class will be a particularly important question for future research.

Student-Faculty Interactions

Probably the most consistent pattern of conditional effects detected in this study relates to students' interactions with and perceptions of faculty. Gender differences in this domain fall into three main categories, the first of which relates to politics and social activism. While interactions with faculty encourage liberalism, political engagement, and a commitment to social activism among students of both genders, relationships of this sort are more common or more pronounced among men. In general, we find that the more time that men spend engaged in one-on-one interactions with faculty, the more liberal they become in their political views and the greater concern they develop about race relations and the welfare of the larger society.

A second theme involving student-faculty interactions has to do with students' attitudes toward gender roles. For men, working with faculty on research or receiving advice, encouragement, and support from faculty relates to more egalitarian views on gender roles. That is, these men become *less* supportive of the notion that "the activities of married women are best confined to the home and family." For women, the opposite is true: those who spend time with faculty, especially in the context of research, become *more* committed to traditional gender roles.

A third noteworthy theme relates to faculty's influence on women's sense of confidence and well-being. Feeling dismissed by faculty in the classroom has negative consequences for women's longer-term academic aspirations, their confidence in math, and even their sense of physical well-being. On the other hand, women who report receiving honest feedback from faculty experience more positive outcomes, such as an improved sense of physical health and a stronger achievement motivation. These dynamics lend support to the theoretical work of Belenky, Clinchy, Goldberger, and Tarule (1997) and Baxter Magolda (1992) because they underscore the importance of validation, support, and sense of connectedness in women's intellectual and personal development. However, it is worth noting that developmental benefits can also arise from nonharmonious interactions with faculty because challenging professors in the classroom—a potentially contentious form of engagement—enhances women's commitment to social activism.

Thus, the study provides significant evidence that men's and women's academic identities, gender role expectations, self-esteem, and community orientation are all sensitive—though in somewhat different ways—to how much time they spend with faculty and how faculty respond to them. The findings—which are further elaborated in Sax, Bryant, and Harper (2005)—clearly underscore Colbeck, Cabrera, and Terenzini's (2001) conclusion that "the nature of faculty-student interactions have differential impact for female and male students" (p. 184).

Implications for Practice. Members of the campus community should be aware of potential gender differences in the student-faculty dynamic—whether in the classroom, during office hours, or in the context of research. Faculty would benefit from a better understanding of the implications of their actions, both overt and subtle, on male and female students. Instructors need to understand that even when they believe they are treating male and female students in the same way, the two genders may internalize those interactions differently. Particular attention should be paid to the fact that dismissive faculty comments can have a deleterious effect on female students' academic confidence and even physical well-being.

Faculty also ought to consider strategies for encouraging women to feel safe speaking up in the classroom. As we have seen, taking the initiative to challenge faculty in the classroom is a precursor to many beneficial outcomes for both genders, including scholarly self-confidence, critical-thinking skills, and leadership orientation; yet it also relates to greater stress and anxiety for women. Faculty are encouraged to reflect on the following questions: Do your teaching practices allow for an open exchange of ideas? How do you respond when students challenge you in the classroom? Do you provide a forum for differing perspectives? Do you encourage students to respect their peers' opinions? Are you aware that women and men may respond differently to your feedback and to classroom dynamics?

Gender differences in the dynamics of student-faculty interaction also have implications for counseling and advising. Knowing that women and men respond differently to their interactions with professors may enable academic advisers and psychological counselors to respond more effectively to students who are having difficulty in college, whether personally or academically. They can help students better understand what to expect from faculty and can help them interpret seemingly negative experiences in a more constructive light.

Directions for Future Research. The findings regarding student-faculty interactions open up a Pandora's box of new questions. Research should study more closely the gender differences in student-faculty interactions in a variety of settings and via multiple forms of data collection, both qualitative and quantitative. Important questions include:

- What are the substantive differences in the nature of men's and women's interactions with their professors? Are there differences in the subject matter discussed?
- How does the nature of student-faculty interactions depend on where the interaction takes place, whether in the classroom, a faculty office, a research lab, or elsewhere?

- Why and how do research experiences influence students' gender role attitudes? What sorts of messages do faculty send—intentionally or not—regarding women's social roles?
- Why do women often negatively internalize their interactions with professors? What specific faculty actions lead them to feel that they are not being taken seriously? What are effective strategies for promoting healthier student-faculty relations and for promoting safe spaces in the classroom?
- How does all this depend on the faculty member's gender? To what extent do the findings observed here reflect students' interactions with the majority male faculty?

Presence of Women Faculty

It is often stated that female students stand to benefit from greater numbers of women in college faculty—and, in fact, attending colleges with more female professors strengthens female students' scholarly confidence, achievement motivation, and college GPA. And yet the presence of women faculty appears to bring a broader range of benefits to male students, including gains in mathematical confidence, scientific orientation, leadership ability, and emotional well-being. Further, the positive effect of female faculty on GPA is even stronger for men than women. Thus, the presence of female faculty appears to provide a particularly positive and supportive environment for men.

Implications for Practice. An obvious implication of these findings would be to hire more women faculty. Women's representation among college faculty has long been a source of concern in higher education because women compose less than 40 percent of full-time faculty nationwide and are further underrepresented at more prestigious institutions and in certain fields, such as the natural sciences and engineering, where the representation of women is 22 and 9 percent, respectively (Cataldi, Bradburn, & Fahimi,

2005). Hiring more female faculty leads to more than just numerical representation for women; it is an opportunity to shape the academic climate, as women faculty have been shown to be more concerned than male faculty with students' emotional development, character development, and self-understanding (Lindholm, Szelenyi, Hurtado, & Korn, 2005). Thus, increasing the numbers of women among faculty also represents a shift in faculty values toward students' holistic development.

Directions for Future Research. Our understanding of these findings would benefit from information on the nature of same-sex versus cross-sex interactions with faculty. Specifically, could the trend observed here result from female faculty more favorably treating their male students than their female students? Or, taking another perspective, might the developmental benefits accrued to men result from having less exposure to male faculty? Research should also question whether these findings are due to a larger climate shift that occurs when an institution employs more women faculty. In other words, how does the representation of women faculty shape the normative culture of departments and institutions, and what impact does this have on male and female students?

Academic Engagement

When they enter college, women have an established record of academic engagement. In their senior year of high school, they devote more time than men to studying, homework, and a range of academic and extracurricular activities. Women also place greater value than men on the intellectual benefits of going to college, such as the opportunity to learn more about what interests them and to prepare themselves for graduate school. Women's superior record of academic achievement and intellectual engagement creates a gender gap that holds steady over the course of college.

Though men are less academically engaged than women, the *influence* of academic engagement is stronger for them. Specifically, time spent preparing for class has a greater impact on men's grades, academic confidence, critical-thinking skills, and achievement motivation. And the more time that men devote to their studies, the more interested they become in the larger political and cultural contexts that surround them; the same is not true for women. Thus, men might view studying not just as a means to improve their grades but as an investment in their broader intellectual and cultural engagement. Certainly, studying matters for women as well, but it seems to make more of a *difference* for men.

Implications for Practice. Clearly, colleges need to consider strategies for facilitating greater academic engagement among male students. This is challenging work because, as mentioned, the gender differences in academic engagement exist well before students set foot on campus and are generally maintained as students move through their undergraduate years. As suggested by Kinzie et al. (2007), colleges should prioritize men's involvement in high-impact practices such as "learning communities, first-year seminars, writing-intensive courses, student-faculty research, study abroad, internships, and capstone seminars" (p. 22). These educational contexts facilitate an investment of intellectual energy among both genders, but they may be especially pivotal for men.

Directions for Future Research. Those suggestions imply that we can raise men's levels of academic engagement by encouraging their involvement in high-impact educational practices. This may be part of the solution. However, this approach presumes that men will benefit at least as much as women from these efforts. Some critics have questioned whether male students might require different educational strategies altogether. With respect to K–12 education, Hoff Sommers (2000) argues,

"The shift away from structured classrooms, competition, strict discipline, and skill-and-fact-based learning has been harmful to all children—but especially boys" (p. 159). The validity of this claim has yet to be tested, though it raises intriguing questions for higher education research: To what extent do colleges consider the differential needs of male and female learners? Should strategies for promoting student engagement be the same for women and men? Does academic engagement yield the same benefits for men as it does for women? As women continue to outnumber men on college campuses, these questions will become increasingly important to answer.

Academic Self-Confidence

Despite the fact that college women earn better grades and exhibit a stronger academic orientation than their male counterparts, they tend to suffer from comparatively low academic confidence. In fact, women rate themselves lower than men on nearly every assessment of their academic abilities. Some of the largest gender gaps are in students' self-assessments of their intellectual and mathematical capabilities, where there is a 17-point difference between the percentages of men and women rating themselves "above average" or in the "highest 10 percent." Gender gaps of this magnitude have a long history on the Freshman Survey—over four decades. Further, these gender differences *grow* during college; gains in intellectual self-confidence are greater for men, and declines in mathematical confidence are more substantial for women.

Implications for Practice. Some may question the practical relevance of women's lower academic confidence relative to men's. After all, if women are getting good grades and graduating from college, why should we worry that their self-assessments are weaker than men's? Perhaps women are just being modest or men too boastful. Indeed, research does show that women tend to underestimate their abilities while men exhibit an outsized sense of self that's not always commensurate with their academic achievement (Sadker & Sadker, 1994). Research also tells us, however, that low academic self-confidence ratings—in and of themselves—can limit students' career aspirations (Sax & Bryant, 2006).

Campus personnel should be aware that getting good grades does not guarantee that women will see themselves as academically strong. This is especially important for faculty, who should take seriously the concerns of successful female students who nonetheless doubt their ability to do well in their classes, thrive in their majors, or get into graduate schools. Such women may rule out academic or career paths that would bring them satisfaction and success. Advisers and others who help students with academic decision making should understand the consequences of low self-confidence and know how to help women assess their abilities more accurately. For example, the adviser of a female student who wants to switch out of engineering should probe more deeply into her reasons. Are her interests changing, or does she lack confidence?

Directions for Future Research. Gender differences in academic self-confidence raise numerous questions for further inquiry. A first step is to develop a better understanding of the validity of self-assessments such as the one used in this study. To what extent do self-ratings measure a student's actual beliefs about her or his abilities? Do women rate themselves lower than men because they *believe* they are less capable, or are they simply reluctant to *describe* themselves as having high ability? Next, research should develop a greater understanding of the conditions that account for the widening gender gap in academic self-confidence during college. To what extent and in what ways do faculty and peers shape students' conceptions of their abilities, and how does this vary by gender, academic major, or other factors?

Future research could also tell us more about the consequences of lower self-confidence. Would grades, graduation rates, and degree aspirations be even higher for women if they possessed a stronger sense of their academic abilities? Does men's relatively greater confidence provide them with any particular advantages in college? Ultimately, though we know that gender differences in college students' academic self-confidence exist, as they have for decades, we need to develop a more nuanced understanding of when and why this matters.

Health and Well-Being

Just as women indicate lower academic self-confidence than men, they also face challenges when it comes to their sense of health and well-being. Compared to men, women enter college with higher levels of self-reported stress and depression and lower ratings of their physical and emotional health. These gender gaps remain significant over four years of college and are in large part a reflection of how women and men allocate their time. Specifically, women devote more time than men to studying, homework, and a range of academic and extracurricular activities, such as community service and ongoing family responsibilities. Men, on the other hand, spend more time than women playing sports, partying, watching television, and playing video games. In other words, men spend more time on activities that can be considered ways to relieve stress, while women devote themselves to a range of responsibilities that tend to induce stress, at least as they attempt to balance these commitments.

Gender differences in time allocation have additional consequences for student development, especially the choice to engage in sports versus academics. Both genders, for example, benefit from sports and exercise, which promote healthier emotional self-concepts, a stronger achievement motivation, and an increased commitment to developing a meaningful philosophy of life. Yet staying physically active also provides unique benefits for women, such as lower stress, higher degree aspirations, competitive self-confidence, and better college grades. (Time devoted to sports and exercise is in fact predictive of *lower* grades for men.) Thus, engagement in physical activity may play a pivotal role for college women by alleviating their higher stress levels while encouraging a competitive spirit that enables them to succeed academically.

Implications for Practice. Campuses must be equipped to handle the growing number of students—especially women—who experience stress and other mental-health concerns during college. Unfortunately, many institutions lack the staff and other resources required to meet the psychological-health needs of students who visit campus clinics, and not every student who could benefit from help seeks it out. Further, as suggested by the National Association of Student Personnel Administrators (2004), students' health concerns must be considered from a holistic perspective—taking into consideration the full range of campus influences, including the role of faculty members, peers, academic policies, and the institution's geographic location and physical layout.

Colleges need to encourage all students to strike a healthier balance between academics, cocurricular engagement, and leisure time. For women, this means encouraging productive forms of stress release, such as exercise, reading for pleasure, or whatever activities provide them with a temporary escape from their ongoing commitments and responsibilities. Getting women involved in sports is particularly important and cannot be accomplished by the mere presence of recreation centers or intramural sports; women need to feel comfortable in these environments. Campus recreation departments should talk with female students about what athletic opportunities are most appealing to them. The University of California, Los Angeles, for example, recently introduced a program called Fitwell, in which student consultants help members of the campus community develop an individualized health and wellness plan. Students choose from a range of services, including independent and group exercise, mind-body fitness, and education related to nutrition, weight management, and stress prevention. A holistic approach to health and well-being may be particularly appealing to women, whose sense of physical well-being is less strongly tied to traditional sports and exercise than it is for men.

Directions for Future Research. We need to develop a better understanding of what it means for a college student to maintain balance. Women's ongoing commitments to their studies, their families, and their communities provide them with numerous developmental benefits, but those same commitments can also contribute to a heightened sense of stress. Similarly, men's devotion to leisure-time activities such as exercise, television, and video games provides them with some release from the pressures of college life but also can impinge on their academic performance. A question for future research is, "How much is too much?" Research on college students' time allocation typically looks at how the amount of time spent on a particular activity affects some aspect of students' development; this will tell us the linear relationship between the activity and the college outcome. Yet we should determine whether there is a numerical tipping point past which the benefits (or consequences) of an activity diminish. Further, how do different *combinations* of activities relate to student development? For example, what is the optimal balance between time spent studying and time spent exercising? How does this differ for women and men?

Impact of Diversity Programming

The role of diversity and student development is complex. Prior research has documented a wide range of benefits on students' values and orientations, and the evidence in this book suggests that experiences with curricular and cocurricular diversity are in fact more liberalizing, motivating, and eye opening for men than women. For example:

- Attending racial or cultural awareness workshops or engaging in social diversity (e.g., dining with, dating, studying with, or living with someone of a different race/ethnicity) contributes more strongly to men's desire to improve race relations.
- Taking ethnic or women's studies courses strengthens political engagement for men more than for women, with women's studies also contributing to social activist orientations more strongly for men.
- Taking ethnic studies courses or engaging in social diversity experiences more strongly relate to the development of men's liberal views on a range of issues, including the environment, health care, and taxation. In addition, taking ethnic studies courses and participating in racial/cultural awareness workshops give rise to more progressive gender role attitudes among male students.

We also have uncovered potential challenges for men who participate in diversity programming, as attitudinal shifts brought about by exposure to diversity also are accompanied by heightened feelings of discomfort in male students. Specifically, men who participate in racial/cultural awareness workshops feel increasingly overwhelmed by all they have to do, and men taking women's studies courses suffer from declines in self-rated physical health. These findings may be testament to the fact that change is not always easy and that stress and self-doubt are some of the consequences of expanding one's awareness about people from historically marginalized groups.

Implications for Practice. The benefits of diversity in the curriculum and cocurriculum have been well documented, and there is every reason to encourage more students, especially men, to seek out these opportunities in college. And yet those engaged in diversity programming should keep in mind that exposure to and awareness of racial and cultural differences can create discomfort and stress, particularly for male students. Campuses should provide appropriate resources for students who may experience heightened stress or self-doubt as a result of these experiences. This could involve following up with students weeks, or even months, after their participation in diversity programming to gauge whether they may need counseling or other support.

Directions for Future Research. Future research ought to explore why the effects of diversity experiences are salient for male students and, in particular, why they sometimes lead to heightened stress for men. Why are men more challenged and conflicted by these experiences than women? What specific aspects of diversity programming lead to which outcomes? Further, to what extent is men's reaction to diversity programming a reflection of the predominantly white sample used in this study? Would similar gender differences in the impact of diversity be observed for women and men across different racial/ethnic groups?

Careers and Majors

Men's and women's major and career selections reflect a mix of long-standing gender differences and contemporary shifts. Consistent with trends observed over several decades, women are more likely than men to pursue majors and careers in elementary education, nursing, and other health professions, whereas men outnumber women in their plans to pursue engineering, computer science, and business. However, historical trends in medicine and law have reversed themselves; these once male-dominated fields are now attracting equal or greater numbers of women. The genders have also moved closer together in their interest in secondary education, a field once dominated by women. Thus, while the gender gap has converged in a number of areas, many major and career choices still reflect historical patterns of occupational sex segregation.

Implications for Practice. When it comes to majors and careers, campuses find it perhaps most difficult to attract more women to pursue the traditionally male fields of engineering and computer science. Large numbers of women opt out of the science and engineering pipeline years before they attend college, due in large part to factors beyond the college's control, such as family influences, early educational experiences, and early impressions regarding science careers. Colleges, however, are in a position to recruit and retain those women who have the necessary ability and preparation for science and engineering careers but who may nevertheless select other career paths. Research has identified informal learning, mentoring, and professional development opportunities as crucial in retaining women in these fields (American Association of University Women Educational Foundation, 2004).

Campuses must also take stock of the climate that exists in science and engineering fields. Women and men majoring in fields such as engineering, physical science, and computer science tend to develop greater emotional health or stress concerns during college and tend to become less interested in broader societal and cultural issues. In fact, a belief that academic science is *disconnected* from society's larger concerns turns many women away from these fields during college (Sax, 2001). Campuses have an opportunity to educate students about the ways in which math and science can help improve society and the human condition, particularly at a time of tremendous progress in computer and biological technologies. Internships and mentorships are potentially useful mechanisms for exposing women to ways in which science transcends the abstract and theoretical by addressing societal issues and needs. The more that we can connect scientific concepts to issues that women tend to care about—such as education, the environment, and human rights—the more likely women will become scientists and effect change in those areas.

Directions for Future Research. The underrepresentation of women in scientific and technical fields has received significant attention in scholarly research. We have learned about the range of individual and structural forces that encourage or discourage women's pursuit of these fields, such as early educational experiences, family expectations, societal messages, and the often unwelcoming climate for women in the sciences. In higher education, strategies aimed at increasing the number of women in science include summer internships, mentorships, professional development workshops, and online networks of women in science. Though such strategies may be successful at retaining more women in science, they are usually viewed as a programmatic *supplement* rather than integrated into mainstream curriculum and programming. In fact, while research has identified numerous strategies for retaining women in science fields, we know far less about how to *transform* the broader culture of academic science. How can we make science more appealing to women? How can we illustrate science's connection to meaningful everyday-life issues and thereby strengthen interest among female students? Future research should identify characteristics of programs that are successful at educating students about the connection between scientific concepts and larger societal concerns. What makes these programs successful? To what extent have they engaged in curricular reform, faculty development, or efforts to alter core departmental values? Does the leadership in these departments place priority on diversifying the scientific and technological workforce? How is this conveyed to faculty, graduate students, and undergraduates?

Beyond Gender: Advancing the Study
of College Impact

Though this book has focused on an exploration of the gendered effects of college, its larger purpose is to increase awareness of the utility of studying the conditional effects of college. The conditional model of college impact, introduced in chapter 4, advances our collective thinking about the impact of college by acknowledging differences in how students respond to their experiences, both on and off campus. Rather than depicting a uniform influence of college as represented by one solitary arrow pointing from college environments to student outcomes, this model incorporates multiple arrows, each representing the unique impact of college for a particular subgroup of students. In this study, these subgroups are defined by gender. However, the model can be used to identify how the impact of college depends on other factors, including race, ethnicity, age, religion, sexual orientation, disability status, socioeconomic status, academic preparation, first-generation status, learning styles, and so forth. Each of these characteristics may influence how a student interfaces with the college environment. Thus, the conditional model of college impact provides a schema not just for research but for the way in which we think about college student programming. It emphasizes that whenever we consider how a particular college environment will affect a student, we ought to think about how that student's background and prior experiences are likely to shape the way in which she or he reacts to that environment. The model emphasizes that there is no normal or deviant pathway to student development, but that students' developmental trajectories are justifiably unique.

The higher education research community has already made progress along these lines, especially when it comes to racial/ethnic differences, yet a broader understanding of how students' various background characteristics shape the impact of college is still in its nascence. As college enrollments have become more diverse, researchers have an opportunity and an obligation to understand what works best and for which students.

Of course, the ability to study conditional college effects, at least from a quantitative perspective, depends on having large enough samples for analysis. In this study, for example, while sample sizes were large enough to divide by gender, further divisions based on race, income, or other factors would have resulted in subsamples far too small given the number of college influences being examined. Thus, to the extent that future research relies on smaller subsamples to test conditional college effects, researchers will need to be more parsimonious in selecting college environments and experiences. Further, researchers must aim to maximize the number of students within specific subgroups of interest, such as women of color, students with disabilities, or low-income students. This is going to be a particular challenge since college student databases traditionally overrepresent students who are high achieving, white, and female (Porter & Whitcomb, 2005). Ongoing efforts to study conditional effects as they relate to nonwhite and/or academically underprepared populations will likely require that students from those groups be oversampled or receive additional response incentives.

Ultimately, with a sufficient number of student samples, such research will further contribute to our understanding of the applicability of long-standing college impact models to students of various sociodemographic backgrounds. Although the basic tenets of college impact models are likely to hold—that is, that student development is shaped by precollege characteristics and engagement with academic, social, and other environments during college—research on conditional college effects can tell us more about the *strength* and *direction* of relationships within these categories. For example, we have seen that the effect of a broad category of college influence such as faculty interaction depends on the nature of the interaction, the particular outcome in question, the student's gender, and quite possibly several other conditions not assessed in the present study. To the extent that research can identify the range of conditions that shape the nature of college impact, the field of higher education will be in a better position to create more nuanced theories and models of college student development.

Implications for Understanding Women's and Men's Development

Though this book does not provide direct tests of feminist developmental theories (due to the nature of the survey data available), results do shed light on whether women's development in college depends more strongly on connections with others than is the case for men. Overall, the evidence does not support the notion that interpersonal relationships are more salient to women's development, as might be expected based on the work of Gilligan, Chodorow, Belenky, and others. To the contrary, interpersonal interactions influence students of *both* genders, yielding effects that are often stronger for men than women. When it comes to faculty interactions, for example, the benefits of talking with faculty outside class and feeling supported by them are generally stronger for men than women. And certain peer interactions—such as socializing with, dining with, dating, or living with individuals from other racial/ethnic groups—also reveal a pattern of effects that is stronger for men than women.

In many cases, interpersonal relations are important for *both* genders—but in different ways. Interactions with faculty, for example, relate more strongly to political engagement and social activism for men, but to perceptions of physical and emotional well-being among women. And socializing with friends is more effective at reducing stress levels for men than women. Some interpersonal interactions even have the *opposite* effect for the two genders, such as working with faculty on research, which accounts for more progressive gender role attitudes among men but more traditional views among women.

Thus, the evidence presented in this book could be used to challenge the notion that women's development during college depends more on interpersonal interactions than men's. However, before drawing that conclusion, it is important to consider the possibility that relations with others are just as important for women—and possibly more so—but are not adequately measured here. We might detect a stronger influence of interpersonal relations if the questionnaires used in this study included more information on the dynamics of different types of relationships, such as those with friends (current and former, on and off campus), romantic partners (in college and long distance, short term and long term), and family members (parents, siblings, and others). In support of the last kind of relationship, this study does suggest that a connection to family plays a more salient role for college women. And yet the specific dynamics of students' interactions with family members are unknown.

While the present study informs developmental theory by revealing hundreds of ways in which college differentially affects women and men, additional research will need to validate these findings and to explore the many complex relationships that could not be examined here.

Concluding Thoughts

One of the challenges of a study of this magnitude and complexity is to answer the perennial question, "So what did you find?" In the spirit of getting to the bottom line, we can draw three major conclusions from this study. First, men and women differ from each other in numerous ways when they arrive at college. Second, though some gender differences converge during the college years, an even greater number are magnified. And finally, in many important ways, college environments and experiences differentially affect women and men.

At a time when national attention is focused on the relative *numbers* of women and men on college campuses, this book has taken stock of the relative *characteristics* of the two genders and how aspects of college further shape those characteristics. As we have seen, though women have a numerical advantage in college, both genders face challenges to their adjustment and development. Just as we need to be concerned about high stress and low self-esteem among women, we must be concerned about growing academic disengagement among men. And while we aim to encourage all students to become engaged and involved, we must be mindful that the dynamics of these experiences can be quite different for the two genders, especially when it comes to students' interactions with their professors. Consequently, institutional efforts aimed at improving the college experience for both genders must consider the unique needs of each.

Though this book offers numerous implications for practice, it also raises several questions for future research. Ideally, this study will pave the way for additional quantitative research on the gender-based conditional effects of college, and for qualitative research that explores in greater depth gender differences that result from college environments and experiences. Ultimately, to the extent that the study of college impact is attuned to differential effects based on gender, race, ethnicity, or other defining characteristics, institutions will be in a better position to provide curricular and cocurricular environments that maximize the developmental potential of all college students.

Appendix A

REVIEW OF PRIOR RESEARCH ON SEPARATE-GENDER COLLEGE EFFECTS

This appendix reviews what prior research reveals about whether and how the impact of college varies by gender. The review is organized by the categories of environmental and experiential variables included in this book, although it extends beyond the particular variables examined in this study. This appendix should be especially useful for higher education researchers because the college impact literature includes no comparable review.

Institutional Characteristics, Faculty Culture, and the Peer Environment

Institutional Characteristics

Studies show that institutional type (university, four-year college, etc.), control (i.e., public or private), and size have implications for both women's and men's development. Public institutions—particularly large ones—have negative consequences for men's and women's social self-concept (Astin & Kent, 1983; Kezar & Moriarty, 2000; Pascarella, Smart, Ethington, & Nettles, 1987) and men's mathematical self-concept (Sax, 1994b). Private institutions relate to gains in women's materialistic goals (Astin & Kent, 1983) and, among women in science fields, declines in the likelihood of entrance into male-dominated science careers (Ethington, Smart, & Pascarella, 1988). When it comes to institutional type, attending a four-year college (versus a university) relates to gains in cognitive abilities for women more than for men (Pascarella, Bohr, Nora, & Terenzini, 1995) but predicts declines in women's social self-confidence (Astin & Kent, 1983). Attending a university, on the other hand, relates to the development of women's sense of leadership ability but has been shown to be detrimental to men's self-perceived leadership skills (Kezar & Moriarty, 2000). All in all, these findings support the notion that institutional contexts can influence men and women differently.

Faculty Culture

Another aspect of the institutional milieu has to do with the faculty culture. For the purposes of this review, faculty culture is considered here as a feature of the college environment; student involvement and interaction with faculty are discussed later. When faculty emphasize liberal arts education and teaching, a number of positive outcomes result for male and female students: women experience higher levels of social self-confidence, and men become more committed to sociopolitical values and humanitarian goals (Astin & Kent, 1983).

Studies on the percentage of women faculty are mixed in terms of whether proportions play a role in women's aspirations and academic choices in college. Although Canes and Rosen (1995) found that an increase in the proportion of women on a department's faculty may not relate to more female students majoring in that field or discipline, others identified the proportion of women faculty on campus as an important catalyst for women's persistence in traditionally male fields even after controlling for the percentage of female students in the field (Astin & Sax, 1996; Sax, 1994a). Beyond women's proportional representation in faculty ranks, it seems that more specific aspects of faculty culture are essential to women's development. According to Astin and Kent (1983), at institutions where faculty are research oriented and socialize with students, women experience gains in academic self-esteem. Conversely, the researchers identified that faculty cultures defined by significant administrative work had negative implications for women students' academic self-confidence. The key element for promoting desirable outcomes among college women appears to hinge on the sociable nature of faculty. Indeed, where faculty are inaccessible or impersonal, women's—and perhaps men's—academic achievement and educational aspirations may suffer (Pascarella, 1984).

The Peer Environment

The peer culture of colleges and universities has long been touted as one of the most dramatic influences on college outcomes (Astin, 1993c). The student body's academic preparation—often used as an indicator of college selectivity—has considerable implications for both women and men. In fact, attending selective institutions is positively associated with men's academic self-esteem (Astin & Kent, 1983) and with women's self-rated leadership ability (Astin & Kent, 1983), sex-atypical career choices (Bielby, 1978; Ethington et al., 1988; Gruca, Ethington, & Pascarella, 1988), and graduate degree aspirations (Tsui, 1995). Attending highly selective institutions also relates to declines in men's self-rated public-speaking ability, perhaps the result of increased personal scrutiny when comparing one's own speaking abilities to talented peers. The conflicting implications of selectivity for men's academic self-esteem and public-speaking self-confidence may reflect the fact that the general academic benefits of selectivity do not necessarily hold true for specific competencies, such as public speaking. For women, moderately selective institutions appear to provide the appropriate balance of high-achieving peers and a less intimidating environment to develop their public-speaking skills and ability to influence others (Kezar & Moriarty, 2000). Finally, average cognitive development of the incoming freshman class positively affects men's first-year reading comprehension but produces mixed effects for women's cognitive outcomes during college (Whitt, Pascarella,

Nesheim, Marth, & Pierson, 2003). Specifically, women's first-year reading comprehension diminishes in the presence of peers with high levels of cognitive competence, whereas their second-year science reasoning improves.

A dimension similar to institutional selectivity—intellectual or academic competition—also bodes differently for men and women: at the same time that men's educational aspirations flourish under such conditions, women's may actually weaken (Pascarella, 1984). In a conflicting report, Sax (1994b) identified competition among students as a positive predictor of women's mathematical self-concept. The fact that the former study used objective measures of achievement and the latter relied on self-perceptions of ability may partly account for the discrepancy.

Another characteristic of the student body—average socio-economic status (SES)—has opposite consequences for men's and women's first-year reading comprehension, with women, but not men, benefiting from an affluent peer group (Whitt et al., 2003). Despite that finding, Whitt et al. (2003) showed that, for women only, average peer SES relates to declines in critical-thinking ability.

The impact of the proportion of women in the student body on college outcomes is rather unclear in the literature to date. Astin and Kent (1983) demonstrated that a low representation of women on campus is predictive of men's humanitarianism, whereas Sax (1994b) provided evidence of women's improved mathematical self-concept when exposed to more women in the student body. Sax (1996) explored the gender composition of the student's major and found little evidence to suggest a direct association between a major's gender composition and cognitive/affective outcomes. Instead, student characteristics, institutional qualities, and the major field mediate the relationship between a major's gender composition and student outcomes. It is likely that the mixed evidence on the role of student and faculty gender composition is due to the variety of approaches used to study those contexts, with some research including more explanatory variables than others.

Major, Academic Involvement and Faculty Interaction

Major

Research on the impact of academic major is difficult to summarize because the varying classification schemes across different studies produce few common themes. Whereas some researchers prefer to group science majors together and compare effects to nonscience majors, others dichotomize male and female fields or abandon such broad groupings, preferring instead long lists of narrowly defined majors as independent variables.

One area that has received considerable attention is the implications of majoring in mathematics, science, and engineering. Two studies confirmed that majoring in the sciences has generally negative consequences for men's social self-confidence (Kezar & Moriarty, 2000; Pascarella et al., 1987), while Astin and Kent (1983) found that declines in social self-concept among science majors extended to members of both sexes. There is some evidence to suggest, however, that majoring in such fields actually strengthens confidence in one's academic and mathematical abilities (Astin & Kent, 1983; Pascarella et al., 1987; Sax, 1994b). For two of these studies (Astin & Kent, 1983; Sax, 1994b), the positive associations between academic or mathematical self-concept and majoring in physical science or engineering were specific to women. Outside of the so-called hard sciences, negative effects on women's overall academic self-concept have been linked to majoring in health science and arts/humanities (Astin & Kent, 1983), while declines in mathematical self-concept have been found among men majoring in social science or the arts/humanities and among women in vocational or technical fields (Sax, 1994b).

Zhao, Carini, and Kuh (2005) examined the consequences of majoring in science, math, engineering, and technology (SMET) for various forms of student involvement, satisfaction, and other outcomes. The authors found that, compared to men in the same fields, women majoring in SMET demonstrated greater academic effort, had higher reading scores, and participated more often in enriching educational experiences (although participated less than men in cocurricular activities). These women were also more likely than men to find their exams challenging but less likely to find time for socializing and leisure. Still, SMET women gained more in terms of personal and social development, though less than men in analyzing quantitative problems, computing, and acquiring work-related skills and knowledge. Women in SMET majors also were somewhat less involved than their male counterparts in collaborative and active learning yet tended to interact more with faculty members through discussions about career plans, course assignments, and grades. Lastly, SMET women thought the campus environment was more supportive than did the men. These findings illuminate women's and men's unique experiences even as they occupy the same academic space.

Field of study affects personal values and goals, although the constellation of effects identified by Astin and Kent (1983) is difficult to summarize into a general theory of impact. One noteworthy finding suggests that men who major in prelaw or business experience gains in materialistic values, while those who major in education experience declines in this area. The influence of major field is different for women: majoring in premed or the social sciences enhances women's materialism, but majoring in the health sciences produces the opposite effect.

Academic Involvement

Numerous studies in the higher education literature focus on academic involvement, and yet, as discussed, we know very little about variations in or comparisons of involvement by gender. Nonetheless, Whitt et al. (2003) established that cognitive outcomes among women are more a function of college environments (e.g., a chilly climate for women, peer cognitive development, peer socioeconomic status, and the institution's vocational emphasis) than actual involvement. On the other hand, the stronger effects for men tend to be grouped around college activities and experiences. In fact, only three academic involvement variables— cumulative credit hours completed, number of term papers written, and number of natural science and engineering courses taken— emerged as positive predictors of various cognitive outcomes for women. The predictive capability of academic involvement measures for men simply proved much more robust than was the case for women. A range of course-taking patterns, in addition to computer use and number of assigned books read, may play a significant role in understanding such outcomes as men's reading comprehension and critical thinking.

Beyond cognitive outcomes, many studies provide evidence of other advantages students enjoy when they are academically involved. Pascarella et al. (1987) identified academic integration as enhancing academic and social self-concept for both genders, while Miller, Finely, and McKinley (1990) suggested that deep processing—an approach indicative of students' full investment in their learning—relates positively to GPA more so for women than men. Others have maintained that being academically focused, successful, and satisfied predicts numerous positive outcomes for male and female college students, including persistence in specific fields, like science and math (Astin & Sax, 1996; Ware, Steckler, & Leserman, 1985), mathematical self-concept (Sax, 1994b), emotional well-being (Sax, Bryant, & Gilmartin, 2004), and even gender role egalitarianism (Bryant, 2003). Measures of disengagement, including feeling bored in class and failing to integrate into the campus structure, have been linked to lower levels of emotional health among women only (Sax et al., 2004).

Specific types of college activities have been linked to college outcomes for men and women. Taking leadership classes, for instance, seems to enhance students' self-perceived leadership abilities, self-assessed public-speaking skills, and self-rated ability to influence others (Kezar & Moriarty, 2000). Similarly, collaborative learning has many positive implications for both women and men, including personal development, understanding of science and technology, appreciation for art, better analytical skills, and openness to diversity (Cabrera et al., 2002). Group projects in class facilitate men's and women's sense of leadership, public-speaking skills, influenceability, and social self-confidence (Kezar & Moriarty, 2000). The number of math and science courses taken impacts women and men in a similar fashion and heightens the mathematical self-concept of students of both genders (Sax, 1994b). Reporting on an effect unique to men, Astin and Kent (1983) showed that belonging to an honor society improves men's leadership, social confidence, and academic self-ratings.

The implications of taking women's studies courses have received a considerable amount of attention in the past two decades. Often such research demonstrates that women's studies courses encourage gender role egalitarianism for both sexes (Bryant, 2003; Harris, Melaas, & Rodacker, 1999)—and, among women, graduate degree aspirations (Tsui, 1995) and feminist identity development (Bargad & Hyde, 1991). The effects of women's studies coursework have also been shown to vary across gender, such that belief in stereotypical gender differences declines among men but not among women (Thomsen, Basu, & Reinitz, 1995). At the same time, men may become less inclined to adopt feminist attitudes, whereas women become more likely to do so as a result of taking women's studies (Thomsen et al., 1995).

Faculty Interaction

The few studies that have examined the effects of student-faculty interactions separately by gender generally point to positive outcomes for both sexes. Student-faculty interaction has been positively associated with students' self-assessed leadership abilities (Kezar & Moriarty, 2000), students' social self-confidence (Kezar & Moriarty, 2000), men's self-rated public-speaking ability (Kezar & Moriarty, 2000), women's perceptions of their capacity to influence others (Kezar & Moriarty, 2000), and men's confidence in their ability to become engineers (Colbeck, Cabrera, & Terenzini, 2001). Furthermore, studies focusing exclusively on women have identified faculty interaction as having a positive impact. Komarovsky (1985) suggested that such interactions result in intellectual exchanges, mentoring relationships, occupational guidance, and increased self-confidence. Likewise, Tsui (1995) found student-faculty interaction to predict women's graduate degree aspirations.

Nonetheless, the mere frequency of students' contact with faculty does not always result in desired outcomes. In fact, Sax (1994b) reported that interacting with faculty contributed to declines in women's mathematical self-concept, and Frost (1991) found no impact of student-faculty contact on critical-thinking skills. In a study with decidedly mixed findings, Bryant (2003) found that sheer time spent interacting with faculty outside class was associated with students growing more traditional in their gender role attitudes, but when the faculty provided intellectual challenge and stimulation, more progressive gender role attitudes ensued.

Taken together, past research appears to suggest that the quantity of student-faculty interactions cannot alone account for the benefits students may incur from them, and that the *quality* of such interactions is critical. For instance, knowing a faculty or administrator personally has been shown to predict men's and women's leadership self-concept and social self-esteem, as well as men's academic self-confidence and humanitarianism (Astin & Kent, 1983). Having faculty role models—also indicative of a personal relationship—promotes students' sense of success in influencing others (Kezar & Moriarty, 2000). Rayman and Brett (1995) identified receiving career advice from advisers or faculty as contributing to women's persistence in science careers following graduation.

In the classroom, professors have considerable opportunities to affect students through their instructional practices. According to Fassinger (1995), classroom participation is a function of numerous factors over which faculty have jurisdiction, including the extent of student-student interaction and rewards (i.e., improved grade) for contributing comments. Student confidence, which also encourages participation, can be fostered by ensuring that the pace of the class is reasonable and that, for men, emphasizing memorization skills is avoided (Fassinger, 1995). Instructor clarity and organization may increase women's confidence in their abilities to enter certain sex-atypical careers, such as engineering (Colbeck et al., 2001). Organization has also been shown to positively impact reading comprehension for both genders, but more so among men (Whitt et al., 2003). Finally, attention to "feeling" versus "thinking" learning styles in the classroom may promote women's "sense of fit" and participation levels (Salter & Persaud, 2003).

A chilly climate and the sex of the instructor also relate to the influence that faculty have on student learning and well-being. The notion of a chilly climate, proposed by Hall and Sandler (1982), suggests that subtle or even overt sexist biases in the classroom and beyond mar women's, and in some cases men's, educational experiences. Surely, faculty are not the only individuals on campus responsible for creating a particular climate, but their part in instituting chilly or warm climates has received a reasonable amount of attention in the literature. It is important to acknowledge the inconsistency of past research regarding the impact of chilly climates. Some studies claim that women suffer educational and personal hardship under chilly circumstances (Fassinger, 1995; Pascarella et al., 1997; Whitt, Edison, Pascarella, Nora, & Terenzini, 1999), while others call the notion of the chilly climate into question (Constantinople, Cornelius, & Gray, 1988; Drew & Work, 1998; Heller, Puff, & Mills, 1985; Whitt et al., 2003).

By some accounts, the instructor's sex is not an issue for student classroom participation (Constantinople et al., 1988); however, other studies suggest that the instructor's sex does matter. Whereas the professor's gender does not affect men's self-perceptions (with the exception that they display greater comprehension in classes with female instructors), Fassinger (1995) observed that women are more confident, are more interested in the subject, exhibit higher levels of participation, and are better able to comprehend material when their professors are female. Not only that, male professors' classrooms may be chillier than female professors' (Fassinger, 1995), perhaps explaining why women with male instructors perceive their professors less favorably compared to women with female instructors or men with instructors of either gender (Crombie, Pyke, Silverthorn, Jones, & Piccinin, 2003). In some cases, interactions with male and female faculty are both viewed as beneficial, but in different ways: Komarovsky (1985) reported that male faculty were viewed as providing intellectual stimulation for women students, whereas female faculty were perceived as encouraging students personally.

Involvement with Peers and the Cocurriculum

Involvement with Peers

Activities involving interactions with peers are central to the college student experience. This section touches on an array of situations that bring students into contact with one another on campus. To begin, it is widely documented that integrating into campus life has a remarkable impact on student success and well-being (Astin, 1993c). Leppel (2002) linked campus integration with persistence for students of both genders. Tomlinson-Clarke and Clarke (1994) reported that levels of campus involvement were by far the strongest predictors of social adjustment in a sample of female college students.

The ramifications of student leadership are numerous and varied. Perhaps not surprisingly, being elected to a student office is associated with self-perceived leadership abilities among both women and men, while the same experience is predictive of men's self-rated public-speaking ability (Kezar & Moriarty, 2000). Serving as resident advisers has a positive impact on women's confidence in their own leadership abilities (Kezar & Moriarty, 2000). Leadership has a hand in self-esteem as well. Although Astin and Kent (1983) found that leadership experiences are more beneficial for women's self-esteem than men's, Pascarella et al. (1987) identified leadership as promoting social self-concept for men and women alike. Others point out that serving as an editor of a campus publication has implications for women's humanitarian and sociopolitical values (Astin & Kent, 1983), and that general leadership involvement encourages women's entrance into male-dominated careers (Ethington et al., 1988). Lastly, there is evidence that men become less traditional in their gender role attitudes upon receiving leadership training (Bryant, 2003).

Another form of involvement—encountering diversity through peer interactions and racial awareness discussions and workshops—is positively associated with various leadership outcomes for both genders (Kezar & Moriarty, 2000), men's egalitarianism (Bryant, 2003), and women's graduate degree aspirations (Tsui, 1995). Also pertinent to understanding leadership outcomes is participation in such activities as intramural sports, intercollegiate athletics, student organizations, and fraternities or sororities, although more white men and women participate in those activities than black men and women (Kezar & Moriarty, 2000).

The type and quality of peer relationships are indicative of how students will develop in college. In fact, for both women and men, a strong support network enhances emotional health, whereas caustic interactions in students' place of residence or in situations involving peer pressure are detrimental to students' sense of psychological well-being (Sax et al., 2004). The amount of time spent socializing with friends each week exerts a positive influence on emotional health, although slightly more so for women than men (Sax et al., 2004). Another differential effect was uncovered in a study of gender role traditionalism: whereas religious peers promote traditional attitudes among men and women, interacting primarily with same-sex peers relates to gains in traditionalism for men only (Bryant, 2003).

Peer relationships also have a hand in influencing academic outcomes. One study reported significant positive associations between non-course-related peer interactions and men's mathematical ability, reading comprehension, and critical thinking (Whitt et al., 2003). However, the study identified Greek affiliation as having negative consequences for men's critical thinking. A number of other studies featuring all-women samples have addressed the effects of peer relationships and testified to the importance of these interactions for women's academic sense of self. Upon critical reflection, Holland and Eisenhart (1990) concluded that the peer system is ultimately responsible for women's focus on romance to the detriment of their career aspirations and academic commitments. Martínez Alemán (1997) expressed an altogether different opinion, suggesting that dialogues with female friends in college provide an outlet for dealing with academic stress, a source of validation, a risk-free opportunity for testing ideas, and a space for gaining unique perspectives and advice.

Place of Residence

Kezar and Moriarty (2000) reported that living on campus in the first year of college positively impacts men's self-rated public-speaking ability. Kezar and Moriarty (2000) also pointed to the detrimental implications for women's self-perceived leadership abilities when they live off campus in the first year. On-campus living arrangements may encourage students to adopt egalitarian gender role attitudes (Buckner, 1981); Bryant (2003) indicated that this is particularly true for women. Finally, the benefits of the residential experience likely extend to women's critical-thinking skills, according to Whitt et al. (2003).

Employment and Financial Aid

Work-related activities also are relevant forces in the lives of college students. While the amount of time spent working has unfavorable consequences for both women's and men's overall college persistence (Leppel, 2002), having an on-campus job positively predicts persistence in science (Astin & Sax, 1996). Further, although working full-time has been shown to predict numerous negative outcomes for combined samples of men and women (Astin, 1993c), Kezar and Moriarty (2000) uncovered advantageous aspects of full-time work, namely improved self-perceived leadership ability (among men) and influenceability (among women). Kezar and Moriarty (2000) also recognized internships and volunteer work as enhancing leadership ability and various self-confidence outcomes for both genders.

The unique effects of financial aid on women's college outcomes relative to men's have not received significant attention in the research literature, but a few authors have disaggregated their results by gender. Receiving financial support for college has been linked to men's persistence in science careers (Farmer, Wardrop, Anderson, & Risinger, 1995). For both women and men, struggling financially—because of credit card debt, excessive spending, and the like—contributes to significant declines in emotional health (Sax et al., 2004).

Appendix B

ANALYTICAL APPROACH USED FOR SEPARATE-GENDER REGRESSIONS

Identification of gender differences in the impact of college involves the study of conditional, or interaction, effects. Uncovering such effects can be accomplished in any number of ways, and Astin (1993a) and Hardy (1993) provide excellent summaries of these approaches. It is useful to illustrate some of these approaches with a hypothetical example. Suppose we are studying how participation in an undergraduate research program predicts students' graduate school aspirations, and we want to know whether this relationship is different for male and female students. One method is to conduct an analysis (via linear regression, structural equation modeling, or other multivariate method) on a combined sample of men and women, where gender is used as an independent variable *and* as a component of an interaction term. For example, the analysis would first control for the independent effects of two variables—gender and program participation—and would then add to the model an interaction term that reflects the *combination* of gender and program participation, such as the cross-product term "gender × program participation." If the interaction term is significantly related to graduate school plans once its main effects (gender and program participation) have been controlled, we would have evidence that the impact of participation in a research program is different for male and female students.

While that approach answers our main question of whether there is an interaction between gender and program participation, it does not clearly tell us about the nature of that interaction. Does the program have stronger or weaker effects on women than men? Are the relationships similar in sign (positive or negative for both genders)? One way to address these questions is to conduct analyses separately for women and men and compare the relative effects of program participation for each gender. Using this approach, participation in an undergraduate research program is an independent variable and gender is a constant within each analysis. In this way, we are able to assess whether the impact of participation in undergraduate research on graduate school aspirations is (a) significant for women; (b) significant for men; and (c) significantly different for women than men (as determined via t-tests). Interaction effects are evident if the t-tests determine that the predictive power of undergraduate research on graduate school aspirations is significantly different for women and men.

Identifying gender-based conditional, or interaction, effects is the focus of chapters 5 through 7. To accomplish this, ordinary least squares regression analyses were employed to assess whether and how the effects of eighty-six college environments and experiences on twenty-six college outcomes differed for women and men. This assessment necessitated controlling for a wide range of student input characteristics, which included fifty-four measures of students' family background, precollege educational experiences, dispositions, and expectations for college and life in general. Given the ease of locating statistically significant relationships in such a large sample, the p-value for entry into the regression was set at .0001 to allow only those variables with a substantial relationship to the outcomes to enter.

Independent variables were organized into the following blocks:

Block 1: Pretest (1 measure, if applicable)

Block 2: Demographic characteristics (10 measures)

Block 3: Precollege characteristics (44 measures[1])

Block 4: Residential and financial variables (7 measures)

Block 5: Institutional characteristics (9 measures)

Block 6: Peer environmental variables (22 measures)

Block 7: Major choice (12 measures)

Block 8: College experiences and involvement (36 measures)

Analysis of differential college effects centers on the relative effects of the eighty-six variables in Blocks 4 through 8. (A complete listing of variables appears later in this appendix.)

Four ordinary least squares regression analyses were conducted for each of the outcome variables (with the exception of career sex-atypicality, which was analyzed using logistic regression). The first two analyses (one for women and one for men) consider all independent variables in the eight blocks, with variables within each block considered for inclusion in the equation in a forward-entry fashion. Forward-entry was necessary to reduce the overall number of variables that would enter the equation for either group. Forcing all 140 independent variables into each analysis would introduce tremendous multicollinearity, making interpreting the gender differences nearly impossible.

As previously mentioned, the p-value for entry into the regression was a fairly stringent .0001, and tolerance was set to .30 as another method of avoiding problems resulting from multicollinearity. Further, careful inspection of correlation matrices for all independent variables ensured that, in nearly all cases, correlations among independent variables did not exceed .70. In some cases, those involving only institutional characteristics and peer aggregates, the intercorrelation did exceed .70. As a result, the predictive power of such variables was examined before the entry of variables highly correlated with them.

Variables that entered the regressions as predictors for *either* men or women were pooled and force-entered one at a time (within each original block) as a common set of independent variables in a second set of regressions (one for women and one for men). Tolerance was not set in the forced-entry regressions to ensure that the same variables would be represented in the equations for men and women. However, due to the exceptional size of the male and female samples and the potential for uncovering significant effects by chance, regression models were cross-validated on randomly drawn subsamples for both women and men. These comparisons confirmed the validity of the regression models for smaller samples.

Tables were then constructed that included regression coefficients for each of the independent variables in the final analysis. The first display focused solely on comparing unstandardized regression coefficients for women and men to gauge whether there was evidence of conditional effects. These comparisons were accomplished via two-tailed t-tests to determine whether the effect of a particular variable was significantly different for women and men. For most of these variables, regression coefficients were compared after all institutional and peer group measures were controlled (at the end of Block 6). However, regression coefficients for institutional characteristics (Block 5) and peer aggregates (Block 6) were considered just before Block 5 to avoid problems resulting from the linear dependence of these variables. While the p-level for consideration as a significant predictor was .0001, significance was set at $p < .01$ for the t-tests, since they did not require as stringent a test. The following t statistic was calculated to compare these variables at the steps just described:

$$t = \frac{b_m - b_w}{\sqrt{S_{bm}^2 + S_{bw}^2}}$$

In addition to examining conditional effects by gender, care was also taken to understand the dynamics of the competing variables within each separate-gender analysis. Specifically, standardized regression coefficients (betas) were examined at the following three stages for each gender: (1) as zero-order correlations; (2) after Block 3; and (3) after Block 6. If any variable experienced a change in sign or an appreciable change in magnitude, the regression output was examined to determine which other independent variable(s) contributed to that change. When relevant, such changes are discussed in the text.

Variables Used in Regressions

This appendix provides a listing of the dependent and independent variables used in regression analyses conducted for this study. An *F* following a variable signifies a factor derived from two or more variables. (See the following section for details on the factor analyses, including factor loadings and reliability coefficients.)

Dependent Variables

Personality and Identity

Scholar (F)

Social activist (F)

Artist (F)

Status striver (F)

Leader (F)

Scientific orientation

Self-rated physical health

Self-rated emotional health

Feeling overwhelmed

Cultural awareness (F)

Religious beliefs and convictions

Political and Social Values

Political engagement (F)

Political orientation

Classic liberalism (F)

Gender role traditionalism

Permissiveness (F)

Raising a family

Developing a meaningful philosophy of life

Promoting racial understanding

Academic Outcomes

College GPA

Self-rated mathematical ability

Self-rated drive to achieve

Self-rated competitiveness

Critical thinking and knowledge (F)

Degree aspirations

Career sex-atypicality (not used in combined sample regression; see chapter 7)

Independent Variables

Independent variables are clustered into blocks and included in the regression analysis based on their presumed order of occurrence. In this way, background characteristics and precollege propensities are controlled before considering the effects of the college environment on student outcomes. As previously mentioned, analyses include a total of 140 independent variables that are divided into eight different blocks. The first three blocks represent student inputs, and the remaining five blocks measure students' exposure to and experiences within the college environment.

Block 1: Pretest

Determined by the outcome for the regression

Block 2: Demographics

First-generation college student

Mother's level of education

Father's level of education

Parents' income

White/Caucasian

Black/African American
American Indian
Asian American
Mexican American/Chicano/Puerto Rican American/Latino
Parents divorced or separated

Block 3: Precollege characteristics

Scholar (F)
Social activist (F)
Artist (F)
Leader (F)
Status striver (F)
Political engagement (F)
Classic liberalism (F)
Permissiveness (F)
Educational reasons for college (F)
Chose college for academic reputation (F)
Expect to drop out of college (F)
Expect change in area of interest (F)
High school: Volunteering (F)
High school: Hedonism (F)
High school GPA
Feeling overwhelmed
Self-rated drive to achieve
Self-rated emotional health
Self-rated physical health
Self-rated mathematical ability
Self-rated competitiveness
Political orientation

Attitudes toward nonconsensual sex

Goal: Raise a family

Goal: Make contribution to science

Goal: Develop meaningful philosophy of life

Goal: Help promote racial understanding

Degree aspirations

Gender role traditionalism

SAT composite (and converted ACT)

Reason for college: Get away from home

Expect to get a job to pay college expenses

Reason for college: Parents' wish

Felt bored in class

Studied with other students

Attended religious services

Hours per week watching television

Hours per week exercising/playing sports

Hours per week socializing

Hours per week studying/homework

Hours per week household/childcare duties

Hours per week student clubs

Hours per week talking with teachers outside class

Hours per week reading for pleasure

Block 4: Residential and Financial Variables

Distance from home

Living on campus

Aid: Family or self

Aid: Work

Aid: Grants and scholarships

Aid: Loans

Concern about financing college

Block 5: Institutional Characteristics

Public university

Private university

Public four-year college

Private nonsectarian four-year college

Private Catholic four-year college

Other religious private four-year college

Number of full-time undergraduates

Student-to-faculty ratio

Percentage of women faculty

Block 6: Peer Environment Variables

To estimate how individual students may be affected by the characteristics of the student body at their institution, peer measures were created based on institutional average responses to selected items on the 1994 Freshman Survey. These institutional aggregates were calculated from all respondents to the Freshman Survey from each campus, not just those for whom there is follow-up data. These peer measures draw heavily from those used in Astin's (1993c) study of college impact. Although these peer mean factors did not exactly replicate those specified by Astin, they were comparable in content. In total, fifteen peer measures were created from the data (seven factors and eight individual variables), which, when assigned to the individual student, reflect the characteristics of the student body at his or her institution. These include:

Peer mean: Intellectual self-esteem (F)

Peer mean: Altruism and social activism (F)

Peer mean: Materialism and social status (F)

Peer mean: Artistic interests (F)

Peer mean: Years of study in math and science (F)

Peer mean: Hedonism (F)

Peer mean: Socioeconomic status (F)

Peer mean: Scientific orientation

Peer mean: Gender role traditionalism

Peer mean: Competitiveness

Peer mean: Expectation to get a job in college

Peer mean: Living on campus

Peer mean: Political views

Peer mean: Understanding of others

College selectivity

Additional peer measures were derived from data provided by the Integrated Postsecondary Education Data Survey. These refer to the composition of the institution's undergraduate student body in terms of gender, race, and fields in which degrees are awarded. These include:

Percentage of nonwhite students

Percentage of bachelor's degrees in business

Percentage of bachelor's degrees in education

Percentage of bachelor's degrees in English, humanities, and fine arts

Percentage of bachelor's degrees in science, math, and engineering

Percentage of bachelor's degrees in history, political science, and social sciences

Percentage of women undergraduates

Block 7: Major Choice

Biological sciences

Business

Physical sciences, math, statistics, or computer science

Education

Engineering

Fine arts

Health profession

History or political science

English or humanities

Journalism or communications

Psychology

Social sciences

Block 8: Environments, Experiences, and Involvement

Involvement with Academics

Enrolled in honors/advanced courses

Worked on independent study project

Hours per week using a personal computer

Hours per week studying/homework

Withdrew from school or took a leave of absence

Felt bored in class

Enrolled in ethnic studies course

Enrolled in women's studies course

Involvement with Faculty

Faculty did not take comments seriously

Challenged a professor's ideas in class

Faculty provided opportunity for research

Faculty provided honest feedback about abilities

Hours per week talking with faculty outside class

General faculty support (F)

Involvement with Peers

Social diversity experiences (F)

Student government (F)

Joined a fraternity or sorority

Hours per week socializing with friends

Hedonism (drinking, smoking, and partying) (F)

Participated in intercollegiate sports

Leadership training

Hours per week student clubs or groups

Took part in demonstrations

Studied with other students

Attended racial/cultural awareness workshop

Involvement in Work

Worked part-time on campus

Had a part-time job off campus

Worked full-time while a student

Other Forms of Involvement

Volunteering or community service (F)

Attended religious services

Hours per week commuting

Tutored another student

Hours per week household/childcare duties

Hours per week watching television

Hours per week exercising/playing sports

Hours per week reading for pleasure

Factor Analyses

Factor analysis was employed to develop ten of the outcome measures and twenty-six independent measures.

Dependent Variable Factors

Five of the dependent variable factors were based on Astin's (1993b) model of student types. Most of the items included in Astin's original typologies were available in the dataset. The validity of these factors was assessed by calculating Cronbach's alphas (a measure of reliability) and running confirmatory factor analyses. These factors are scholar, social activist, artist, leader, and status striver.

Scholar (α = .67 A; .65 M; .68 W)

Item	Loading		
	All	Men	Women
Self-rated: Academic ability	.81	.80	.80
Self-rated: Intellectual self-confidence	.79	.78	.80
Self-rated: Writing ability	.74	.73	.75

Social activist (α = .72 A; .74 M; .72 W)

Item	Loading		
	All	Men	Women
Goal: Influence social values	.81	.82	.79
Goal: Participate in a community action program	.76	.76	.76
Goal: Help others in difficulty	.69	.69	.69
Goal: Influence the political structure	.69	.74	.69

Artist (α = .77 A; .78 M; .76 W)

	Loading		
Item	All	Men	Women
Goal: Create artistic work	.80	.81	.79
Self-rated: Artistic ability	.78	.76	.79
Self-rated: Creativity	.71	.66	.74
Goal: Write original works	.66	.71	.62
Goal: Become accomplished in the performing arts	.66	.71	.62

Leader (α = .73 A; .73 M; .72 W)

	Loading		
Item	All	Men	Women
Self-rated: Leadership ability	.84	.84	.83
Self-rated: Public-speaking ability	.81	.80	.81
Self-rated: Social self-confidence	.77	.79	.76

Status striver (α = .72 A; .73 M; .71 W)

	Loading		
Item	All	Men	Women
Goal: Obtain recognition from colleagues	.73	.73	.74
Goal: Be very well-off financially	.71	.71	.70
Goal: Have administrative responsibility for work of others	.71	.70	.71
Goal: Become authority in my field	.69	.69	.69
Goal: Be successful in a business of my own	.60	.63	.55

An additional personality factor, political engagement, consisted of two items that are closely related to one another, although this factor was not based on previous research.

Political engagement ($\alpha = .66$ A; .66 M; .67 W)

Item	Loading		
	All	Men	Women
Goal: Keep up to date with political affairs	.87	.86	.87
Frequency: Discussed politics	.87	.86	.87

The remaining dependent variable factors were derived from two clusters of questions included on the College Student Survey: self-changes and views. Each of these clusters was submitted to a factor analysis using varimax rotation. This process resulted in two self-change factors and two view factors, which were submitted in their final form to confirmatory factor analysis.

Self-change: Critical thinking and knowledge ($\alpha = .77$ A; .77 M; .76 W)

Item	Loading		
	All	Men	Women
Self-change: Ability to think critically	.80	.80	.79
Self-change: Analytical and problem-solving skills	.76	.76	.75
Self-change: General knowledge	.71	.73	.70
Self-change: Writing skills	.63	.61	.64
Self-change: Knowledge of a particular field or discipline	.61	.63	.59
Self-change: Reading speed and comprehension	.60	.59	.60

Self-change: Cultural awareness ($\alpha = .76$ A; .77 M; .76 W)

Item	Loading		
	All	Men	Women
Self-change: Understanding of the problems facing my community	.81	.81	.81
Self-change: Understanding social problems facing the nation	.77	.78	.77
Self-change: Ability to get along with people of other races/cultures	.75	.76	.74
Self-change: Knowledge of people from other races/cultures	.72	.72	.72

Views: Classic liberalism ($\alpha = .71$ A; .74 M; .66 W)

Item	Loading		
	All	Men	Women
View: Federal government is not doing enough to control pollution	.71	.71	.70
View: National health care plan is needed	.67	.70	.63
View: Wealthy people should pay a larger share of taxes	.60	.65	.55
View: Federal government should do more to control sale of handguns	.60	.60	.56
View: Federal government should do more to discourage energy consumption	.60	.60	.59
View: Federal government is not protecting consumers from bad goods/services	.56	.56	.55
View: Federal government should raise taxes to help reduce the deficit	.48	.55	.44

Views: Permissiveness ($\alpha = .73$ A; .72 M; .76 W)

Item	Loading		
	All	Men	Women
View: Abortion should be legal	.79	.80	.80
View: Sex is OK if two people like each other	.70	.69	.71
View: Marijuana should be legalized	.82	.83	.82
View: Homosexual relationships should be permitted	.65	.61	.70

Independent Variable Factors

Several approaches were taken to create the twenty-six factors used as independent variables. Seven of these factors were modeled after the dependent variables to create exact pretests. Confirmatory factor analyses were used to assess factor loadings and Cronbach's alphas for the following seven variables:

Scholar pretest (α = .65 A; .65 M; .65 W)

	Loading		
Item	All	Men	Women
Self-rated: Academic ability	.80	.80	.80
Self-rated: Self-confidence (intellectual)	.80	.80	.80
Self-rated: Writing	.71	.73	.71

Social activist pretest (α = .69 A; .72 M; .67 W)

	Loading		
Item	All	Men	Women
Goal: Influence social values	.80	.82	.78
Goal: Participate in a community action program	.71	.71	.71
Goal: Influence the political structure	.68	.74	.68
Goal: Help others in difficulty	.67	.68	.65

Artist pretest (α = .73 A; .75 M; .73 W)

	Loading		
Item	All	Men	Women
Goal: Create artistic work	.77	.79	.76
Self-rated: Artistic ability	.75	.72	.77
Self-rated: Creativity	.71	.66	.74
Goal: Write original works	.65	.70	.62
Goal: Become accomplished in the performing arts	.61	.66	.58

Leader pretest (α = .72 A; .72 M; .73 W)

	Loading		
Item	All	Men	Women
Self-rated: Leadership ability	.84	.84	.84
Self-rated: Public-speaking ability	.81	.80	.82
Self-rated: Social self-confidence	.76	.76	.76

Status striver pretest (α = .72 A; .73 M; .71 W)

	Loading		
Item	All	Men	Women
Goal: Obtain recognition from colleagues	.75	.76	.75
Goal: Have administrative responsibility for work of others	.72	.72	.72
Goal: Become authority in my field	.69	.70	.69
Goal: Be very well-off financially	.68	.67	.68
Goal: Be successful in a business of my own	.61	.62	.59

Political engagement pretest (α = .66 A; .64 M; .66 W)

	Loading		
Item	All	Men	Women
Frequency: Discussed politics	.86	.86	.86
Goal: Keep up to date with political affairs	.86	.86	.86

Classic liberalism pretest (α = .66 A; .70 M; .62 W)

	Loading		
Item	All	Men	Women
View: Federal government is not doing enough to control pollution	.68	.69	.66
View: National health care plan is needed	.67	.68	.65
View: Federal government should do more to control sale of handguns	.64	.63	.63
View: Wealthy people should pay a larger share of taxes	.58	.64	.53
View: Federal government should do more to discourage energy consumption	.54	.56	.52
View: Federal government is not protecting consumers from bad goods/services	.47	.47	.46
View: Federal government should raise taxes to help reduce the deficit	.43	.48	.42

Two college choice factors were created through exploratory factor analyses (using varimax rotation) that considered all thirty-one reasons why students attend college and why they chose their particular college. These analyses resulted in the following two factors:

Educational reasons for college (α = .70 A; .71 M; .69 W)

Item	Loading		
	All	Men	Women
Gain general education	.78	.78	.77
Become more cultured	.76	.76	.75
Improve study skills	.73	.73	.72
Learn more things	.66	.67	.65

Chose college for academic reputation (α = .72 A; .73 M; .71 W)

Item	Loading		
	All	Men	Women
Graduates get good jobs	.86	.86	.86
Graduates go to top grad schools	.83	.84	.83
Good academic reputation	.72	.73	.70

A similar exploratory approach was used to develop the following two factors related to students' expectations for college:

Expect to drop out of college (α = .74 A; .75 M; .72 W)

Item	Loading		
	All	Men	Women
Drop out temporarily	.89	.90	.89
Drop out permanently	.89	.90	.89

Expect change in area of interest (α = .87 A; .85 M; .88 W)

| Item | Loading | | |
	All	Men	Women
Change career choice	.94	.93	.94
Change major field	.94	.93	.94

The following three factors were also derived from the Freshman Survey:

High school: Volunteering (α = .76 A; .76 M; .76 W)

| Item | Loading | | |
	All	Men	Women
Performed volunteer work	.90	.90	.90
Hours per week: Volunteering	.90	.90	.90

High school: Hedonism (α = .80 A; .79 M; .80 W)

| Item | Loading | | |
	All	Men	Women
Drank beer	.89	.89	.88
Drank wine or liquor	.85	.86	.84
Hours per week: Partying	.75	.74	.76
Smoked cigarettes	.67	.65	.69

Permissiveness pretest (α = .68 A; .66 M; .71 W)

| Item | Loading | | |
	All	Men	Women
View: Abortion should be legal	.80	.80	.80
View: Sex is OK if two people like each other	.74	.77	.75
View: Marijuana should be legalized	.70	.68	.70
View: Homosexual relationships should be permitted	.61	.56	.68

The remaining five student factors were derived from exploratory factor analysis considering all the college involvement variables that were of interest to the research team. The team assessed the resulting scales for their theoretical sensibility and modified some as a result. The final versions of each of these factors were then submitted to confirmatory factor analyses to obtain factor loadings and Cronbach's alphas. These variables include:

Social diversity experiences (α = .79 A; .78 M; .80 W)

| | Loading | | |
Item	All	Men	Women
Dined with someone of another ethnic group	.83	.82	.83
Studied with someone of another ethnic group	.79	.78	.80
Interacted with someone of another ethnic group	.72	.74	.72
Socialized with someone of different ethnic group	.72	.71	.72
Dated someone of another ethnic group	.58	.55	.60
Had roommate of different ethnic group	.54	.52	.55

Volunteering or community service (α = .74 A; .74 M; .73 W)

| | Loading | | |
Item	All	Men	Women
Performed volunteer work	.89	.89	.88
Hours per week: Volunteer work	.82	.81	.83
Any community service/volunteering	.73	.74	.71

Hedonism (α = .82 A; .81 M; .82 W)

| | Loading | | |
Item	All	Men	Women
Drank beer	.89	.89	.89
Drank wine or liquor	.85	.86	.85
Hours per week: Partying	.84	.83	.84
Smoked cigarettes	.64	.61	.66

Student government (α = .71 A; .75 M; .68 W)

	Loading		
Item	All	Men	Women
Elected to student office	.88	.89	.87
In student government	.88	.89	.87

General faculty support (α = .84 A; .83 M; .84 W)

	Loading		
Item	All	Men	Women
Advice about educational program	.74	.74	.74
Respect	.71	.71	.71
Emotional support	.71	.66	.72
Intellectual challenge/stimulation	.68	.68	.67
Faculty took interest in progress	.68	.66	.68
Opportunity to discuss homework	.67	.66	.68
Encouragement for graduate school	.66	.67	.64
Letter of recommendation	.64	.64	.64

The study also includes seven peer environmental factors characterizing the peer group at the student's own institution, as this information shows:

Peer mean: Intellectual self-esteem (α = .95)

Item	Loading: All
Self-rated: Self confidence (intellectual)	.94
Self-rated: Academic ability	.93
Self-rated: Drive to achieve	.93
Self-rated: Public-speaking ability	.87
Self-rated: Writing ability	.82
Expectation: Elect to honor society	.81
Self-rated: Mathematical ability	.80
Self-rated: Leadership ability	.71

Peer mean: Altruism and social activism ($\alpha = .82$)

Item	Loading: All
Goal: Participate in a community action program	.91
Goal: Promote racial understanding	.91
Goal: Help with environmental clean-up	.76
Goal: Become a community leader	.67

Peer mean: Materialism and social status ($\alpha = .93$)

Item	Loading: All
Goal: Be very well-off financially	.96
Reason college: Make more money	.89
Goal: Obtain recognition	.86
Goal: Be successful in a business of my own	.86
Goal: Have administrative responsibility for work of others	.81
Goal: Become authority in my field	.76

Peer mean: Artistic interests ($\alpha = .91$)

Item	Loading: All
Goal: Be accomplished in the performing arts	.91
Goal: Create artistic work	.91
Self-rated: Artistic ability	.88
Career goal: Artist	.85

Peer mean: Years of study in math and science ($\alpha = .69$)

Item	Loading: All
Years in high school physical science	.89
Years in high school math	.87
Years in high school biology	.60

Peer mean: Hedonism ($\alpha = .96$)

Item	Loading: All
Drank beer	.98
Drank wine/liquor	.97
Hours per week: Partying	.93
Smoked cigarettes	.89

Peer mean: Socioeconomic status ($\alpha = .91$)

Item	Loading: All
Father's education	.98
Mother's education	.96
Parents' income	.91

Cronbach's Alphas

To enhance the reliability of the dependent and independent variable factors and to prevent any one item from dominating the factor, final factor scales were created using standardized z-scores (if factor components were based on different scales of measurement). For factors in which all items are measured on the same scale, scores were left unstandardized.

All together, variable factor loadings for dependent and independent variables ranged from a low of .43 to a high of .98, while Cronbach's alphas ranged from .65 to .96. Factor loadings greater than .40 were considered acceptable for this study, as were Cronbach's alphas of at least .65. Cronbach's alphas and factor loadings were also computed separately by gender to ensure that the factors were reliable scales for both men and women. In so doing, women's Cronbach's alphas ranged from .62 to .88, while men's ranged from .64 to .85. Women's factor loadings ranged from .42 to .94, and men's ranged from .47 to .93.

Weighting and Substitutions

One of the most important questions that arise in any survey is whether the sample is representative of the student population it is designed to reflect. Quite simply, some people are more inclined to fill out and return surveys than are others, and these differences in the tendency to respond introduce a nonresponse bias to the resulting dataset. Further, as college student survey response rates have declined over the years, it is increasingly difficult to achieve a representative sample of respondents (Dey, 1997b). It is the researcher's responsibility to assess the extent of this bias and determine whether to adjust the data to make them better reflect the student population at hand.

In surveys of college students, response rates tend to be highest among women and high-achieving students, and this study was no exception. Further, some institutions are more likely than others to participate in the Freshman Survey and College Student Survey, with Catholic institutions and other private colleges better represented than public institutions. In an attempt to correct for sampling and nonresponse bias, a multistage weighting procedure was used to bring the sample of 17,637 respondents up to the population of 792,569 men and women who had entered coeducational baccalaureate institutions as first-time, full-time students in fall 1994.

First, a classification scheme was created based on 152 different combinations of gender; high school GPA; and institutional type, control, and selectivity (i.e., 2 genders × 4 grade-level categories × 19 institutional classifications = 152 categories). For example, one cell would include women attending medium-selectivity public universities whose average high school grade was a B+. The next step was to distribute the sample of 17,637 across the 152 cells and to compare that to the distribution of the study population across those same cells. The ratio of the two numbers in each cell (sample count and population count) were then used to calculate a weight for students in each cell. For example, if cell 21 refers to women in medium-selectivity public institutions with average high school grades of B+, then:

$$\text{Weight}_{cell21} = \frac{\#\ cell21\ \text{students in population}}{\#\ cell21\ \text{students in sample}}$$

Calculated this way, students in cells with a very high representation in the sample would receive the lowest weights while students in cells with low representation would receive the highest weights. The median weight across all cases was 15.7. When the weights are applied to the data, analyses then reflect the responses we would expect if all students in the population had responded to both surveys.

The final step in the weighting procedure was to deflate the weights. This was necessary because the weighted counts of 426,673 women and 365,896 men would be too large for any meaningful tests of significance. In samples that large, even the most trivial of relationships would be deemed significant. To deflate, or normalize, the weights, each original weight (described earlier) was divided by the ratio of the weighted to unweighted total samples: $792,569 \div 17,637 = 44.94$. This process enabled us to maintain the proportions provided by weighting and prevented the exaggeration of significant differences brought on by a large sample size.

To check the accuracy of the weights, the weighted 1994–1998 data was compared with the weighted national norms from the 1994 Freshman Survey. The more accurate the weights are, the more closely the weighted longitudinal subset will match with the national freshman data. Frequency distributions were compared on several key demographic variables, including sex, high school GPA, family income, father's education, mother's education, and race. The first two—sex and grades—provided identical distributions between the two datasets. This confirmed that the weights were calculated correctly. The distributions were also nearly identical for family income and parents' education, demonstrating that by removing the bias introduced by gender and grades, we also corrected for the fact that respondents typically came from families with higher income and educational levels.

With respect to race, however, the weighted longitudinal data did not match the national normative data. Specifically, the longitudinal file overrepresents white and Asian American students, and it underrepresents African American, Latino, and other non-white groups. This pattern of racial/ethnic differences in response rates is common in surveys of college students (Dey, 1997b). Adjusting the data to account for differences in high school grades did improve the racial/ethnic balance in the data, but it did not eliminate the bias completely. An attempt was made to incorporate race/ethnicity into the original weighting scheme; however, the distribution of racial/ethnic groups across the categories of sex, grades, and institutional type was not broad enough to calculate reliable weights. In other words, some cells would have contained only one or two students of a particular racial/ethnic category, meaning that the resulting weights would be unacceptably high; other cells contained no members of a particular racial/ethnic group, and in that case, a weight could not even be calculated.

In sum, the weights were designed to reduce bias in the sample in terms of students' gender; academic achievement; and institutional type, control, and selectivity. All analyses were performed using the weighted student data.

Substitutions for Missing Data

When the final sample was selected, each variable was checked for skewness and the number of missing cases using non-mean-replaced, unweighted data. Skewness was deemed problematic when it was greater than 2.0 (or less than –2.0). Regarding missing data, it was determined that variables missing greater than 15 percent of the total number of cases (or 2,646 cases) were not eligible for data replacement. When variables were missing fewer than

15 percent of cases, the mean was substituted when the variable was normally distributed, and the median was substituted when the variable was skewed, as suggested in McDermeit, Funk, and Dennis (1999). Although McDermeit et al. also recommend that the mode be used for substitution when the variable is dichotomous, none of the dichotomous variables in this study were missing cases. Values for mean and median replacements were calculated and applied separately by gender; however, for SAT composite, mean replacement considered both gender and race.

A number of the variables for this study were factors composed of many variables. Missing cases and skewness were assessed for each of the items in the factor scales and replaced with means and medians (as described) before computing each of the factor scales. The peer mean variables did not require replacement of missing data because they were based on institutional aggregates; each person in the sample received a score on these measures, and so there were no missing values. Two databases were created: one included replaced data, and the other did not. The former was used for regressions; the latter was used for descriptive analyses such as frequencies and cross-tabulations.

Note

1. Of these forty-four precollege characteristics, only forty-three are considered in this block when a direct pretest for the dependent variable is available. In such a case, the pretest variable appears in Block 1.

Appendix C

CHANGES IN THE GENDER GAP DURING COLLEGE

This appendix reports on gender differences observed across each of the twenty-six college outcomes presented in chapters 5, 6, and 7. The majority of these outcomes have direct pretests from the 1994 survey, so in most cases, the tables allow for an examination of how the gender gap changed over time. Outcomes are presented in the order that they appear in each chapter, and when the outcome is a factor, gender differences are reported for the items composing that factor. For the last outcome, career sex-atypicality, students' actual career aspirations are included.

The following tables report on the significance of gender differences in three ways: (1) between women and men at college entry (1994); (2) between women and men as college seniors (1998); and (3) between the gender gap in 1994 and the gender gap in 1998. For most items, pre- and posttest comparisons are based on frequency distributions and cross-tabulations. Tests of significance were employed depending on the type of comparison being made. The test of gender differences in 1994 and 1998 (items 1 and 2) relied on independent sample z-tests of the standard error of the gender gap. To test whether there was a significant *change* in the gender gap over four years (item 3), the McNemar test for dependent proportions was employed (Agresti & Finlay, 1997). In all cases, differences are only considered significant at $p < .001$.

Table C.1 Personality and Identity: Change in the Gender Gap During College

	1994			1998			Significant change in gender difference?[a]
	Women (%)	Men (%)	Diff. (W − M)	Women (%)	Men (%)	Diff. (W − M)	
Scholar personality							
Self-ratings (above average or highest 10%)							
Intellectual self-confidence	48.8	63.1*	−14.3	59.4	78.1*	−18.7	Widens
Writing ability	47.1*	40.5	+6.6	58.2	56.8	+1.4	Narrows
Academic ability	68.2	73.9*	−5.7	70.5	75.9*	−5.4	
Social activist personality							
Goals (very important or essential)							
Influence the political structure	16.0	21.8*	−5.8	12.7	15.0*	−2.3	Narrows
Help others in difficulty	69.3*	51.8	+17.5	75.4*	60.2	+15.2	
Influence social values	44.7*	36.8	+7.9	47.3*	38.6	+8.7	
Participate in community program	30.0*	21.0	+9.0	29.2*	18.3	+10.9	
Artist personality							
Self-ratings (above average or highest 10%)							
Creativity	44.2	52.4*	−8.2	50.7	61.0*	−10.3	
Artistic ability	20.7	25.7*	−5.0	24.4	28.8*	−4.4	
Goals (very important or essential)							
Write original works	10.3	10.8	−0.5	12.0	15.3*	−3.3	Widens
Create artistic work	10.7	10.4	+0.3	14.3	13.0	+1.3	
Achieve in performing arts	10.7	11.8	−1.1	10.3	11.9*	−1.6	

Status striver personality

Goals (very important or essential)

Obtain recognition from colleagues	52.4	59.5*	−7.1	51.9	70.3*	−18.4	Widens
Be successful in own business	28.8	38.4*	−9.6	21.6	35.5*	−13.9	Widens
Have administrative responsibility over others	35.3	37.2	−1.9	37.7	41.6*	−3.9	
Become authority in field	62.7	61.5	+1.2	64.3	62.8	+1.5	
Be well-off financially	64.4	70.8*	−6.4	53.3	58.9*	−5.6	

Leader personality

Self-ratings (above average or highest 10%)

Public-speaking ability	32.0	34.1	−2.1	41.8	51.5*	−9.7	Widens
Leadership ability	54.6	59.5*	−4.9	61.0	70.3*	−9.3	Widens
Social self-confidence	40.2	43.8*	−3.6	56.3	60.8*	−4.5	

Scientific orientation

Goal (very important or essential)

Make a contribution to science	14.7	18.5*	−3.8	9.6	13.6*	−4.0	

Table C.1 (Continued)

	1994			1998			Significant change in gender difference?[a]
	Women (%)	Men (%)	Diff. (W − M)	Women (%)	Men (%)	Diff. (W − M)	
Physical health							
Self-rating (above average or highest 10%)							
Physical health	50.2	66.2*	−16.0	51.4	63.8*	−12.4	Narrows
Emotional health							
Self-rating (above average or highest 10%)							
Emotional health	56.6	63.2*	−6.6	56.1	66.3*	−10.2	Widens
Felt overwhelmed frequently	35.8*	14.9	+20.9	36.9*	19.8	+17.1	Narrows
Cultural awareness							
Self-change (much stronger or stronger)							
Understand problems of community	n/a	n/a	n/a	66.9	65.6	+1.3	n/a
Understand social problems of nation	n/a	n/a	n/a	77.6	76.1	+1.5	n/a
Ability to get along with other races	n/a	n/a	n/a	59.3	58.9	+0.4	n/a
Knowledge of people from other races	n/a	n/a	n/a	69.2	67.2	+2.0	n/a
Religious beliefs and convictions							
Self-change (much stronger or stronger)							
Religious beliefs	n/a	n/a	n/a	39.9*	35.2	+4.7	n/a

[a] Only changes significant at $p < .001$ are designated as widening or narrowing.

* Percentage is significantly larger ($p < .001$) for that group.

Table C.2 Political and Social Values: Change in the Gender Gap During College

	1994			1998			Significant change in gender difference?[a]
	Women (%)	Men (%)	Diff. (W − M)	Women (%)	Men (%)	Diff. (W − M)	
Political engagement							
Goal (very important or essential)							
Keep up to date with political affairs	33.4	39.5*	−6.1	32.5	37.5*	−5.0	
Discussed politics frequently	15.3	21.7*	−6.4	11.3	18.9*	−7.6	
Political orientation							
Far right	1.1	2.7*	−1.6	0.5	1.4*	−0.9	
Conservative	19.8	29.1*	−9.3	21.2	30.8*	−9.6	
Middle of the road	50.1*	45.0	+5.1	47.6*	42.6	+5.0	
Liberal	22.5*	16.8	+5.7	26.3*	21.4	+4.9	
Far left	0.7	1.5*	−0.8	1.8	1.9	−0.1	
Classic liberalism							
Views (agree somewhat or strongly)							
Federal government is not doing enough to control pollution	87.6*	80.2	+7.4	80.8*	73.5	+7.3	
National health care plan is needed	70.5*	63.2	+7.3	73.7*	63.4	+10.3	Widens

(Continued)

Table C.2 (Continued)

	1994			1998			Significant change in gender difference?[a]
	Women (%)	Men (%)	Diff. (W – M)	Women (%)	Men (%)	Diff. (W – M)	
Wealthy people should pay larger share of taxes	67.6*	64.5	+3.1	61.7*	57.1	+4.6	
Federal government should do more to control sale of guns	89.8*	73.3	+16.5	90.9*	74.2	+16.7	
Federal government should discourage energy consumption	78.4*	70.7	+7.7	74.4*	70.1	+4.3	Narrows
Federal government is not protecting consumers	73.5*	63.9	+9.6	58.3*	50.9	+7.4	
Federal government should raise taxes to reduce deficit	26.1	28.3	–2.2	17.0	22.5*	–5.5	Widens
Gender role traditionalism							
View (agree somewhat or strongly)							
Activities of married woman confined to the home	17.3	27.3*	–10.0	11.4	18.8*	–7.4	Narrows
Permissiveness							
Views (agree somewhat or strongly)							
Abortion should be legal	58.9	57.7	+1.2	64.9*	60.4	+4.5	Widens

If two people really like each other; it's OK
for them to have sex even if they've known

each other for only a very short time	28.8	49.0*	−20.2	45.3	56.4*	−11.1	Narrows
Marijuana should be legalized	24.3	31.0*	−6.7	33.4	37.6*	−4.2	
Homosexual relations should be prohibited	22.1	41.0*	−18.9	13.7	29.0*	−15.3	Narrows
Raising a family							
Goal (very important or essential)							
Raise a family	72.1	72.0	+0.1	78.0*	71.3	+6.7	Widens
Developing meaningful philosophy of life							
Goal (very important or essential)							
Develop a meaningful philosophy of life	43.1	45.6*	−2.5	53.5	53.6	−0.1	
Promoting racial understanding							
Goal (very important or essential)							
Help promote racial understanding	36.5*	29.5	+7.0	36.2*	26.3	+9.9	Widens

[a] Only changes significant at $p < .001$ are designated as widening or narrowing.

* Percentage is significantly larger ($p < .001$) for that group.

Table C.3 Academic Outcomes: Change in the Gender Gap During College

	1994			1998			Significant change in gender difference?[a]
	Women (%)	Men (%)	Diff. (W – M)	Women (%)	Men (%)	Diff. (W – M)	
Mathematical ability							
Self-rating (above average or highest 10%) Mathematical ability	43.6	54.6*	–11.0	37.3	51.4*	–14.1	Widens
Drive to achieve							
Self-rating (above average or highest 10%) Drive to achieve	71.2	72.7	–1.5	73.6	73.0	+0.6	
Competitiveness							
Self-rating (above average or highest 10%) Competitiveness	44.4	69.8*	–25.4	48.7	71.8*	–23.1	
Critical thinking and knowledge							
Self-change (much stronger or stronger)							
Ability to think critically	n/a	n/a	n/a	93.4	93.2	+0.2	
Analytic/problem-solving skills	n/a	n/a	n/a	92.1	92.6	–0.5	
General knowledge	n/a	n/a	n/a	98.3	97.6	+0.7	
Writing skills	n/a	n/a	n/a	82.2	80.7	+1.5	
Knowledge of a particular field	n/a	n/a	n/a	98.6	97.8	+0.8	
Reading speed and comprehension	n/a	n/a	n/a	68.0	66.4	+1.6	

College GPA						
A or A+	22.1*	16.7	+5.4	11.4*	9.1	+2.3	Narrows
B+ or A−	42.1*	37.9	+4.2	37.4*	30.0	+7.4	Widens
B	26.4	30.5*	−4.1	34.9	37.0	−2.1	
C+ or B−	8.7	13.2*	−4.5	13.3	18.4*	−5.1	
C or lower	0.6	1.6*	−1.0	2.3	4.4*	−2.1	Widens
Degree aspirations						
BA or other	24.1	25.2	−1.1	21.9	29.6*	−7.7	Widens
MA or MDiv	39.7	40.4	−0.7	44.9*	37.2	7.7	Reverses
PhD	13.4	14.0	−0.6	13.0	11.8	+1.2	
MD	8.5	8.3	+0.2	3.1	4.6	−1.5	
JD	3.5	4.4	−0.9	3.5	4.2	−0.7	
Career aspirations						
Engineer	3.3	11.8*	−8.5	2.2	8.0*	−5.8	Narrows
Business professional	11.6	16.5*	−4.9	16	21.1*	−5.1	
Computer programmer	0.9	3.4*	−2.5	1.9	7.3*	−5.4	Widens
Law enforcement officer	0.4	2.2*	−1.8	0.7	2.6*	−1.9	
Doctor/dentist/physician	6.8	7.9	−1.1	2.7	4.1*	−1.4	
Farmer/forester	0.8	1.9*	−1.1	0.6	1.0	−0.4	Narrows
Lawyer	3.5	4.4	−0.9	2.7	3.5	−0.8	
Clergy	0.2	1.0*	−0.8	0.3	1.2*	−0.9	
Military	0.3	1.0*	−0.7	0.5	1.6*	−1.1	

(Continued)

Table C.3 (Continued)

	1994			1998			Significant change in gender difference?[a]
	Women (%)	Men (%)	Diff. (W − M)	Women (%)	Men (%)	Diff. (W − M)	
Secondary teacher	4.8	5.5	−0.7	4.8	4.7	+0.1	
Artist	4.9	5.6	−0.7	5.3*	4.2	+1.1	Reverses
Architect	1.0	1.6*	−0.6	0.9	1.1	−0.2	
Research scientist	2.0	2.5	−0.5	3.2	3.0	+0.2	
College teacher	0.4	0.6	−0.2	1.2	1.8*	−0.6	
Homemaker	0.2*	0.0	+0.2	0.3*	0.0	+0.3	
Business clerk	1.2*	0.4	+0.8	0.5	0.3	+0.2	Narrows
Social worker	1.7*	0.7	+1.0	6.5*	1.0	+5.5	Widens
Undecided	13.7	12.6	+1.1	3.9	3.5	+0.4	
Psychologist	2.2*	0.7	+1.5	1.7*	0.5	+1.2	
Nurse	3.2*	0.4	+2.8	3.2*	0.3	+2.9	
Health professional	11.7*	4.7	+7.0	5.9*	2.2	+3.7	Narrows
Elementary teacher	10.7*	2.8	+7.9	11.9*	2.8	+9.1	Widens

[a] Only changes significant at $p < .001$ are designated as widening or narrowing.

* Percentage is significantly larger ($p < .001$) for that group.

Appendix D

SQUARED MULTIPLE CORRELATIONS, BY GENDER

Table D.1 Squared Multiple Correlations, by Gender

Outcome	R^2 for women		R^2 for men	
	After inputs	Final	After inputs	Final
Personality and identity				
Scholar	.39	.47	.40	.47
Social activist	.26	.38	.27	.41
Artist	.48	.53	.47	.54
Status striver	.25	.31	.31	.41
Leader	.41	.53	.47	.55
Scientific orientation	.17	.33	.16	.33
Self-rated physical health	.21	.29	.31	.43
Self-rated emotional health	.20	.25	.22	.27
Feeling overwhelmed	.09	.18	.10	.18
Self-change: Cultural awareness	.11	.23	.13	.27
Self-change: Religious beliefs and convictions	.12	.28	.14	.32
Political and social values				
Political engagement	.30	.37	.30	.41
Political orientation	.40	.43	.35	.40
Classic liberalism	.31	.37	.40	.45
Gender role traditionalism	.12	.17	.20	.25
Permissiveness	.56	.65	.58	.66
Raising a family	.23	.28	.27	.32
Developing a meaningful philosophy of life	.20	.24	.23	.29
Promoting racial understanding	.26	.35	.23	.36

(Continued)

Table D.1 (Continued)

Outcome	R^2 for women		R^2 for men	
	After inputs	Final	After inputs	Final
Academics				
College GPA	.31	.47	.31	.48
Self-rated mathematical ability	.49	.53	.51	.56
Self-rated drive to achieve	.20	.31	.28	.41
Self-rated competitiveness	.28	.35	.38	.43
Self-change: Critical thinking and knowledge	.10	.23	.14	.33
Degree aspirations	.18	.29	.20	.32

Note: Results for career a typicality are excluded from this table due to differences in analytical approach.

References

Agliata, D., & Tantleff-Dunn, S. (2004). The impact of media exposure on males' body image. *Journal of Social and Clinical Psychology, 23*(1), 7–22.

Agresti, A., & Finlay, B. (1997). *Statistical methods for the social sciences* (3rd ed.). Englewood Cliffs, NJ: Prentice Hall.

American Association of University Women Educational Foundation. (1992). *How schools shortchange girls—The AAUW report: A study of major findings on girls and education.* New York: Marlowe.

American Association of University Women Educational Foundation. (1998). *Gender gaps: Where schools still fail our children.* Washington, DC: Author.

American Association of University Women Educational Foundation. (2004). *Under the microscope: A decade of gender equity programs in the sciences.* Washington, DC: Author.

Astin, A. W. (1968). *The college environment.* Washington, DC: American Council on Education.

Astin, A. W. (1977). *Four critical years: Effects of college on beliefs, attitudes, and knowledge.* San Francisco: Jossey-Bass.

Astin, A. W. (1993a). *Assessment for excellence: The philosophy and practice of assessment and evaluation in higher education.* Westport, CT: American Council on Education and Oryx Press.

Astin, A. W. (1993b). An empirical typology of college students. *Journal of College Student Development, 34*(1), 36–46.

Astin, A. W. (1993c). *What matters in college? Four critical years revisited.* San Francisco: Jossey-Bass.

Astin, A. W. (1999). Student involvement: A developmental theory for higher education. *Journal of College Student Development, 40*(5), 518–529.

Astin, A. W. (2003). Studying how college affects students: A personal history of the CIRP. *About Campus, 8*(3), 21–28.

Astin, A. W., & Denson, N. (2006). *Long-term effects of college on students' political orientation.* Los Angeles: Higher Education Research Institute, University of California, Los Angeles.

Astin, A. W., Oseguera, L., Sax, L. J., & Korn, W. S. (2002). *The American freshman: Thirty-five year trends, 1966–2001.* Los Angeles: Higher Education Research Institute, University of California, Los Angeles.

Astin, A. W., & Sax, L. J. (1998). How undergraduates are affected by service participation. *Journal of College Student Development, 39*(3), 251–263.

Astin, A. W., Sax, L. J., & Avalos, J. (1999). The long-term effects of volunteerism during the undergraduate years. *Review of Higher Education, 21*(2), 187–202.

Astin, A. W., Vogelgesang, L. J., Ikeda, E. K., & Yee, J. A. (2000). *How service learning affects students.* Los Angeles: Higher Education Research Institute, University of California, Los Angeles.

Astin, H. S. (1990). Educating women: A promise and a vision for the future. *American Journal of Education, 4,* 479–493.

Astin, H. S., & Kent, L. (1983). Gender roles in transition: Research and policy implications for higher education. *Journal of Higher Education, 54,* 309–324.

Astin, H. S., & Sax, L. J. (1996). Developing scientific talent in undergraduate women. In C. Davis, A. Ginorio, C. Hollenshead, B. Lazarus, & P. Rayman (Eds.), *The equity equation: Women in science, mathematics, and engineering* (pp. 96–121). San Francisco: Jossey-Bass.

Bargad, A., & Hyde, J. S. (1991). Women's studies: A study of feminist identity development in women. *Psychology of Women Quarterly, 15*(2), 181–201.

Baxter Magolda, M. B. (1992). *Knowing and reasoning in college: Gender-related patterns in students' intellectual development.* San Francisco: Jossey Bass.

Belenky, M. F., Clinchy, B. M., Goldberger, N. R., & Tarule, J. M. (1997). *Women's ways of knowing: The development of self, voice, and mind.* New York: Basic Books.

Bielby, D.D.V. (1978). Career sex-atypicality and career involvement of college educated women: Baseline evidence from the 1960s. *Sociology of Education, 51*(1), 7–28.

Biocca, F., & Myers, P. (1992). The elastic body image: The effect of television advertising and programming on body image distortions in young women. *Journal of Communication, 42*(3), 108–133.

Bowen, W. G., & Bok, D. (1998). *The shape of the river: Long-term consequences of considering race in college and university admissions.* Princeton, NJ: Princeton University Press.

Box-Steffensmeier, J. M., De Boef, S., & Lin, T. (2004). The dynamics of the partisan gender gap. *American Political Science Review, 98,* 515–528.

Branscombe, N. R. (1998). Thinking about gender privilege or disadvantage: Consequences for well-being in women and men. *British Journal of Social Psychology, 37,* 167–184.

Bryant, A. N. (2003). Changes in attitudes toward women's roles: Predicting gender-role traditionalism among college students. *Sex Roles, 48,* 131–142.

Buckner, D. R. (1981). Developing coed residence hall programs for sex-role exploration. *Journal of College Student Personnel, 22,* 52–54.

Cabrera, A. F., Crissman, J. L., Bernal, E. M., Nora, A., Terenzini, P. T., & Pascarella, E. T. (2002). Collaborative learning: Its impact on college students' development and diversity. *Journal of College Student Development, 43*(1), 20–34.

Canes, B. J., & Rosen, H. (1995). Following in her footsteps? Faculty gender composition and women's choices of college majors. *Industrial and Labor Relations Review, 48,* 486–504.

Catalani, R. (2006). A CSI writer on the CSI effect. *Yale Law Journal Pocket Part, 115.* Retrieved March 17, 2008, from http://www.thepocketpart. org/2006/02/catalani.htm.

Cataldi, E. F., Bradburn, E. M., & Fahimi, M. (2005). *2004 national study of postsecondary faculty: Background characteristics, work activities, and compensation of instructional faculty and staff.* Washington, DC: National Center for Education Statistics.

Chodorow, N. (1978). *The reproduction of mothering.* Berkeley: University of California Press.

Colbeck, C. L., Cabrera, A. F., & Terenzini, P. T. (2001). Learning professional confidence: Linking teaching practices, students' self-perceptions, and gender. *Review of Higher Education, 24*(2), 173–191.

Constantinople, A., Cornelius, R., & Gray, J. (1988). The chilly climate: Fact or artifact? *Journal of Higher Education, 59,* 527–550.

Crombie, G., Pyke, S. W., Silverthorn, N., Jones, A., & Piccinin, S. (2003). Students' perceptions of their classroom participation and instructor as a function of gender and context. *Journal of Higher Education, 74,* 51–76.

Davis, J. A. (1966). The campus as a frog pond: An application of the theory of relative deprivation to career decisions of college men. *American Journal of Sociology, 72*(1), 17–31.

Deak, J. (2002). *Girls will be girls: Raising confident and courageous daughters.* New York: Hyperion.

Dey, E. L. (1996). Undergraduate political attitudes: An examination of peer, faculty, and social influences. *Research in Higher Education, 37*(5), 535–554.

Dey, E. L. (1997a). Undergraduate political attitudes: Peer influence in changing social contexts. *Journal of Higher Education, 68,* 398–413.

Dey, E. L. (1997b). Working with low survey response rates: The efficacy of weighting adjustments. *Research in Higher Education, 38*(2), 215–227.

Drew, T. L., & Work, G. G. (1998). Gender-based differences in perception of experiences in higher education. *Journal of Higher Education, 69,* 542–555.

Edlund, L., & Pande, R. (2002). Why have women become left-wing? The political gender gap and the decline in marriage. *Quarterly Journal of Economics, 117*(3), 917–961.

Erikson, E. H. (1968). *Identity: Youth and crisis*. New York: W. W. Norton.

Ethington, C. A., Smart, J. C., & Pascarella, E. T. (1988). Influences on women's entry into male-dominated occupations. *Higher Education, 17*, 545–562.

Ex, C., Janssens, J., & Korzilius, H. (2002). Young females' images of motherhood in relation to television viewing. *Journal of Communication, 52*(4), 955–971.

Farmer, H. S., Wardrop, J. L., Anderson, M. Z., & Risinger, R. (1995). Women's career choices: Focus on science, math, and technology careers. *Journal of Counseling Psychology, 42*, 155–170.

Fassinger, P. A. (1995). Understanding classroom interaction: Students' and professors' contributions to students' silence. *Journal of Higher Education, 66*, 82–96.

Feldman, K. A., & Newcomb, T. M. (1969). *The impact of college on students*. San Francisco: Jossey-Bass.

Frost, S. H. (1991). Fostering the critical thinking of college women through academic advising and faculty contact. *Journal of College Student Development, 32*(4), 259–366.

Gati, I., Osipow, S. H., & Givon, M. (1995). Gender differences in career decision making: The content and structure of preferences. *Journal of Counseling Psychology, 42*, 204–216.

Gilligan, C. (1982). *In a different voice: Psychological theory and women's development*. Cambridge, MA: Harvard University Press.

Gruca, J. M., Ethington, C. A., & Pascarella, E. T. (1988). Intergenerational effects of college graduation on career sex-atypicality in women. *Research in Higher Education, 29*(2), 99–124.

Gurin, P., Dey, E. L., Hurtado, S., & Gurin, G. (2002). Diversity and higher education: Theory and impact on educational outcomes. *Harvard Educational Review, 72*(3), 332–366.

Hall, R. M., & Sandler, B. R. (1982). *The classroom climate: A chilly one for women?* Washington, DC: Association of American Colleges.

Hardy, M. A. (1993). Regression with dummy variables. In M. S. Lewis-Beck (Series Ed.), *Quantitative applications in the social sciences* (pp. 1–90). Newbury Park, CA: Sage Publications.

Harper, C. E., Wolf, D., & Sax, L. J. (2007, November). *The relationship between parental involvement and college students' personal, academic, and social development*. Paper presented at the annual meeting of the Association for the Study of Higher Education, Louisville, KY.

Harris, K. L., Melaas, K., & Rodacker, E. (1999). The impact of women's studies courses on college students of the 1990s. *Sex Roles, 40*, 969–977.

Heller, J. F., Puff, C. R., & Mills, C. J. (1985). Assessment of the chilly college climate for women. *Journal of Higher Education, 56,* 446–461.

Higher Education Research Institute. (2006). *The spiritual life of college students: A national study of college students' search for meaning and purpose.* Los Angeles: Higher Education Research Institute, University of California, Los Angeles.

Hoff Sommers, C. (2000). *The war against boys: How misguided feminism is harming our young men.* New York: Simon & Schuster.

Holland, D. C., & Eisenhart, M. A. (1990). *Educated in romance: Women, achievement, and college culture.* Chicago: University of Chicago Press.

Holland, J. L. (1973). *Making vocational choices: A theory of careers.* Englewood Cliffs, NJ: Prentice Hall.

Holmbeck, G. N., & Wandrei, M. L. (1993). Individual and relational predictors of adjustment in first-year college students. *Journal of Counseling Psychology, 40,* 73–78.

Hooghe, M. (2002). Watching television and civic engagement: Disentangling the effects of time, programs, and stations. *Press/Politics, 7*(2), 84–104.

Hyde, J. S. (2005). The gender similarities hypothesis. *American Sociologist, 60*(6), 581–592.

Jacobs, J. A. (1986). The sex-segregation of fields of study: Trends during the college years. *Journal of Higher Education, 57,* 134–154.

Jacobs, J. A. (1996). Gender inequality and higher education. *Annual Review of Sociology, 22,* 153–185.

Josselson, R. (1987). *Finding herself: Pathways to identity development in women* San Francisco: Jossey-Bass.

Kanter, R. M. (1977). *Men and women of the corporation.* New York: Basic Books.

Kenny, M. E., & Donaldson, G. A. (1991). Contributions of parental attachment and family structure to the social and psychological functioning of first-year college students. *Journal of Counseling Psychology, 38,* 479–486.

Kezar, A., & Moriarty, D. (2000). Expanding our understanding of student leadership development: A study exploring gender and ethnic identity. *Journal of College Student Development, 41*(1), 55–69.

Kim, M. M. (2001). Institutional effectiveness of women-only colleges: Cultivating students' desire to influence social conditions. *Journal of Higher Education, 72,* 287–321.

Kim, M. M. (2002). Cultivating intellectual development: Comparing women-only colleges and coeducational colleges for educational effectiveness. *Research in Higher Education, 43*(4), 447–481.

Kindlon, D. J., & Thompson, M. (1999). *Raising Cain: Protecting the emotional life of boys.* New York: Ballantine Books.

King, J. (2006). *Gender equity in higher education*. Washington, DC: American Council on Education.

Kinzie, J., Gonyea, R., Kuh, G. D., Umbach, P. D., Blaich, C., & Korkmaz, A. (2007, November). *The relationship between gender and student engagement in college*. Paper presented at the annual meeting of the Association for the Study of Higher Education, Louisville, KY.

Kitzrow, M. A. (2003). The mental health needs of today's college students: Challenges and recommendations. *NASPA Journal, 41*, 167–181.

Kohlberg, L. (1975). The cognitive-developmental approach to moral education. *Phi Delta Kappan, 56*, 670–677.

Komarovsky, M. (1985). *Women in college: Shaping new feminine identities*. New York: Basic Books.

Kuh, G. D. (2001). Assessing what really matters to student learning: Inside the National Survey of Student Engagement. *Change, 33*, 10–17, 66.

Lapsley, D. K., Rice, K. G., & Shadid, G. E. (1989). Psychological separation and adjustment to college. *Journal of Counseling Psychology, 36*, 286–294.

Lease, S. H. (2003). Testing a model of men's nontraditional occupational choices. *Career Development Quarterly, 51*, 244–258.

Lemaine, A. (2004, September 13). "CSI" spurs campus forensics scene. *San Diego Union Tribune*. Retrieved July 18, 2006, from http://www.signonsandiego.com/uniontrib/20040913/news_1c13csi.html

Leppel, K. (2002). Similarities and differences in the college persistence of men and women. *Review of Higher Education, 25*(4), 433–450.

Lindholm, J. A., Astin, H. S., Choi, J. Y., & Gutierrez-Zamano, E. (2002). *The educational paths of recent high school graduates: College, work, and future plans*. Los Angeles: Higher Education Research Institute, University of California, Los Angeles.

Lindholm, J. A., Szelenyi, K., Hurtado, S., & Korn, W. S. (2005). *The American college teacher: National norms for the 2004–05 HERI Faculty Survey*. Los Angeles: Higher Education Research Institute, University of California, Los Angeles.

Little, C. A. (2002). Curricular and professional choices. In A. M. Martínez Alemán & K. A. Renn (Eds.), *Women in higher education: An encyclopedia* (pp. 292–294). Santa Barbara, CA: ABC-CLIO.

Lopez, F. G., Campbell, V. L., & Watkins, C. E. (1986). Depression, psychological separation, and college adjustment: An investigation of sex differences. *Journal of Counseling Psychology, 33*, 52–56.

Lovgren, S. (2004, September 23). "CSI" effect is mixed blessing for real crime labs. *National Geographic*. Retrieved July 18, 2006, from http://news.nationalgeographic.com/news/2004/09/0923_040923_csi.html

Lundgren, D., & Rudawsky, D. (1998). Female and male college students' responses to negative feedback from parents and peers. *Sex Roles, 39*(5/6), 409–429.

Marcia, J. (1966). Development and validation of ego-identity status. *Journal of Personality and Social Psychology, 3,* 551–558.

Margolis, J., & Fisher, A. (2002). *Unlocking the clubhouse: Women in computing.* Cambridge, MA: MIT Press.

Marsh, H. W., Smith, I. D., & Barnes, J. (1985). Multidimensional self-concepts: Relations with sex and academic achievement. *Journal of Educational Psychology, 77*(5), 581–596.

Martínez Alemán, A. M. (1997). Understanding and investigating female friendship's educative value. *Journal of Higher Education, 68,* 119–159.

McDermeit, M., Funk, R., & Dennis, M. (1999). *Data cleaning and replacement of missing values.* Bloomington, IL: Chestnut Health Systems.

McGrath, E., Keita, G. P., Strickland, B. R., & Russo, N. F. (Eds.).(1990). *Women and depression: Risk factors and treatment issues.* Washington, DC: American Psychological Association.

Mead, S. (2006). *The truth about boys and girls.* Washington, DC: Education Sector.

Miller, C. D., Finely, J., & McKinley, D. L. (1990). Learning approaches and motives: Male and female differences and implications for learning assistance programs. *Journal of College Student Development, 31*(2), 147–154.

Miller-Bernal, L. (1989). College experiences and sex-role attitudes: Does a women's college make a difference? *Youth and Society, 20,* 363–387.

Morgan, C., Isaac, J. D., & Sansone, C. (2001). The role of interest in understanding the career choices of female and male college students. *Sex Roles, 44,* 295–320.

Mortenson, T. G. (2003). *Fact sheet: What's wrong with the guys?* Oskaloosa, IA: Postsecondary Education Opportunity.

National Association of Student Personnel Administrators. (2004). *Leadership for a healthy campus: An ecological approach for student success.* Washington, DC: Author.

Nolen-Hoeksema, S., & Girgus, J. S. (1994). The emergence of gender differences in depression during adolescence. *Psychological Bulletin, 115,* 424–443.

Orenstein, P. (1994). *School girls: Young women, self-esteem, and the confidence gap.* New York: Doubleday.

Pascarella, E. T. (1984). College environmental influences on students' educational aspirations. *Journal of Higher Education, 55,* 751–771.

Pascarella, E. T. (1985). College environmental influences on learning and cognitive development: A critical review and synthesis. In J. C. Smart (Ed.), *Higher education: Handbook of theory and research* (Vol. 1, pp. 1–61). New York: Agathon Press.

Pascarella, E. T. (2006). How college affects students: Ten directions for future research. *Journal of College Student Development*, 47(5), 508–520.

Pascarella, E. T., Bohr, L, Nora, A., & Terenzini, P. T. (1995). Cognitive effects of 2-year and 4-year colleges: New evidence. *Educational Evaluation and Policy Analysis*, 17, 83–96.

Pascarella, E. T., Edison, M., Nora, A., Hagedorn, L. S., & Terenzini, P. T. (1996). Influences on students' openness to diversity and challenge in the first year of college. *Journal of Higher Education*, 67, 174–195.

Pascarella, E. T., Smart, J. C., Ethington, C. A., & Nettles, M. T. (1987). The influence of college on self-concept: A consideration of race and gender differences. *American Educational Research Journal*, 24, 49–77.

Pascarella, E. T., & Terenzini, P. T. (1991). *How college affects students: Findings and insights from twenty years of research*. San Francisco: Jossey-Bass.

Pascarella, E. T., & Terenzini, P. T. (1998). Studying college students in the 21st century: Meeting new challenges. *Review of Higher Education*, 21(2), 151–165.

Pascarella, E. T., & Terenzini, P. T. (2005). *How college affects students: A third decade of research*. San Francisco: Jossey-Bass.

Pascarella, E. T., Whitt, E. J., Edison, M. I., Nora, A., Hagedorn, L. S., Yeager, P. M., et al. (1997). Women's perceptions of a "chilly climate" and their cognitive outcomes during the first year of college. *Journal of College Student Development*, 38(2), 109–124.

Perkins, W. H. (1999). Stress-motivated drinking in collegiate and postcollegiate young adulthood: Life course and gender patterns. *Journal of Studies on Alcohol*, 60(2), 219–227.

Perry, W. G. (1970). *Forms of intellectual and ethical development in the college years: A scheme*. Troy, MO: Holt, Rinehart, & Winston.

Pipher, M. (1995). *Reviving Ophelia: Saving the selves of adolescent girls*. New York: Ballantine Books.

Pollack, W. (1999). *Real boys: Rescuing our sons from the myths of boyhood*. New York: Henry Holt.

Porter, S. R., & Whitcomb, M. E. (2005). Non-response in student surveys: The role of demographics, engagement and personality. *Research in Higher Education*, 46(2), 127–152.

Pryor, J. H., Hurtado, S., Saenz, V. B., Korn, J. S., Santos, J. L., & Korn, W. S. (2006). *The American freshman: National norms for fall 2006*. Los Angeles: Higher Education Research Institute, University of California, Los Angeles.

Pryor, J. H., Hurtado, S., Saenz, V. B., Santos, J. L., & Korn, W. S. (2007). *Forty year trends*. Los Angeles: Higher Education Research Institute, University of California, Los Angeles.

Putnam, R. (2000). *Bowling alone: The collapse and revival of American community.* New York: Simon & Schuster.

Rada, J. A., & Wulfemeyer, K. T. (2005). Color coded: Racial descriptors in television coverage of intercollegiate sports. *Journal of Broadcasting & Electronic Media, 49*(1), 65–85.

Rainville, R., & McCormick, E. (1977). Extent of covert racial prejudice in pro football announcers' speech. *Journalism Quarterly, 54,* 20–26.

Rayman, P., & Brett, B. (1995). Women science majors: What makes a difference in persistence after graduation? *Journal of Higher Education, 66,* 388–414.

Riordan, C. (1992). Single- and mixed-gender colleges for women: Educational, attitudinal, and occupational outcomes. *Review of Higher Education, 15*(3), 327–346.

Riordan, C. (1994). The value of attending a women's college: Education, occupation and income benefits. *Journal of Higher Education, 65,* 486–510.

Rosovsky, H., & Hartley, M. (2002). *Evaluation and the academy: Are we doing the right thing? Grade inflation and letters of recommendation.* Cambridge, MA: American Academy of Arts and Sciences.

Rowell, G. H., Perhac, D. G., Hankins, J. A., Parker, B. C., Pettey, C. C., & Iriarte-Gross, J. M. (2003, February 19–23). *Computer-related gender differences.* Paper presented at the ACM Special Interest Group on Computer Science Education, Reno, NV.

Sadker, M., & Sadker, D. (1994). *Failing at fairness: How America's schools cheat girls.* New York: Charles Scribner's Sons.

Salter, D. W., & Persaud, A. (2003). Women's views of the factors that encourage and discourage classroom participation. *Journal of College Student Development, 44*(6), 831–844.

Sanday, P. (1990). *Fraternity gang rape: Sex, brotherhood, and privilege on campus.* New York: New York University Press.

Sax, L. J. (1994a). The dynamics of "tokenism": How college students are affected by the proportion of women in their major. Unpublished doctoral dissertation, University of California, Los Angeles.

Sax, L. J. (1994b). Mathematical self-concept: How college reinforces the gender gap. *Research in Higher Education, 35*(2), 141–166.

Sax, L. J. (1994c). Predicting gender and major-field differences in mathematical self-concept during college. *Journal of Women and Minorities in Science and Engineering, 1,* 291–307.

Sax, L. J. (1994d). Retaining tomorrow's scientists: Exploring the factors that keep male and female college students interested in science careers. *Journal of Women and Minorities in Science and Engineering, 1,* 45–61.

Sax, L. J. (1996). The dynamics of "tokenism": How college students are affected by the proportion of women in their major. *Research in Higher Education, 37*(4), 389–425.

Sax, L. J. (2001). Undergraduate science majors: Gender differences in who goes to graduate school. *Review of Higher Education, 24*(2), 153–172.

Sax, L. J. (2003). Our incoming students: What are they like? *About Campus, 8*(3), 15–20.

Sax, L. J., & Bryant, A. N. (2006). The impact of college on sex-atypical career choices of men and women. *Journal of Vocational Behavior, 68,* 52–63.

Sax, L. J., Bryant, A. N., & Gilmartin, S. K. (2004). A longitudinal investigation of emotional health among male and female first-year college students. *Journal of the First-Year Experience and Students in Transition, 16*(2), 39–65.

Sax, L. J., Bryant, A. N., & Harper, C. E. (2005). The differential effects of student-faculty interaction on college outcomes for women and men. *Journal of College Student Development, 46*(6), 642–659.

Sax, L. J., & Harper, C. E. (2007). Origins of the gender gap: Pre-college and college influences on differences between men and women. *Research in Higher Education, 48*(6), 669–694.

Serex, C. P., & Townsend, B. K. (1999). Student perceptions of chilling practices in sex-atypical majors. *Research in Higher Education, 40*(5), 527–538.

Seymour, E., & Hewitt, N. M. (1997). *Talking about leaving: Why undergraduates leave the sciences.* Boulder, CO: Westview Press.

Sherman, J. (1983). Factors predicting girls' and boys' enrollment in college preparatory mathematics. *Psychology of Women Quarterly, 7*(3), 272–281.

Simons, H. D., Van Rheenen, D., & Covington, M. B. (1999). Academic motivation and the student athlete. *Journal of College Student Development, 40*(2), 151–161.

Smart, J. C., Feldman, K. A., & Ethington, C. A. (2000). *Academic disciplines: Holland's theory and the study of college students and faculty.* Nashville, TN: Vanderbilt University Press.

Smith, D. G. (1990). Women's colleges and coed colleges: Is there a difference for women? *Journal of Higher Education, 61,* 181–197.

Smith, D. G., Morrison, D. E., & Wolf, L. E. (1994). College as a gendered experience: An empirical analysis using multiple lenses. *Journal of Higher Education, 65,* 696–725.

Smith, D. G., Wolf, L. E., & Morrison, D. E. (1995). Paths to success: Factors related to the impact of women's colleges. *Journal of Higher Education, 66,* 245–266.

Stage, F. K., & Anaya, G. L. (1996). A transformational view of college student research. In F. K. Stage, G. L. Anaya, J. P. Bean, D. Hossler, & G. D. Kuh (Eds.), *College students: The evolving nature of research* (pp. xi–xxii). Needham Heights, MA: Simon & Schuster.

Stake, J., & Hoffman, F. (2001). Changes in student social attitudes, activism, and personal confidence in higher education: The role of women's studies. *American Educational Research Journal, 38,* 411–436.

Stake, J., Roades, L., Rose, S., Ellis, L., & West, C. (1994). The women's studies experience: Impetus for feminist activism. *Psychology of Women Quarterly, 18*(1), 17–24.

Stickel, S. A., & Bonett, R. M. (1991). Gender differences in career self-efficacy: Combining a career with home and family. *Journal of College Student Development, 32*(4), 297–301.

Stipek, D. (2001). Academic achievement and social behaviors associated with age of entry into kindergarten. *Journal of Applied Developmental Psychology, 22,* 175–189.

Stoecker, J. L., & Pascarella, E. T. (1991). Women's colleges and women's career attainments revisited. *Journal of Higher Education, 62,* 394–406.

Tatum, B. D. (1992). Talking about race, learning about racism: The application of racial identity development theory in the classroom. *Harvard Educational Review, 62*(1), 1–24.

Tavris, C. (1992). *The mismeasure of women.* New York: Touchstone.

Thomsen, C. J., Basu, A. M., & Reinitz, M. T. (1995). Effects of women's studies courses on gender-related attitudes of women and men. *Psychology of Women Quarterly, 19*(3), 419–426.

Tinto, V. (1987). *Leaving college: Rethinking the causes and cures of student attrition.* Chicago: University of Chicago Press.

Tomlinson-Clarke, S., & Clarke, D. (1994). Predicting social adjustment and academic achievement for college women with and without pre-college leadership. *Journal of College Student Development, 35*(2), 120–124.

Trent, J. W., & Medsker, L. L. (1968). *Beyond high school.* San Francisco: Jossey-Bass.

Tsui, L. (1995, November). *Boosting female ambition: How college diversity impacts graduate degree aspirations of women.* Paper presented at the annual meeting of the Association for the Study of Higher Education, Orlando, FL.

Umbach, P. D., Palmer, M. M., Kuh, G. D., & Hannah, S. J. (2006). Intercollegiate athletics and effective educational practices: Winning combination or losing effort? *Research in Higher Education, 47*(6), 709–733.

U.S. Department of Education. (2003). *Degrees and other formal awards conferred.* Washington, DC: National Center for Education Statistics.

U.S. Department of Education. (2004). *Trends in educational equity of girls and women.* Washington, DC: National Center for Education Statistics.

Ware, N. C., Steckler, N. A., & Leserman, J. (1985). Undergraduate women: Who chooses a science major? *Journal of Higher Education, 56,* 73–84.

Wechsler, H., & Rohman, M. (1981). Extensive users of alcohol among college students. *Journal of Studies on Alcohol, 42*(1), 149–155.

Weidman, J. C. (1989). Undergraduate socialization: A conceptual approach. In J. C. Smart (Ed.), *Higher education: Handbook of theory and research* (Vol. 5, pp. 289–322). New York: Agathon Press.

West, J., Meek, A., & Hurst, D. (2000). *Children who enter kindergarten late or repeat kindergarten: Their characteristics and later school performance* (NCES No. 2000–039). Washington, DC: U.S. Department of Education.

Whitt, E. J., Edison, M. I., Pascarella, E. T., Nora, A., & Terenzini, P. T. (1999). Women's perceptions of a "chilly climate" and cognitive outcomes in college: Additional evidence. *Journal of College Student Development, 40*(2), 163–177.

Whitt, E. J., Pascarella, E. T., Nesheim, B.S.E., Marth, B. P., & Pierson, C. T. (2003). Differences between women and men in objectively measured outcomes, and the factors that influence those outcomes, in the first three years of college. *Journal of College Student Development, 44,* 587–610.

Wolf, D., Harper, C. E., & Sax, L. J. (2007, November). *An exploratory study of parent involvement in the academic lives of college students.* Paper presented at the annual meeting of the Association for the Study of Higher Education, Louisville, KY.

Zhao, C., Carini, R. M., & Kuh, G. D. (2005). Searching for the peach blossom Shangri-La: Student engagement of men and women SMET majors. *Review of Higher Education, 28*(4), 503–525.

Index

A

Absolute knowing, 57
Academic engagement, 227–228; directions for future research in, 228–229; implications for practice in, 228
Academic involvement, 248–250
Academic outcomes, 179–215; and career sex-atypicality, 208–213; changes in gender gap in, during college, 292–294; and college GPA, 179–185; and competitiveness (self-rated), 195–199; and degree aspirations, 204–208; and drive to achieve, 191–195; and mathematical ability (self-rated), 185–190; and self change: critical thinking and knowledge, 200–204
Academic self-confidence: gender differences in, 25–29; gender differences in, among first-year students, 26
Age, gender differences in, 15
Agliata, D., 110
Agresti, A., 285
American Association of University Women (AAUW), 30, 32; Educational Foundation, 236, 237
American Council on Education and the Education Sector, 1, 10
Anaya, G. L., 58
Anderson, M. Z., 256
Artist personality, 89–92; aspects of college that influence both genders in, 89–91; factors influencing men only in, 92; factors influencing women only in, 92; gender differences in college-level predictors of, 90–91; opposing differences for women and men in, 91–92

B

Astin, A. W., 2–4, 10–12, 37, 43–44, 67, 70, 91, 93, 94, 96, 114, 122, 125, 135, 145, 146, 149, 156, 181–182, 200, 245, 253, 256, 257, 265, 269
Astin, H. S., 17–18, 62, 63, 66, 93, 100–101, 243–251, 254, 256
"At Colleges, Women Are Leaving Men in the Dust" (*New York Times*), 1
Avalos, J., 43–44

Bargad, A., 120, 128, 250
Barnes, J., 25
Basu, A. M., 110, 250
Baxter Magolda, M. B., 57, 224
Belenky, M. F., 42, 53, 57, 63, 224, 240
Bernal, E. M., 250
Bible study, 133
Bielby, D.D.V., 245
Biocca, F., 110
Biological sciences, 37
Blaich, C., 228
Bohr, L., 223–224
Bok, D., 10
Bonett, R. M., 37
Bowen, W. G., 10
Box-Steffenmeier, J. M., 44
Bradburn, E. M., 226–227
Branscombe, N. R., 121
Brett, B., 251–252
Bryant, A. N., 24, 63, 82, 153, 157, 215, 224, 230, 249–251, 254–256
Buckner, D. R., 255–256

C

Cabrera, A. F., 104, 224, 250, 251
Campbell, V. L., 49